Lectionary Texts
Year A

The Church Hymnal Corporation
800 Second Avenue, New York, N.Y. 10017

*The Church Hymnal Corporation wishes to express its
appreciation to The National Council of Churches for permission
to use the texts, to the Reverend Leo Malania for editing this
volume and to Nelson Gruppo for the layout and design.*

ISBN 0-89869-090-0 Reader's Edition
       0-89869-091-9 Pew Edition

Introduction

Lectionary Texts is published in three separate volumes for Years A, B, and C. The selection of the readings is in strict accordance with The Lectionary of *The Book of Common Prayer* pages 889-925, and pages 288-291 for the Great Vigil of Easter. The texts of the readings have been drawn from *The Common Bible* (Revised Standard Version, an Ecumenical Edition), whose accuracy and wide ecumenical acceptance are generally recognized. The texts in this book may, of course, be replaced by corresponding passages from any of the other versions of the Bible authorized for public worship in this Church.

This edition of *Lectionary Texts: Year A* has been extensively revised in the light of many comments received from those who used the original edition first published in 1977. The readings have been edited for liturgical use in accordance with the suggestions in *The Book of Common Prayer,* page 888. All alternatives cited have been included. In only a very few cases where exactly the same passages are to be read, rather than reprinting an entire passage, page references to a preceding or following page are given.

All optional passages have also been included. Those which may be omitted (cited in parentheses in the Lectionary), have been set off in separate indented paragraphs, and marked with a vertical bar line at the margin. In some of the passages, an opening phrase needed to clarify the context is printed in italics and set off in brackets. These italicized words or passages should be omitted when the preceding section is read and the continuity of the entire reading is clear. Examples will be found on pages 60, and 64, where an optional passage contains matter needed to clarify the meaning of the subsequent passage. Unless otherwise indicated, all page numbers refer to *The Book of Common Prayer*.

Citations from the Psalter are placed at the point where psalmody is normally used in the celebration of the Holy Eucharist, following the Old Testament Lesson. When the readings are used at a principal service of Morning or Evening Prayer, the Psalm is read at the place appointed in the service, before the Lessons. When used at the Office, the longer version of the Psalm is to be preferred. The shorter form is intended to be sung at the Eucharist.

The Church Hymnal Corporation wishes to record its deep appreciation to all who welcomed the publication of the first edition of *Lectionary Texts: Year A* and of the subsequent editions of *Lectionary Texts: Year B* and *Lectionary Texts: Year C*. The publishers are especially grateful to all who took the trouble to write and make valuable suggestions for improving this series. To the extent possible, these suggestions have been incorporated in the present volume. As in *Lectionary Texts: Year C*, the day or week is identified in the footlines for easier reference.

The publishers hope that this book will enrich participation in worship by all the people, and will assist the clergy and other ministers in worthily proclaiming the Word of God at the principal service of Sundays and major Holy Days.

Lectionary Texts: Year A

First Sunday of Advent

A Reading (Lesson) from the Book of Isaiah [2:1-5]

The word which Isaiah the son of Amoz saw concerning Judah and Jerusalem. It shall come to pass in the latter days that the mountain of the house of the Lord shall be established as the highest of the mountains, and shall be raised above the hills; and all the nations shall flow to it, and many peoples shall come, and say: "Come, let us go up to the mountain of the Lord, to the house of the God of Jacob; that he may teach us his ways and that we may walk in his paths." For out of Zion shall go forth the law, and the word of the Lord from Jerusalem. He shall judge between the nations, and shall decide for many peoples; and they shall beat their swords into plowshares, and their spears into pruning hooks; nation shall not lift up sword against nation, neither shall they learn war any more. O house of Jacob, come, let us walk in the light of the Lord.

Psalm 122 [page 779]

A Reading (Lesson) from the Letter of Paul to the Romans [13:8-14]

Owe no one anything, except to love one another; for he who loves his neighbor has fulfilled the law. The commandments, "You shall not commit adultery, You shall not kill, You shall not steal, You shall not covet," and any other commandment, are summed up in this sentence, "You shall love your neighbor as yourself." Love does no wrong to a neighbor; therefore love is the fulfilling of the law. Besides this you know what hour it is, how it is full time now for you to wake from sleep. For salvation is nearer to us now than when we first believed; the night is far gone, the day is at hand. Let us then cast off the works of darkness and put on the armor of light; let us conduct ourselves becomingly as in the day, not in reveling and drunkenness, not in debauchery and licentiousness, not in quarreling and jealousy. But put on the Lord Jesus Christ, and make no provision for the flesh, to gratify its desires.

✝ *The Holy Gospel of Our Lord Jesus Christ
According to Matthew* [24:37-44]

On the Mount of Olives, Jesus said to his disciples privately, "As were the days of Noah, so will be the coming of the Son of man. For as in those days before the flood they were eating and drinking, marrying and giving in marriage, until the day when Noah entered the ark, and they did not know until the flood came and swept them all away, so will be the coming of the Son of man. Then two men will be in the field; one is taken and one is left. Two women will be grinding at the mill; one is taken and one is left. Watch therefore, for you do not know on what day your Lord is coming. But know this, that if the householder had known in what part of the night the thief was coming, he would have watched and would not have let his house be broken into. Therefore you also must be ready; for the Son of man is coming at an hour you do not expect."

Second Sunday of Advent

A Reading (Lesson) from the Book of Isaiah [11:1-10]

There shall come forth a shoot from the stump of Jesse, and a branch shall grow out of his roots. And the Spirit of the Lord shall rest upon him, the spirit of wisdom and understanding, the spirit of counsel and might, the spirit of knowledge and the fear of the Lord. And his delight shall be in the fear of the Lord. He shall not judge by what his eyes see, or decide by what his ears hear; but with righteousness he shall judge the poor, and decide with equity for the meek of the earth; and he shall smite the earth with the rod of his mouth, and with the breath of his lips he shall slay the wicked. Righteousness shall be the girdle of his waist, and faithfulness the girdle of his loins. The wolf shall dwell with the lamb, and the leopard shall lie down with the kid, and the calf and the lion and the fatling together, and a little child shall lead them. The cow and the bear shall feed; their young shall lie down together; and the lion shall eat straw like the ox. The sucking child shall play over the hole of the asp, and the weaned child shall put his hand on the adder's den. They shall not hurt or destroy in all my holy mountain; for the earth shall be full of the knowledge of the Lord as the waters cover the sea. In that day the root of Jesse shall stand as an ensign to the peoples; him shall the nations seek, and his dwelling shall be glorious.

Psalm 72 [page 685]   or   *72:1-8* [page 685]

A Reading (Lesson) from the Letter of Paul to the Romans [15:4-13]

Whatever was written in former days was written for our instruction, that by steadfastness and by the encouragement of the scriptures we might have hope. May the God of steadfastness and encouragement grant you to live in such harmony with one another, in accord with Christ Jesus, that together you may with one voice glorify the God and Father of our Lord Jesus Christ. Welcome one another, therefore, as Christ has welcomed you, for the glory of God. For I tell you that Christ became a servant to the circumcised to show God's truthfulness, in order to confirm the promises given to the patriarchs, and in order that the Gentiles might glorify God for his mercy. As it is written,"Therefore I will praise thee among the Gentiles, and sing to thy name"; and again it is said,"Rejoice, O Gentiles, with his people"; and again,"Praise the Lord, all Gentiles, and let all the peoples praise him"; and further Isaiah says,"The root of Jesse shall come, he who rises to rule the Gentiles; in him shall the Gentiles hope." May the God of hope fill you with all joy and peace in believing, so that by the power of the Holy Spirit you may abound in hope.

✝ *The Holy Gospel of Our Lord Jesus Christ*
According to Matthew [3:1-12]

In those days came John the Baptist, preaching in the wilderness of Judea,"Repent, for the kingdom of heaven is at hand." For this is he who was spoken of by the prophet Isaiah when he said,"The voice of one crying in the wilderness: Prepare the way of the Lord, make his paths straight." Now John wore a garment of camel's hair, and a leather girdle around his waist; and his food was locusts and wild honey. Then went out to him Jerusalem and all Judea and all the region about the Jordan, and they were baptized by him in the river Jordan, confessing their sins. But when he saw many of the Pharisees and Sad'ducees coming for baptism he said to them,"You brood of vipers! Who warned you to flee from the wrath to come? Bear fruit that befits repentance, and do not presume to say to yourselves, 'We have Abraham as our father'; for I tell you, God is able from these stones to raise up children to Abraham. Even now the axe is laid to the root of the trees; every tree therefore that does not bear good fruit is cut down and thrown into the fire. I baptize you with water for repentance, but he who is coming after me is mightier than I, whose sandals I am not worthy to carry; he will baptize you with the Holy Spirit and with fire. His winnowing fork is in his hand, and he will clear his threshing floor and gather his wheat into the granary, but the chaff he will burn with unquenchable fire."

Third Sunday of Advent

A Reading (Lesson) from the Book of Isaiah [35:1-10]

The wilderness and the dry land shall be glad, the desert shall rejoice and blossom; like the crocus it shall blossom abundantly, and rejoice with joy and singing. The glory of Lebanon shall be given to it, the majesty of Carmel and Sharon. They shall see the glory of the Lord, the majesty of our God. Strengthen the weak hands, and make firm the feeble knees. Say to those who are of a fearful heart, "Be strong, fear not! Behold, your God will come with vengeance, with the recompense of God. He will come and save you." Then the eyes of the blind shall be opened, and the ears of the deaf unstopped; then shall the lame man leap like a hart, and the tongue of the dumb sing for joy. For waters shall break forth in the wilderness, and streams in the desert; the burning sand shall become a pool, and the thirsty ground springs of water; the haunt of jackals shall become a swamp, the grass shall become reeds and rushes. And a highway shall be there, and it shall be called the Holy Way; the unclean shall not pass over it, and fools shall not err therein. No lion shall be there, nor shall any ravenous beast come up on it; they shall not be found there, but the redeemed shall walk there. And the ransomed of the Lord shall return, and come to Zion with singing; everlasting joy shall be upon their heads; they shall obtain joy and gladness, and sorrow and sighing shall flee away.

Psalm 146 [page 803]   or   *146:4-9* [page 803]

A Reading (Lesson) from the Letter of James [5:7-10]

Be patient, brethren, until the coming of the Lord. Behold, the farmer waits for the precious fruit of the earth, being patient over it until it receives the early and the late rain. You also be patient. Establish your hearts, for the coming of the Lord is at hand. Do not grumble, brethren, against one another, that you may not be judged; behold, the Judge is standing at the doors. As an example of suffering and patience, brethren, take the prophets who spoke in the name of the Lord.

✝ *The Holy Gospel of Our Lord Jesus Christ According to Matthew* [11:2-11]

Now when John heard in prison about the deeds of the Christ, he sent word by his disciples and said to him, "Are you he who is to come, or shall we look for another?" And Jesus answered them, "Go and tell John what you hear and see: the blind receive their sight and the lame walk, lepers are cleansed and the deaf hear, and the dead are raised up, and the poor have good news preached to them. And blessed is he who takes no offense at me." As they went away, Jesus began to speak to the crowds concerning John: "What did you go out into the wilderness to behold? A reed shaken by the wind? Why then did you go out? To see a man clothed in soft raiment? Behold, those who wear soft raiment are in kings' houses. Why then did you go out? To see a prophet? Yes, I tell you, and more than a prophet. This is he of whom it is written,'Behold, I send my messenger before thy face, who shall prepare thy way before thee.' Truly, I say to you, among those born of women there has risen no one greater than John the Baptist; yet he who is least in the kingdom of heaven is greater than he."

Fourth Sunday of Advent

A Reading (Lesson) from the Book of Isaiah [7:10-17]

The Lord spoke to Ahaz,"Ask a sign of the Lord your God; let it be deep as Sheol or high as heaven."But Ahaz said,"I will not ask, and I will not put the Lord to the test."And he said,"Hear then, O House of David! Is it too little for you to weary men, that you weary my God also? Therefore the Lord himself will give you a sign. Behold, a young woman shall conceive and bear a son, and shall call his name Imman'u-el. He shall eat curds and honey when he knows how to refuse the evil and choose the good. For before the child knows how to refuse the evil and choose the good, the land before whose two kings you are in dread will be deserted. The Lord will bring upon you and upon your people and upon your father's house such days as have not come since the day that E'phraim departed from Judah— the King of Assyria."

Psalm 24 [page 613]   or   *24:1-7* [page 613]

A Reading (Lesson) from the Letter of Paul to the Romans [1:1-7]

Paul, a servant of Jesus Christ, called to be an apostle, set apart for the gospel of God which he promised beforehand through his prophets in the holy scriptures, the gospel concerning his Son, who was descended from David according to the flesh and designated Son of God in power according to the Spirit of holiness by his resurrection from the dead, Jesus Christ our Lord, through whom we have received grace and apostleship to bring about the obedience of faith for the sake of his name among all the nations, including yourselves who are called to belong to Jesus Christ; To all God's beloved in Rome, who are called to be saints: Grace to you and peace from God our Father and the Lord Jesus Christ.

✝ *The Holy Gospel of Our Lord Jesus Christ According to Matthew* [1:18-25]

Now the birth of Jesus Christ took place in this way. When his mother Mary had been betrothed to Joseph, before they came together she was found to be with child of the Holy Spirit; and her husband Joseph, being a just man and unwilling to put her to shame, resolved to divorce her quietly. But as he considered this, behold, an angel of the Lord appeared to him in a dream, saying, "Joseph, son of David, do not fear to take Mary your wife, for that which is conceived in her is of the Holy Spirit; she will bear a son, and you shall call his name Jesus, for he will save his people from their sins." All this took place to fulfill what the Lord had spoken by the prophet: "Behold, a virgin shall conceive and bear a son, and his name shall be called Emman'u-el" (which means, God with us). When Joseph woke from sleep, he did as the angel of the Lord commanded him; he took his wife, but knew her not until she had borne a son; and he called his name Jesus.

The Nativity of Our Lord: Christmas Day I

A Reading (Lesson) from the Book of Isaiah [9:2-4, 6-7]

The people who walked in darkness have seen a great light; those who dwelt in a land of deep darkness, on them has light shined. Thou hast multiplied the nation, thou hast increased its joy; they rejoice before thee as with joy at the harvest, as men rejoice when they divide the spoil. For the yoke of his burden, and the staff for his shoulder, the rod of his oppressor, thou hast broken as on the day of Mid'ian. For to us a child is born, to us a son is given; and the government will be upon his shoulder, and his name will be called"Wonderful Counselor, Mighty God, Everlasting Father, Prince of Peace."Of the increase of his government and of peace there will be no end, upon the throne of David, and over his kingdom, to establish it, and to uphold it with justice and with righteousness, from this time forth and for evermore. The zeal of the Lord of hosts will do this.

Psalm 96 [page 725]   or   *96:1-4, 11-12* [page 725]

A Reading (Lesson) from the Letter of Paul to Titus [2:11-14]

The grace of God has appeared for the salvation of all men, training us to renounce irreligion and worldly passions, and to live sober, upright, and godly lives in this world, awaiting our blessed hope, the appearing of the glory of our great God and Savior Jesus Christ, who gave himself for us to redeem us from all iniquity and to purify for himself a people of his own who are zealous for good deeds.

✝ *The Holy Gospel of Our Lord Jesus Christ According to Luke* [2:1-14 (15-20)]

In those days a decree went out from Caesar Augustus that all the world should be enrolled. This was the first enrollment, when Quirin'i-us was governor of Syria. And all went to be enrolled, each to his own city. And Joseph also went up from Galilee, from the city of Nazareth, to

Judea, to the city of David, which is called Bethlehem, because he was of the house and lineage of David, to be enrolled with Mary, his betrothed, who was with child. And while they were there, the time came for her to be delivered. And she gave birth to her first-born son and wrapped him in swaddling cloths, and laid him in a manger, because there was no place for them in the inn. And in that region there were shepherds out in the field, keeping watch over their flock by night. And an angel of the Lord appeared to them, and the glory of the Lord shone around them, and they were filled with fear. And the angel said to them, "Be not afraid; for behold, I bring you good news of a great joy which will come to all the people; for to you is born this day in the city of David a Savior, who is Christ the Lord. And this will be a sign for you: you will find a babe wrapped in swaddling cloths and lying in a manger." And suddenly there was with the angel a multitude of the heavenly host praising God and saying, "Glory to God in the highest, and on earth peace among men with whom he is pleased!"

When the angels went away from them into heaven, the shepherds said to one another, "Let us go over to Bethlehem and see this thing that has happened, which the Lord has made known to us." And they went with haste, and found Mary and Joseph, and the babe lying in a manger. And when they saw it they made known the saying which had been told them concerning this child; and all who heard it wondered at what the shepherds told them. But Mary kept all these things, pondering them in her heart. And the shepherds returned, glorifying and praising God for all they had heard and seen, as it had been told them.

Christmas Day II

A Reading (Lesson) from the Book of Isaiah
[62:6-7, 10-12]

Upon your walls, O Jerusalem, I have set watchmen; all the day and all the night they shall never be silent. You who put the Lord in remembrance, take no rest, and give him no rest until he establishes Jerusalem and makes it a praise in the earth. Go through, go through the gates, prepare the way for the people; build up, build up the highway, clear it of stones, lift up an ensign over the peoples. Behold, the Lord has proclaimed to the end of the earth: Say to the daughter of Zion,"Behold, your salvation comes; behold, his reward is with him, and his recompense before him." And they shall be called The holy people, The redeemed of the Lord; and you shall be called Sought out, a city not forsaken.

Psalm 97 [page 726]   or   *97:1-4, 11-12* [page 726]

A Reading (Lesson) from the Letter of Paul to Titus [3:4-7]

When the goodness and loving kindness of God our Savior appeared, he saved us, not because of deeds done by us in righteousness, but in virtue of his own mercy, by the washing of regeneration and renewal in the Holy Spirit, which he poured out upon us richly through Jesus Christ our Savior, so that we might be justified by his grace and become heirs in hope of eternal life.

✝ *The Holy Gospel of Our Lord Jesus Christ According to Luke* [2:(1-14)15-20]

In those days a decree went out from Caesar Augustus that all the world should be enrolled. This was the first enrollment, when Quirin'i-us was governor of Syria.

And all went to be enrolled, each to his own city. And
Joseph also went up from Galilee, from the city of
Nazareth, to Judea, to the city of David, which is called
Bethlehem, because he was of the house and lineage of
David, to be enrolled with Mary, his betrothed, who
was with child. And while they were there, the time
came for her to be delivered. And she gave birth to her
first-born son and wrapped him in swaddling cloths,
and laid him in a manger, because there was no place for
them in the inn. And in that region there were shepherds
out in the field, keeping watch over their flock by night.
And an angel of the Lord appeared to them, and the
glory of the Lord shone around them, and they were
filled with fear. And the angel said to them,"Be not
afraid; for behold, I bring you good news of a great joy
which will come to all the people; for to you is born this
day in the city of David a Savior, who is Christ the Lord.
And this will be a sign for you: You will find a babe
wrapped in swaddling cloths and lying in a
manger." And suddenly there was with the angel a
multitude of the heavenly host praising God and
saying,"Glory to God in the highest, and on earth peace
among men with whom he is pleased!"

When the angels went away from them into heaven, the
shepherds said to one another,"Let us go over to
Bethlehem and see this thing that has happened, which the
Lord has made known to us." And they went with haste,
and found Mary and Joseph, and the babe lying in a
manger. And when they saw it they made known the
saying which had been told them concerning this child;
and all who heard it wondered at what the shepherds told
them. But Mary kept all these things, pondering them in
her heart. And the shepherds returned, glorifying and
praising God for all they had heard and seen, as it had been
told them.

Christmas Day III

A Reading (Lesson) from the Book of Isaiah [52:7-10]

How beautiful upon the mountains are the feet of him who
brings good tidings, who publishes peace, who brings good
tidings of good, who publishes salvation, who says to
Zion, "Your God reigns." Hark, your watchmen lift up
their voice, together they sing for joy; for eye to eye they
see the return of the Lord to Zion. Break forth together
into singing, you waste places of Jerusalem; for the Lord
has comforted his people, he has redeemed Jerusalem. The
Lord has bared his holy arm before the eyes of all the
nations; and all the ends of the earth shall see the salvation
of our God.

Psalm 98 [page 727] or 98:1-6 [page 727]

A Reading (Lesson) from the Letter to the Hebrews
[1:1-12]

In many and various ways God spoke of old to our fathers
by the prophets; but in these last days he has spoken to us
by a son, whom he appointed the heir of all things, through
whom also he created the world. He reflects the glory of
God and bears the very stamp of his nature, upholding the
universe by his word of power. When he had made
purification for sins, he sat down at the right hand of the
Majesty on high, having become as much superior to
angels as the name he has obtained is more excellent than
theirs. For to what angel did God ever say, "Thou art my
Son, today I have begotten thee"? Or again, "I will be to
him a father, and he shall be to me a son"? And again,
when he brings the firstborn into the world, he says, "Let
all God's angels worship him." Of the angels he says, "Who
makes his angels winds, and his servants flames of fire."
But of the Son he says, "Thy throne, O God, is for ever and

ever, the righteous scepter is the scepter of thy kingdom. Thou hast loved righteousness and hated lawlessness; therefore God, thy God, has anointed thee with the oil of gladness beyond thy comrades." And, "Thou, Lord, didst found the earth in the beginning, and the heavens are the work of thy hands; they will perish, but thou remainest; they will all grow old like a garment, like a mantle thou wilt roll them up, and they will be changed. But thou art the same, and thy years will never end."

✠ *The Holy Gospel of Our Lord Jesus Christ According to John* [1:1-14]

In the beginning was the Word, and the Word was with God, and the Word was God. He was in the beginning with God; all things were made through him, and without him was not anything made that was made. In him was life, and the life was the light of men. The light shines in the darkness, and the darkness has not overcome it. There was a man sent from God, whose name was John. He came for testimony, to bear witness to the light, that all might believe through him. He was not the light, but came to bear witness to the light. The true light that enlightens every man was coming into the world. He was in the world, and the world was made through him, yet the world knew him not. He came to his own home, and his own people received him not. But to all who received him, who believed in his name, he gave power to become children of God; who were born, not of blood nor of the will of the flesh nor of the will of man, but of God. And the Word became flesh and dwelt among us, full of grace and truth; we have beheld his glory, glory as of the only Son from the Father.

First Sunday after Christmas

A Reading (Lesson) from the Book of Isaiah [61:10—62:3]

I will greatly rejoice in the Lord, my soul shall exult in my God; for he has clothed me with the garments of salvation, he has covered me with the robe of righteousness, as a bridegroom decks himself with a garland, and as a bride adorns herself with her jewels. For as the earth brings forth its shoots, and as a garden causes what is sown in it to spring up, so the Lord God will cause righteousness and praise to spring forth before all the nations. For Zion's sake I will not keep silent, and for Jerusalem's sake I will not rest, until her vindication goes forth as brightness, and her salvation as a burning torch. The nations shall see your vindication, and all the kings your glory; and you shall be called by a new name which the mouth of the Lord will give. You shall be a crown of beauty in the hand of the Lord, and a royal diadem in the hand of your God.

Psalm 147 [page 804]   or   *147:13-21* [page 805]

A Reading (Lesson) from the Letter of Paul to the Galatians [3:23-25; 4:4-7]

Now before faith came, we were confined under the law, kept under restraint until faith should be revealed. So that the law was our custodian until Christ came, that we might be justified by faith. But now that faith has come, we are no longer under a custodian. But when the time had fully come, God sent forth his Son, born of woman, born under the law, to redeem those who were under the law, so that we might receive adoption as sons. And because you are sons, God has sent the Spirit of his Son into our hearts, crying, "Abba! Father!" So through God you are no longer a slave but a son, and if a son then an heir.

✠ *The Holy Gospel of Our Lord Jesus Christ According to John* [1:1-18]

In the beginning was the Word, and the Word was with God, and the Word was God. He was in the beginning with God; all things were made through him, and without him was not anything made that was made. In him was life, and the life was the light of men. The light shines in the darkness, and the darkness has not overcome it. There was a man sent from God, whose name was John. He came for testimony, to bear witness to the light, that all might believe through him. He was not the light, but came to bear witness to the light. The true light that enlightens every man was coming into the world. He was in the world, and the world was made through him, yet the world knew him not. He came to his own home, and his own people received him not. But to all who received him, who believed in his name, he gave power to become children of God; who were born, not of blood nor of the will of the flesh nor of the will of man, but of God. And the Word became flesh and dwelt among us, full of grace and truth; we have beheld his glory, glory as of the only Son from the Father. (John bore witness to him, and cried, "This was he of whom I said, 'He who comes after me ranks before me, for he was before me.' ") And from his fullness have we all received, grace upon grace. For the law was given through Moses; grace and truth came through Jesus Christ. No one has ever seen God; the only Son, who is in the bosom of the Father, he has made him known.

The Holy Name of Our Lord Jesus Christ   *January 1*

A Reading (Lesson) from the Book of Exodus [34:1-8]

The Lord said to Moses, "Cut two tables of stone like the first; and I will write upon the tables the words that were on the first tables, which you broke. Be ready in the morning, and come up in the morning to Mount Sinai, and present yourself there to me on the top of the mountain. No man shall come up with you, and let no man be seen throughout all the mountain; let no flocks or herds feed before the mountain." So Moses cut two tables of stone like the first; and he rose early in the morning and went up on Mount Sinai, as the Lord had commanded him, and took in his hand two tables of stone. And the Lord descended in the cloud and stood with him there, and proclaimed the name of the Lord. The Lord passed before him, and proclaimed,"The Lord, the Lord, a God merciful and gracious, slow to anger, and abounding in steadfast love and faithfulness, keeping steadfast love for thousands, forgiving iniquity and transgression and sin, but who will by no means clear the guilty, visiting the iniquity of the fathers upon the children and the children's children, to the third and fourth generation." And Moses made haste to bow his head toward the earth, and worshiped.

Psalm 8 [page 592]

A Reading (Lesson) from the Letter of Paul to the Romans [1:1-7]

Paul, a servant of Jesus Christ, called to be an apostle, set apart for the gospel of God which he promised beforehand through his prophets in the holy scriptures, the gospel concerning his Son, who was descended from David according to the flesh, and designated Son of God in power according to the Spirit of holiness by his resurrection from the dead, Jesus Christ our Lord, through whom we have received grace and apostleship to bring about the obedience of faith for the sake of his name among all the nations, including yourselves who are called to belong to Jesus Christ; to all God's beloved in Rome, who are called to be saints: Grace to you and peace from God our Father and the Lord Jesus Christ

or the following

*A Reading (Lesson) from the Letter of Paul
to the Philippians* [2:9-13]

Therefore God has highly exalted Christ Jesus and
bestowed on him the name which is above every name,
that at the name of Jesus every knee should bow, in heaven
and on earth and under the earth, and every tongue confess
that Jesus Christ is Lord, to the glory of God the Father.
Therefore, my beloved, as you have always obeyed, so
now, not only as in my presence but much more in my
absence, work out your own salvation with fear and
trembling; for God is at work in you, both to will and to
work for his good pleasure.

✝ *The Holy Gospel of Our Lord Jesus Christ
According to Luke* [2:15-21]

When the angels went away from them into heaven, the
shepherds said to one another,"Let us go over to
Bethlehem and see this thing that has happened, which the
Lord has made known to us." And they went with haste,
and found Mary and Joseph, and the babe lying in a
manger. And when they saw it they made known the
saying which had been told them concerning this child;
and all who heard it wondered at what the shepherds told
them. But Mary kept all these things, pondering them in
her heart. And the shepherds returned, glorifying and
praising God for all they had heard and seen, as it had been
told them. And at the end of eight days, when he was
circumcised, he was called Jesus, the name given by the
angel before he was conceived in the womb.

Second Sunday after Christmas Day

A Reading (Lesson) from the Book of Jeremiah [31:7-14]

Thus says the Lord: "Sing aloud with gladness for Jacob, and raise shouts for the chief of the nations; proclaim, give praise, and say, 'The Lord has saved his people, the remnant of Israel.' Behold, I will bring them from the north country, and gather them from the farthest parts of the earth, among them the blind and the lame, the woman with child and her who is in travail, together; a great company, they shall return here. With weeping they shall come, and with consolations I will lead them back, I will make them walk by brooks of water, in a straight path in which they shall not stumble; for I am a father to Israel, and E'phraim is my first-born. Hear the word of the Lord, O nations, and declare it in the coastlands afar off; say, 'He who scattered Israel will gather him, and will keep him as a shepherd keeps his flock.' For the Lord has ransomed Jacob, and has redeemed him from hands too strong for him. They shall come and sing aloud on the height of Zion, and they shall be radiant over the goodness of the Lord, over the grain, the wine, and the oil, and over the young of the flock and the herd; their life shall be like a watered garden, and they shall languish no more. Then shall the maidens rejoice in the dance, and the young men and the old shall be merry. I will turn their mourning into joy, I will feast the soul of the priests with abundance, and my people shall be satisified with my goodness, says the Lord."

Psalm 84 [page 707]   or   *84:1-8* [page 707]

A Reading (Lesson) from the Letter of Paul to the Ephesians [1:3-6, 15-19a]

Blessed be the God and Father of our Lord Jesus Christ, who has blessed us in Christ with every spiritual blessing in the heavenly places, even as he chose us in him before the foundation of the world, that we should be holy and blameless before him. He destined us in love to be his sons through Jesus Christ, according to the purpose of his will, to the praise of his glorious grace which he freely bestowed on us in the Beloved. For this reason, because I have heard of your faith in the Lord Jesus and your love toward all the saints, I do not cease to give thanks for you, remembering you in my prayers, that the God of our Lord Jesus Christ, the Father of glory, may give you a spirit of wisdom and revelation in the knowledge of him, having the eyes of your hearts enlightened, that you may know what is the hope to which he has called you, what are the riches of his glorious inheritance in the saints, and what is the immeasurable greatness of his power in us who believe.

✝ *The Holy Gospel of Our Lord Jesus Christ According to Matthew* [2:13-15, 19-23]

Now when the wise men had departed, behold, an angel of the Lord appeared to Joseph in a dream and said, "Rise, take the child and his mother, and flee to Egypt, and remain there till I tell you; for Herod is about to search for the child, to destroy him." And he rose and took the child and his mother by night, and departed to Egypt, and remained there until the death of Herod. This was to fulfill what the Lord had spoken by the prophet, "Out of Egypt have I called my son." But when Herod died, behold, an angel of the Lord appeared in a dream to Joseph in Egypt, saying, "Rise, take the child and his mother, and go to the land of Israel, for those who sought the child's life are dead." And he rose and took the child and his mother, and went to the land of Israel. But when he heard that Archela'us reigned over Judea in place of his father Herod, he was afraid to go there, and being warned in a dream he withdrew to the district of Galilee. And he went and dwelt in a city called Nazareth, that what was spoken by the prophets might be fulfilled, "He shall be called a Nazarene."

or this

✝ *The Holy Gospel of Our Lord Jesus Christ According to Luke* [2:41-52]

Now the parents of Jesus went to Jerusalem every year at the feast of the Passover. And when he was twelve years old, they went up according to custom; and when the feast was ended, as they were returning, the boy Jesus stayed behind in Jerusalem. His parents did not know it, but supposing him to be in the company they went a day's journey, and they sought him among their kinsfolk and acquaintances; and when they did not find him, they returned to Jerusalem, seeking him. After three days they found him in the temple, sitting among the teachers, listening to them and asking them questions; and all who heard him were amazed at his understanding and his answers. And when they saw him they were astonished; and his mother said to him, "Son, why have you treated us so? Behold, your father and I have been looking for you anxiously." And he said to them, "How is it that you sought me? Did you not know that I must be in my Father's house?" And they did not understand the saying which he spoke to them. And he went down with them and came to Nazareth, and was obedient to them; and his mother kept all these things in her heart. And Jesus increased in wisdom and in stature, and in favor with God and man.

or this

Matthew 2:1-12 [page 27 below]

The Epiphany   *January 6*

A Reading (Lesson) from the Book of Isaiah [60:1-6,9]

Arise, shine; for your light has come, and the glory of the
Lord has risen upon you. For behold, darkness shall cover
the earth, and thick darkness the peoples; but the Lord will
arise upon you, and his glory will be seen upon you.
And nations shall come to your light, and kings to the
brightness of your rising. Lift up your eyes round about,
and see; they all gather together, they come to you; your
sons shall come from far, and your daughters shall be
carried in the arms. Then you shall see and be radiant, your
heart shall thrill and rejoice; because the abundance of the
sea shall be turned to you, the wealth of the nations shall
come to you. A multitude of camels shall cover you, the
young camels of Mid'ian and Ephah; all those from Sheba
shall come. They shall bring gold and frankincense, and
shall proclaim the praise of the Lord. For the coastlands
shall wait for me, the ships of Tarshish first, to bring your
sons from far, their silver and gold with them, for the name
of the Lord your God, and for the Holy One of Israel,
because he has glorified you.

Psalm 72 [page 685]   or   *72:1-2, 10-17* [page 685]

*A Reading (Lesson) from the Letter of Paul
to the Ephesians* [3:1-12]

I, Paul, a prisoner for Christ Jesus on behalf of you
Gentiles, assume that you have heard of the stewardship of
God's grace that was given to me for you, how the mystery
was made known to me by revelation, as I have written
briefly. When you read this you can perceive my insight
into the mystery of Christ, which was not made known to
the sons of men in other generations as it has now been
revealed to his holy apostles and prophets by the Spirit;

that is, how the Gentiles are fellow heirs, members of the same body, and partakers of the promise in Christ Jesus through the gospel. Of this gospel I was made a minister according to the gift of God's grace which was given me by the working of his power. To me, though I am the very least of all the saints, this grace was given, to preach to the Gentiles the unsearchable riches of Christ, and to make all men see what is the plan of the mystery hidden for ages in God who created all things; that through the church the manifold wisdom of God might now be made known to the principalities and powers in the heavenly places. This was according to the eternal purpose which he has realized in Christ Jesus our Lord, in whom we have boldness and confidence of access through our faith in him.

✝ *The Holy Gospel of Our Lord Jesus Christ According to Matthew* [2:1-12]

Now when Jesus was born in Bethlehem of Judea in the days of Herod the king, behold, wise men from the East came to Jerusalem, saying, "Where is he who has been born king of the Jews? For we have seen his star in the East, and have come to worship him." When Herod the king heard this, he was troubled, and all Jerusalem with him; and assembling all the chief priests and scribes of the people, he inquired of them where the Christ was to be born. They told him, "In Bethlehem of Judea; for so it is written by the prophet: 'And you, O Bethlehem, in the land of Judah, are by no means least among the rulers of Judah; for from you shall come a ruler who will govern my people Israel.'" Then Herod summoned the wise men secretly and ascertained from them what time the star appeared; and he sent them to Bethlehem, saying, "Go and search diligently for the child, and when you have found him bring me word, that I too may come and worship him." When they had heard the king they went their way; and lo, the star

which they had seen in the East went before them till it
came to rest over the place where the child was. When they
saw the star, they rejoiced exceedingly with great joy; and
going into the house they saw the child with Mary his
mother, and they fell down and worshiped him. Then,
opening their treasures, they offered him gifts, gold and
frankincense and myrrh. And being warned in a dream not
to return to Herod, they departed to their own country by
another way.

First Sunday after the Epiphany

A Reading (Lesson) from the Book of Isaiah [42:1-9]

Behold my servant, whom I uphold, my chosen, in whom
my soul delights; I have put my Spirit upon him, he will
bring forth justice to the nations. He will not cry or lift up
his voice, or make it heard in the street; a bruised reed he
will not break, and a dimly burning wick he will not
quench; he will faithfully bring forth justice. He will not
fail or be discouraged till he has established justice in the
earth; and the coastlands wait for his law. Thus says God,
the Lord, who created the heavens and stretched them out,
who spread forth the earth and what comes from it, who
gives breath to the people upon it and spirit to those
who walk in it: "I am the Lord, I have called you in
righteousness, I have taken you by the hand and kept you;
I have given you as a covenant to the people, a light to the
nations, to open the eyes that are blind, to bring out the
prisoners from the dungeon, from the prison those who sit
in darkness. I am the Lord, that is my name; my glory I give
to no other, nor my praise to graven images. Behold, the
former things have come to pass, and new things I now
declare; before they spring forth, I tell you of them."

Psalm 89:1-29 [page 713]   or   *89:20-29* [page 715]

A Reading (Lesson) from the Acts of the Apostles
[10:34-38]

Peter opened his mouth and said: "Truly I perceive that
God shows no partiality, but in every nation any one who
fears him and does what is right is acceptable to him. You
know the word which he sent to Israel, preaching good
news of peace by Jesus Christ (he is Lord of all), the word
which was proclaimed throughout all Judea, beginning
from Galilee after the baptism which John preached: how
God anointed Jesus of Nazareth with the Holy Spirit and
with power; how he went about doing good and healing all
that were oppressed by the devil, for God was with him."

✝ *The Holy Gospel of Our Lord Jesus Christ*
According to Matthew [3:13-17]

Jesus came from Galilee to the Jordan to John, to be
baptized by him. John would have prevented him,
saying,"I need to be baptized by you, and do you come to
me?" But Jesus answered him,"Let it be so now; for thus
it is fitting for us to fulfill all righteousness." Then he
consented. And when Jesus was baptized, he went up
immediately from the water, and behold, the heavens were
opened and he saw the Spirit of God descending like a
dove, and alighting on him; and lo, a voice from heaven,
saying,"This is my beloved Son, with whom I am well
pleased."

Second Sunday after the Epiphany

A Reading (Lesson) from the Book of Isaiah [49:1-7]

Listen to me, O coastlands, and hearken, you peoples from
afar. The Lord called me from the womb, from the body of
my mother he named my name. He made my mouth like a
sharp sword, in the shadow of his hand he hid me; he made

me a polished arrow, in his quiver he hid me away. And he said to me,"You are my servant, Israel, in whom I will be glorified." But I said,"I have labored in vain, I have spent my strength for nothing and vanity; yet surely my right is with the Lord, and my recompense with my God." And now the Lord says, who formed me from the womb to be his servant, to bring Jacob back to him, and that Israel might be gathered to him, for I am honored in the eyes of the Lord, and my God has become my strength—he says: "It is too light a thing that you should be my servant to raise up the tribes of Jacob and to restore the preserved of Israel; I will give you as a light to the nations, that my salvation may reach to the end of the earth." Thus says the Lord, the Redeemer of Israel and his Holy One, to one deeply despised, abhorred by the nations, the servant of rulers: "Kings shall see and arise; princes, and they shall prostrate themselves; because of the Lord, who is faithful, the Holy One of Israel, who has chosen you."

Psalm 40:1-10 [page 640]

A Reading (Lesson) from the First Letter of Paul to the Corinthians [1:1-9]

Paul, called by the will of God to be an apostle of Christ Jesus, and our brother Sos'thenes, to the church of God which is at Corinth, to those sanctified in Christ Jesus, called to be saints together with all those who in every place call on the name of our Lord Jesus Christ, both their Lord and ours: grace to you and peace from God our Father and the Lord Jesus Christ. I give thanks to God always for you because of the grace of God which was given you in Christ Jesus, that in every way you were enriched in him with all speech and all knowledge—even as the testimony to Christ was confirmed among you—so that you are not lacking in any spiritual gift, as you wait for the revealing of our Lord Jesus Christ; who will sustain you to the end, guiltless in the day of our Lord Jesus Christ. God is faithful, by whom you were called into the fellowship of his Son, Jesus Christ our Lord.

✝ *The Holy Gospel of Our Lord Jesus Christ According to John* [1:29-41]

John saw Jesus coming toward him, and said,"Behold, the Lamb of God, who takes away the sin of the world! This is he of whom I said, 'After me comes a man who ranks before me, for he was before me.' I myself did not know him; but for this I came baptizing with water, that he might be revealed to Israel." And John bore witness,"I saw the Spirit descend as a dove from heaven, and it remained on him. I myself did not know him; but he who sent me to baptize with water said to me, 'He on whom you see the Spirit descend and remain, this is he who baptizes with the Holy Spirit.' And I have seen and have borne witness that this is the Son of God." The next day again John was standing with two of his disciples; and he looked at Jesus as he walked, and said,"Behold, the Lamb of God!" The two disciples heard him say this, and they followed Jesus. Jesus turned, and saw them following, and said to them,"What do you seek?" And they said to him, "Rabbi" (which means Teacher),"where are you staying?" He said to them,"Come and see." They came and saw where he was staying; and they stayed with him that day, for it was about the tenth hour. One of the two who heard John speak, and followed him, was Andrew, Simon Peter's brother. He first found his brother Simon, and said to him,"We have found the Messiah" (which means Christ).

Third Sunday after the Epiphany

A Reading (Lesson) from the Book of Amos [3:1-8]

Hear this word that the Lord has spoken against you, O people of Israel, against the whole family which I brought up out of the land of Egypt: "You only have I known of all the families of the earth; therefore I will punish you for all your iniquities. Do two walk together, unless they have made an appointment? Does a lion roar in the forest, when he has no prey? Does a young lion cry out from his den, if he has taken nothing? Does a bird fall in a snare on the earth, when there is no trap for it? Does a snare spring up from the ground, when it has taken nothing? Is a trumpet blown in a city, and the people are not afraid? Does evil befall a city, unless the Lord has done it? Surely the Lord God does nothing, without revealing his secret to his servants the prophets. The lion has roared; who will not fear? The Lord God has spoken; who can but prophesy?"

Psalm 139:1-17 [page 794]   or   *139:1-11* [page 794]

A Reading (Lesson) from the First Letter of Paul to the Corinthians [1:10-17]

I appeal to you, brethren, by the name of our Lord Jesus Christ, that all of you agree and that there be no dissensions among you, but that you be united in the same mind and the same judgment. For it has been reported to me by Chlo'e's people that there is quarreling among you, my brethren. What I mean is that each one of you says, "I belong to Paul," or "I belong to Apol'los," or "I belong to Cephas," or "I belong to Christ." Is Christ divided? Was Paul crucified for you? Or were you baptized in the name of Paul? I am thankful that I baptized none of you except Crispus and Ga'ius; lest any one should say that you were baptized in my name. (I did baptize also the household of Steph'anas. Beyond that, I do not know whether I baptized any one else.) For Christ did not send me to baptize but to preach the gospel, and not with eloquent wisdom, lest the cross of Christ be emptied of its power.

✝ *The Holy Gospel of Our Lord Jesus Christ According to Matthew* [4:12-23]

When Jesus heard that John had been arrested, he withdrew into Galilee; and leaving Nazareth he went and dwelt in Caper'na-um by the sea, in the territory of Zeb'ulun and Naph'tali, that what was spoken by the prophet Isaiah might be fulfilled: "The land of Zeb'ulun and the land of Naph'tali, toward the sea, across the Jordan, Galilee of the Gentiles—the people who sat in darkness have seen a great light, and for those who sat in the region and shadow of death light has dawned." From that time Jesus began to preach, saying, "Repent, for the kingdom of heaven is at hand." As he walked by the Sea of Galilee, he saw two brothers, Simon who is called Peter and Andrew his brother, casting a net into the sea; for they were fishermen. And he said to them, "Follow me, and I will make you fishers of men." Immediately they left their nets and followed him. And going on from there he saw two other brothers, James the son of Zeb'edee and John his brother, in the boat with Zeb'edee their father, mending their nets, and he called them. Immediately they left the boat and their father, and followed him. And he went about all Galilee, teaching in their synagogues and preaching the gospel of the kingdom and healing every disease and every infirmity among the people.

Fourth Sunday after the Epiphany

A Reading (Lesson) from the Book of Micah [6:1-8]

Hear what the Lord says: Arise, plead your case before the mountains, and let the hills hear your voice. Hear, you mountains, the controversy of the Lord, and you enduring foundations of the earth; for the Lord has a controversy with his people, and he will contend with Israel. "O my people, what have I done to you? In what have I wearied you? Answer me! For I brought you up from the land of Egypt, and redeemed you from the house of bondage; and I sent before you Moses, Aaron, and Miriam. O my people, remember what Balak king of Moab devised, and what Balaam the son of Beor answered him, and what happened from Shittim to Gilgal, that you may know the saving acts of the Lord." — "With what shall I come before the Lord, and bow myself before God on high? Shall I come before him with burnt offerings, with calves a year old? Will the Lord be pleased with thousands of rams, with ten thousands of rivers of oil? Shall I give my first-born for my transgression, the fruit of my body for the sin of my soul?" He has showed you, O man, what is good; and what does the Lord require of you but to do justice, and to love kindness, and to walk humbly with your God?

Psalm 37: 1-18 [page 633]   or   *37:1-6* [page 633]

A Reading (Lesson) from the First Letter of Paul to the Corinthians [1:(18-25) 26-31]

The word of the cross is folly to those who are perishing, but to us who are being saved it is the power of God. For it is written, "I will destroy the wisdom of the wise, and the cleverness of the clever I will thwart." Where is the wise man? Where is the scribe? Where is the debater of this age? Has not God made foolish the wisdom of the world? For since, in the wisdom of God, the world did not know God through wisdom, it pleased God through the folly of what we preach to save those who believe. For Jews demand signs and Greeks seek wisdom, but we preach Christ crucified, a stumbling block to Jews and folly to Gentiles, but to those who are called, both Jews and Greeks, Christ the power of God and the wisdom of God. For the foolishness of God is wiser than men, and the weakness of God is stronger than men.

[*For*] consider your call, brethren; not many of you were wise according to worldly standards, not many were powerful, not many were of noble birth; but God chose what is foolish in the world to shame the wise, God chose what is weak in the world to shame the strong, God chose what is low and despised in the world, even things that are not, to bring to nothing things that are, so that no human being might boast in the presence of God. He is the source of your life in Christ Jesus, whom God made our wisdom, our righteousness and sanctification and redemption; therefore, as it is written, "Let him who boasts, boast of the Lord."

✝ *The Holy Gospel of Our Lord Jesus Christ
According to Matthew* [5:1-12]

Seeing the crowds, Jesus went up on the mountain, and when he sat down his disciples came to him. And he opened his mouth and taught them, saying: "Blessed are the poor in spirit, for theirs is the kingdom of heaven. Blessed are those who mourn, for they shall be comforted. Blessed are the meek, for they shall inherit the earth. Blessed are those who hunger and thirst for righteousness, for they shall be satisfied. Blessed are the merciful, for they shall obtain mercy. Blessed are the pure in heart, for they shall see God. Blessed are the peacemakers, for they shall be called sons of God. Blessed are those who are persecuted for righteousness' sake, for theirs is the kingdom of heaven. Blessed are you when men revile you and persecute you and utter all kinds of evil against you falsely on my account. Rejoice and be glad, for your reward is great in heaven, for so men persecuted the prophets who were before you."

Fifth Sunday after the Epiphany

A Reading (Lesson) from the Book of Habakkuk
[3:2-6, 17-19]

O Lord, I have heard the report of thee, and thy work, O Lord, do I fear. In the midst of the years renew it; in the midst of the years make it known; in wrath remember mercy. God came from Teman, and the Holy One from Mount Paran. His glory covered the heavens, and the earth was full of his praise. His brightness was like the light, rays flashed from his hand; and there he veiled his power. Before him went pestilence, and plague followed close behind. He stood and measured the earth; he looked and shook the nations; then the eternal mountains were scattered, the everlasting hills sank low. His ways were as of old. Though the fig tree do not blossom, nor fruit be on the vines, the produce of the olive fail and the fields yield no food, the flock be cut off from the fold and there be no herd in the stalls, yet I will rejoice in the Lord, I will joy in the God of my salvation. God, the Lord, is my strength; he makes my feet like hinds' feet, he makes me tread upon my high places.

Psalm 27 [page 617]   or   *27:1-7* [page 617]

*A Reading (Lesson) from the First Letter of Paul
to the Corinthians* [2:1-11]

When I came to you, brethren, I did not come proclaiming
to you the testimony of God in lofty words or wisdom. For
I decided to know nothing among you except Jesus Christ
and him crucified. And I was with you in weakness and in
much fear and trembling; and my speech and my message
were not in plausible words of wisdom, but in
demonstration of the Spirit and of power, that your faith
might not rest in the wisdom of men but in the power of
God. Yet among the mature we do impart wisdom,
although it is not a wisdom of this age or of the rulers of
this age, who are doomed to pass away. But we impart a
secret and hidden wisdom of God, which God decreed
before the ages for our glorification. None of the rulers of
this age understood this; for if they had, they would not
have crucified the Lord of glory. But, as it is written, "What
no eye has seen, nor ear heard, nor the heart of man
conceived, what God has prepared for those who love
him", God has revealed to us through the Spirit. For the
Spirit searches everything, even the depths of God. For
what person knows a man's thoughts except the spirit of
the man which is in him? So also no one comprehends the
thoughts of God except the Spirit of God.

✝ *The Holy Gospel of Our Lord Jesus Christ
According to Matthew* [5:13-20]

Jesus said, "You are the salt of the earth; but if salt has lost
its taste, how shall its saltness be restored? It is no longer
good for anything except to be thrown out and trodden
under foot by men. You are the light of the world. A city
set on a hill cannot be hid. Nor do men light a lamp and
put it under a bushel, but on a stand, and it gives light to all
in the house. Let your light so shine before men, that they
may see your good works and give glory to your Father

who is in heaven. Think not that I have come to abolish the law and the prophets; I have come not to abolish them but to fulfill them. For truly, I say to you, till heaven and earth pass away, not an iota, not a dot, will pass from the law until all is accomplished. Whoever then relaxes one of the least of these commandments and teaches men so, shall be called least in the kingdom of heaven; but he who does them and teaches them shall be called great in the kingdom of heaven. For I tell you, unless your righteousness exceeds that of the scribes and Pharisees, you will never enter the kingdom of heaven."

Sixth Sunday after the Epiphany

A Reading (Lesson) from the Book of Ecclesiasticus [15:11-20]

Do not say, "Because of the Lord I left the right way"; for he will not do what he hates. Do not say, "It was he who led me astray"; for he has no need of a sinful man. The Lord hates all abominations, and they are not loved by those who fear him. It was he who created man in the beginning, and he left him in the power of his own inclination. If you will, you can keep the commandments, and to act faithfully is a matter of your own choice. He has placed before you fire and water: stretch out your hand for whichever you wish. Before a man are life and death, and whichever he chooses will be given to him. For great is the wisdom of the Lord; he is mighty in power and sees everything; his eyes are on those who fear him, and he knows every deed of man. He has not commanded any one to be ungodly, and he has not given any one permission to sin.

Psalm 119:1-16 [page 763] or *119:9-16* [page 764]

A Reading (Lesson) from the First Letter of Paul to the Corinthians [3:1-9]

I, brethren, could not address you as spiritual men, but as men of the flesh, as babes in Christ. I fed you with milk, not solid food; for you were not ready for it; and even yet you are not ready, for you are still of the flesh. For while there is jealousy and strife among you, are you not of the flesh, and behaving like ordinary men? For when one says, "I belong to Paul," and another, "I belong to Apol'los," are you not merely men? What then is Apol'los? What is Paul? Servants through whom you believed, as the Lord assigned to each. I planted, Apol'los watered, but God gave the growth. So neither he who plants nor he who waters is anything, but only God who gives the growth. He who plants and he who waters are equal, and each shall receive his wages according to his labor. For we are God's fellow workers; you are God's field, God's building.

✠ *The Holy Gospel of Our Lord Jesus Christ According to Matthew* [5:21-24, 27-30, 33-37]

Jesus said, "You have heard that it was said to the men of old, 'You shall not kill; and whoever kills shall be liable to judgment.' But I say to you that every one who is angry with his brother shall be liable to judgment; whoever insults his brother shall be liable to the council, and whoever says, 'You fool!' shall be liable to the hell of fire. So if you are offering your gift at the altar, and there remember that your brother has something against you, leave your gift there before the altar and go; first be reconciled to your brother, and then come and offer your gift. You have heard that it was said, 'You shall not commit adultery.' But I say to you that every one who looks at a woman lustfully has already committed adultery with her in his heart. If your right eye causes you to sin, pluck it out and throw it away; it is better that you lose one of your members than that your whole body be thrown into hell. And if your right hand causes you to sin, cut it off and throw it away; it is better that you lose one of your members than that your whole body go into hell. Again you have heard that it was said to the men of old, 'You shall not swear falsely, but shall perform to the Lord what you have sworn.' But I say to you, Do not swear at all, either by heaven, for it is the throne of God, or by the earth, for it is his footstool, or by Jerusalem, for it is the city of the great King. And do not swear by your head, for you cannot make one hair white or black. Let what you say be simply 'Yes' or 'No'; anything more than this comes from evil."

Seventh Sunday after the Epiphany

A Reading (Lesson) from the Book of Leviticus
[19:1-2, 9-18]

The Lord said to Moses, "Say to all the congregation of the people of Israel, You shall be holy; for I the Lord your God am holy. When you reap the harvest of your land, you shall not reap your field to its very border, neither shall you gather the gleanings after your harvest. And you shall not strip your vineyard bare, neither shall you gather the fallen grapes of your vineyard; you shall leave them for the poor and for the sojourner: I am the Lord your God. You shall not steal, nor deal falsely, nor lie to one another. And you shall not swear by my name falsely, and so profane the name of your God: I am the Lord. You shall not oppress your neighbor or rob him. The wages of a hired servant shall not remain with you all night until the morning. You shall not curse the deaf or put a stumbling block before the blind, but you shall fear your God: I am the Lord. You shall do no injustice in judgment; you shall not be partial to the poor or defer to the great, but in righteousness shall you judge your neighbor. You shall not go up and down as a slanderer among your people, and you shall not stand forth against the life of your neighbor: I am the Lord. You shall not hate your brother in your heart, but you shall reason with your neighbor, lest you bear sin because of him. You shall not take vengeance or bear any grudge against the sons of your own people, but you shall love your neighbor as yourself: I am the Lord."

Psalm 71 [page 683]   or   *71:16-24* [page 684]

A Reading (Lesson) from the First Letter of Paul to the Corinthians [3:10-11, 16-23]

According to the grace of God given to me, like a skilled master builder I laid a foundation, and another man is building upon it. Let each man take care how he builds upon it. For no other foundation can any one lay than that which is laid, which is Jesus Christ. Do you not know that you are God's temple and that God's Spirit dwells in you? If any one destroys God's temple, God will destroy him. For God's temple is holy, and that temple you are. Let no one deceive himself. If any one among you thinks that he is wise in this age, let him become a fool that he may become wise. For the wisdom of this world is folly with God. For it is written, "He catches the wise in their craftiness," and again, "The Lord knows that the thoughts of the wise are futile." So let no one boast of men. For all things are yours, whether Paul or Apol'los or Cephas or the world or life or death or the present or the future, all are yours; and you are Christ's; and Christ is God's.

✝ *The Holy Gospel of Our Lord Jesus Christ*
According to Matthew [5:38-48]

Jesus said, "You have heard that it was said, 'An eye for an eye and a tooth for a tooth.' But I say to you, Do not resist one who is evil. But if any one strikes you on the right cheek, turn to him the other also; and if any one would sue you and take your coat, let him have your cloak as well; and if any one forces you to go one mile, go with him two miles. Give to him who begs from you, and do not refuse him who would borrow from you. You have heard that it was said, 'You shall love your neighbor and hate your enemy.' But I say to you, Love your enemies and pray for those who persecute you, so that you may be sons of your Father who is in heaven; for he makes his sun rise on the evil and on the good, and sends rain on the just and on the unjust. For if you love those who love you, what reward have you? Do not even the tax collectors do the same? And if you salute only your brethren, what more are you doing than others? Do not even the Gentiles do the same? You, therefore, must be perfect, as your heavenly Father is perfect."

Eighth Sunday after the Epiphany

A Reading (Lesson) from the Book of Isaiah [49:8-18]

Thus says the Lord: "In a time of favor I have answered you, in a day of salvation I have helped you; I have kept you and given you as a covenant to the people, to establish the land, to apportion the desolate heritages; saying to the prisoners, 'Come forth,' to those who are in darkness, 'Appear.' They shall feed along the ways, on all bare heights shall be their pasture; they shall not hunger or thirst, neither scorching wind nor sun shall smite them, for he who has pity on them will lead them, and by springs of water will guide them. And I will make all my mountains a way, and my highways shall be raised up. Lo, these shall come from afar, and lo, these from the north and from the west, and these from the land of Syene." Sing for joy, O heavens, and exult, O earth; break forth, O mountains, into singing! For the Lord has comforted his people, and will have compassion on his afflicted. But Zion said, "The Lord has forsaken me, my Lord has forgotten me." — "Can a woman forget her sucking child, that she should have no compassion on the son of her womb? Even these may forget, yet I will not forget you. Behold, I have graven you on the palms of my hands; your walls are continually before me. Your builders outstrip your destroyers, and those who laid you waste go forth from you. Lift up your eyes round about and see; they all gather, they come to you. As I live, says the Lord, you shall put them all on as an ornament, you shall bind them on as a bride does."

Psalm 62 [page 669] or *62:6-14* [page 669]

A Reading (Lesson) from the First Letter of Paul to the Corinthians [4:1-5 (6-7) 8-13]

This is how one should regard us, as servants of Christ and stewards of the mysteries of God. Moreover it is required of stewards that they be found trustworthy. But with me it is a very small thing that I should be judged by you or by any human court. I do not even judge myself. I am not aware of anything against myself, but I am not thereby acquitted. It is the Lord who judges me. Therefore do not pronounce judgment before the time, before the Lord comes, who will bring to light the things now hidden in darkness and will disclose the purposes of the heart. Then every man will receive his commendation from God.

I have applied all this to myself and Apol'los for your benefit, brethren, that you may learn by us not to go beyond what is written, that none of you may be puffed up in favor of one against another. For who sees anything different in you? What have you that you did not receive? If then you received it, why do you boast as if it were not a gift?

Already you are filled! Already you have become rich! Without us you have become kings! And would that you did reign, so that we might share the rule with you! For I think that God has exhibited us apostles as last of all, like men sentenced to death; because we have become a spectacle to the world, to angels and to men. We are fools for Christ's sake, but you are wise in Christ. We are weak, but you are strong. You are held in honor, but we in disrepute. To the present hour we hunger and thirst, we are ill-clad and buffeted and homeless, and we labor, working with our own hands. When reviled, we bless; when persecuted, we endure; when slandered, we try to conciliate; we have become, and are now, as the refuse of the world, the offscouring of all things.

✝ *The Holy Gospel of Our Lord Jesus Christ*
According to Matthew [6:24-34]

Jesus said, "No one can serve two masters; for either he will hate the one and love the other, or he will be devoted to the one and despise the other. You cannot serve God and mammon. Therefore I tell you, do not be anxious about your life, what you shall eat or what you shall drink, nor about your body, what you shall put on. Is not life more than food, and the body more than clothing? Look at the birds of the air: they neither sow nor reap nor gather into barns, and yet your heavenly Father feeds them. Are you not of more value than they? And which of you by being anxious can add one cubit to his span of life? And why are you anxious about clothing? Consider the lilies of the field, how they grow; they neither toil nor spin; yet I tell you, even Solomon in all his glory was not arrayed like one of these. But if God so clothes the grass of the field, which today is alive and tomorrow is thrown into the oven, will he not much more clothe you, O men of little faith? Therefore do not be anxious, saying, 'What shall we eat?' or 'What shall we drink?' or 'What shall we wear?' For the Gentiles seek all these things; and your heavenly Father knows that you need them all. But seek first his kingdom and his righteousness, and all these things shall be yours as well. Therefore do not be anxious about tomorrow, for tomorrow will be anxious for itself. Let the day's own trouble be sufficient for the day."

Last Sunday after the Epiphany

A Reading (Lesson) from the Book of Exodus
[24:12 (13-14) 15-18]

The Lord said to Moses, "Come up to me on the mountain, and wait there; and I will give you the tables of stone, with the law and the commandment, which I have written for their instruction."

> So Moses rose with his servant Joshua, and Moses went up into the mountain of God. And he said to the elders, "Tarry here for us, until we come to you again; and behold, Aaron and Hur are with you; whoever has a cause, let him go to them."

Then Moses went up on the mountain, and the cloud covered the mountain. The glory of the Lord settled on Mount Sinai, and the cloud covered it six days; and on the seventh day he called to Moses out of the midst of the cloud. Now the appearance of the glory of the Lord was like a devouring fire on the top of the mountain in the sight of the people of Israel. And Moses entered the cloud, and went up on the mountain. And Moses was on the mountain forty days and forty nights.

Psalm 99 [page 728]

A Reading (Lesson) from the Letter of Paul to the Philippians [3:7-14]

Whatever gain I had, I counted as loss for the sake of Christ. Indeed I count everything as loss because of the surpassing worth of knowing Christ Jesus my Lord. For his sake I have suffered the loss of all things, and count them as refuse, in order that I may gain Christ and be found in him, not having a righteousness of my own, based on law, but that which is through faith in Christ, the righteousness from God that depends on faith; that I may know him and the power of his resurrection, and may share his sufferings, becoming like him in his death, that if possible I may attain the resurrection from the dead. Not that I have already obtained this or am already perfect; but I press on to make it my own, because Christ Jesus has made me his own. Brethren, I do not consider that I have made it my own; but one thing I do, forgetting what lies behind and straining forward to what lies ahead, I press on toward the goal for the prize of the upward call of God in Christ Jesus.

✝ *The Holy Gospel of Our Lord Jesus Christ According to Matthew* [17:1-9]

Six days after Peter had acknowledged Jesus as the Christ, the Son of the living God, Jesus took with him Peter and James and John his brother, and led them up a high mountain apart. And he was transfigured before them, and his face shone like the sun, and his garments became white as light. And behold, there appeared to them Moses and Eli′jah, talking with him. And Peter said to Jesus, "Lord, it is well that we are here; if you wish, I will make three booths here, one for you and one for Moses and one for Eli'jah." He was still speaking, when lo, a bright cloud overshadowed them, and a voice from the cloud said, "This is my beloved Son, with whom I am well pleased; listen to him." When the disciples heard this, they fell on their faces, and were filled with awe. But Jesus came and touched them, saying, "Rise, and have no fear." And when they lifted up their eyes, they saw no one but Jesus only. And as they were coming down the mountain, Jesus commanded them, "Tell no one the vison, until the Son of man is raised from the dead."

Ash Wednesday

A Reading (Lesson) from the Book of Joel [2:1-2, 12-17]

Blow the trumpet in Zion; sound the alarm on my holy mountain! Let all the inhabitants of the land tremble, for the day of the Lord is coming, it is near, a day of darkness and gloom, a day of clouds and thick darkness! Like blackness there is spread upon the mountains a great and powerful people; their like has never been from of old, nor will be again after them through the years of all generations. "Yet even now," says the Lord, "return to me with all your heart, with fasting, with weeping, and with mourning; and rend your hearts and not your garments." Return to the Lord, your God, for he is gracious and merciful, slow to anger, and abounding in steadfast love, and repents of evil. Who knows whether he will not turn and repent, and leave a blessing behind him, a cereal offering and a drink offering for the Lord, your God? Blow the trumpet in Zion; sanctify a fast; call a solemn assembly; gather the people. Sanctify the congregation; assemble the elders; gather the children, even nursing infants. Let the bridegroom leave his room, and the bride her chamber. Between the vestibule and the altar let the priests, the ministers of the Lord, weep and say,"Spare thy people, O Lord, and make not thy heritage a reproach, a byword among the nations. Why should they say among the peoples,'Where is their God?' "

or this

A Reading (Lesson) from the Book of Isaiah [58:1-12]

Thus says the high and lofty One who inhabits eternity, whose name is Holy: "Cry aloud, spare not, lift up your voice like a trumpet; declare to my people their transgression, to the house of Jacob their sins. Yet they seek me daily, and delight to know my ways, as if they were a nation that did righteousness and did not forsake the ordinance of their God; they ask of me righteous judgments, they delight to draw near to God. 'Why have we fasted, and thou seest it not? Why have we humbled ourselves, and thou takest no knowledge of it?' Behold, in the day of your fast you seek your own pleasure, and oppress all your workers. Behold, you fast only to quarrel and to fight and to hit with wicked fist. Fasting like yours this day will not make your voice to be heard on high. Is such the fast that I choose, a day for a man to humble himself? Is it to bow down his head like a rush, and to spread sackcloth and ashes under him? Will you call this a fast, and a day acceptable to the Lord? Is not this the fast that I choose: to loose the bonds of wickedness, to undo the thongs of the yoke, to let the oppressed go free, and to break every yoke? Is it not to share your bread with the hungry, and bring the homeless poor into your house; when you see the naked, to cover him, and not to hide yourself from your own flesh? Then shall your light break forth like the dawn, and your healing shall spring up speedily; your righteousness shall go before you, the glory of the Lord shall be your rear guard. Then you shall call, and the Lord will answer; you shall cry, and he will say, Here I am. If you take away from the midst of you the yoke, the pointing of the finger, and speaking wickedness, if you pour yourself out for the hungry and satisfy the desire of the afflicted, then shall your light rise in the darkness and your gloom be as the noonday. And the Lord will guide you continually, and satisfy your desire with good things, and make your bones strong; and you shall be like a watered garden, like a spring of water, whose waters fail not. And your ancient ruins shall be rebuilt; you shall raise up the foundations of many generations; you shall be called the repairer of the breach, the restorer of streets to dwell in."

Psalm 103 [page 733]   or   *103:8-14* [page 733]

A Reading (Lesson) from the Second Letter of Paul to the Corinthians [5:20b—6:10]

We beseech you on behalf of Christ, be reconciled to God. For our sake he made him to be sin who knew no sin, so that in him we might become the righteousness of God. Working together with him, then, we entreat you not to accept the grace of God in vain. For he says,"At the acceptable time I have listened to you, and helped you on the day of salvation." Behold, now is the acceptable time; behold, now is the day of salvation. We put no obstacle in any one's way, so that no fault may be found with our ministry, but as servants of God we commend ourselves in every way: through great endurance, in afflictions, hardships, calamities, beatings, imprisonments, tumults, labors, watching, hunger; by purity, knowledge, forbearance, kindness, the Holy Spirit, genuine love, truthful speech, and the power of God; with the weapons of righteousness for the right hand and for the left; in honor and dishonor, in ill repute and good repute. We are treated as impostors, and yet are true; as unknown, and yet well known; as dying, and behold we live; as punished, and yet not killed; as sorrowful, yet always rejoicing; as poor, yet making many rich; as having nothing, and yet possessing everything.

✝ *The Holy Gospel of Our Lord Jesus Christ According to Matthew* [6:1-6,16-21]

Jesus said, "Beware of practicing your piety before men in order to be seen by them; for then you will have no reward from your Father who is in heaven. Thus, when you give alms, sound no trumpet before you, as the hypocrites do in the synagogues and in the streets, that they may be praised by men. Truly, I say to you, they have received their reward. But when you give alms, do not let your left hand know what your right hand is doing, so that your alms may be in secret; and your Father who sees in secret will reward you. And when you pray, you must not be like the hypocrites; for they love to stand and pray in the synagogues and at the street corners, that they may be seen by men. Truly, I say to you, they have received their reward. But when you pray, go into your room and shut the door and pray to your Father who is in secret; and your Father who sees in secret will reward you. And when you fast, do not look dismal, like the hypocrites, for they disfigure their faces that their fasting may be seen by men. Truly, I say to you, they have received their reward. But when you fast, anoint your head and wash your face, that your fasting may not be seen by men but by your Father who is in secret; and your Father who sees in secret will reward you. Do not lay up for yourselves treasures on earth, where moth and rust consume and where thieves break in and steal, but lay up for yourselves treasure in heaven, where neither moth nor rust consumes and where thieves do not break in and steal. For where your treasure is, there will your heart be also."

First Sunday in Lent

A Reading (Lesson) from the Book of Genesis
[2:4b-9, 15-17, 25 – 3:7]

In the day that the Lord God made the earth and the heavens, when no plant of the field was yet in the earth and no herb of the field had yet sprung up—for the Lord God had not caused it to rain upon the earth, and there was no man to till the ground; but a mist went up from the earth and watered the whole face of the ground—then the Lord God formed man of dust from the ground, and breathed into his nostrils the breath of life; and man became a living being. And the Lord God planted a garden in Eden, in the east; and there he put the man whom he had formed. And out of the ground the Lord God made to grow every tree that is pleasant to the sight and good for food, the tree of life also in the midst of the garden, and the tree of the knowledge of good and evil. The Lord God took the man and put him in the garden of Eden to till it and keep it. And the Lord God commanded the man, saying,"You may freely eat of every tree of the garden; but of the tree of the knowledge of good and evil you shall not eat, for in the day that you eat of it you shall die." And the man and his wife were both naked, and were not ashamed. Now the serpent was more subtle than any other wild creature that the Lord God had made. He said to the woman,"Did God say, 'You shall not eat of any tree of the garden'?" And the woman said to the serpent,"We may eat of the fruit of the trees of the garden; but God said, 'You shall not eat of the fruit of the tree which is in the midst of the garden, neither shall you touch it, lest you die.' " But the serpent said to the woman,"You will not die. For God knows that when you eat of it your eyes will be opened, and you will be like God, knowing good and evil." So when the woman saw that the tree was good for food, and that it was a delight to the eyes, and that the tree was to be desired to make one wise, she took of its fruit and ate; and she also gave some to her husband, and he ate. Then the eyes of both were opened, and they knew that they were naked; and they sewed fig leaves together and made themselves aprons.

Psalm 51 [page 656]   or   *51:1-13* [page 656]

A Reading (Lesson) from the Letter of Paul to the Romans [5:12-19 (20-21)]

As sin came into the world through one man and death through sin, and so death spread to all men because all men sinned—sin indeed was in the world before the law was given, but sin is not counted where there is no law. Yet death reigned from Adam to Moses, even over those whose sins were not like the transgression of Adam, who was a type of the one who was to come. But the free gift is not like the trespass. For if many died through one man's trespass, much more have the grace of God and the free gift in the grace of that one man Jesus Christ abounded for many. And the free gift is not like the effect of that one man's sin. For the judgment following one trespass brought condemnation, but the free gift following many trespasses brings justification. If, because of one man's trespass, death reigned through that one man, much more will those who receive the abundance of grace and the free gift of righteousness reign in life through the one man Jesus Christ. Then as one man's trespass led to condemnation for all men, so one man's act of righteousness leads to acquittal and life for all men. For as by one man's disobedience many were made sinners, so by one man's obedience many will be made righteous.

Law came in, to increase the trespass; but where sin increased, grace abounded all the more, so that, as sin reigned in death, grace also might reign through righteousness to eternal life through Jesus Christ our Lord.

✝ *The Holy Gospel of Our Lord Jesus Christ According to Matthew* [4:1-11]

After Jesus was baptized, he was led up by the Spirit into the wilderness to be tempted by the devil. And he fasted forty days and forty nights, and afterward he was hungry. And the tempter came and said to him, "If you are the Son of God, command these stones to become loaves of bread." But he answered, "It is written, 'Man shall not live by bread alone, but by every word that proceeds from the mouth of God.'" Then the devil took him to the holy city, and set him on the pinnacle of the temple, and said to him, "If you are the Son of God, throw yourself down; for it is written, 'He will give his angels charge of you', and 'On their hands they will bear you up, lest you strike your foot against a stone.'" Jesus said to him, "Again it is written, 'You shall not tempt the Lord your God.'" Again, the devil took him to a very high mountain, and showed him all the kingdoms of the world and the glory of them; and he said to him, "All these I will give you, if you will fall down and worship me." Then Jesus said to him, "Begone, Satan! for it is written, 'You shall worship the Lord your God and him only shall you serve.'" Then the devil left him, and behold, angels came and ministered to him.

Second Sunday in Lent

A Reading (Lesson) from the Book of Genesis [12:1-8]

The Lord said to Abram, "Go from your country and your kindred and your father's house to the land that I will show you. And I will make of you a great nation, and I will bless you, and make your name great, so that you will be a blessing. I will bless those who bless you, and him who curses you I will curse; and by you all the families of the earth shall bless themselves." So Abram went, as the Lord had told him; and Lot went with him. Abram was seventy-five years old when he departed from Haran. And Abram took Sar'ai his wife, and Lot his brother's son, and all their possessions which they had gathered, and the persons that they had gotten in Haran; and they set forth to go to the land of Canaan. When they had come to the land of Canaan, Abram passed through the land to the place at Shechem, to the oak of Moreh. At that time the Canaanites were in the land. Then the Lord appeared to Abram, and said, "To your descendants I will give this land." So he built there an altar to the Lord, who had appeared to him. Thence he removed to the mountain on the east of Bethel, and pitched his tent, with Bethel on the west and Ai on the east; and there he built an altar to the Lord and called on the name of the Lord.

Psalm 33:12-22 [page 626]

A Reading (Lesson) from the Letter of Paul to the Romans
[4:1-5 (6-12) 13-17]

What then shall we say about Abraham, our forefather according to the flesh? For if Abraham was justified by works, he has something to boast about, but not before God. For what does the scripture say? "Abraham believed God, and it was reckoned to him as righteousness." Now to one who works, his wages are not reckoned as a gift but as his due. And to one who does not work but trusts him who justifies the ungodly, his faith is reckoned as righteousness.

So also David pronounces a blessing upon the man to whom God reckons righteousness apart from works: "Blessed are those whose iniquities are forgiven, and whose sins are covered; blessed is the man against whom the Lord will not reckon his sin." Is this blessing pronounced only upon the circumcised, or also upon the uncircumcised? We say that faith was reckoned to Abraham as righteousness. How then was it reckoned to him? Was it before or after he had been circumcised? It was not after, but before he was circumcised. He received circumcision as a sign or seal of the righteousness which he had by faith while he was still uncircumcised. The purpose was to make him the father of all who believe without being circumcised and who thus have righteousness reckoned to them, and likewise the father of the circumcised who are not merely circumcised but also follow the example of the faith which our father Abraham had before he was circumcised.

The promise to Abraham and his descendants, that they should inherit the world, did not come through the law but through the righteousness of faith. If it is the adherents of the law who are to be the heirs, faith is null and the promise is void. For the law brings wrath, but where there is no law there is no transgression. That is why it depends on faith, in order that the promise may rest on grace and be guaranteed to all his descendants—not only to the adherents of the law but also to those who share the faith of Abraham, for he is the father of us all, as it is written, "I have made you the father of many nations"—in the presence of the God in whom he believed, who gives life to the dead and calls into existence the things that do not exist.

✝ *The Holy Gospel of Our Lord Jesus Christ According to John* [3:1-17]

There was a man of the Pharisees, named Nicode′mus, a ruler of the Jews. This man came to Jesus by night and said to him, "Rabbi, we know that you are a teacher come from God; for no one can do these signs that you do, unless God is with him." Jesus answered him, "Truly, truly, I say to you, unless one is born anew, he cannot see the kingdom of God." Nicode'mus said to him, "How can a man be born when he is old? Can he enter a second time into his mother's womb and be born?" Jesus answered, "Truly, truly, I say to you, unless one is born of water and the Spirit, he cannot enter the kingdom of God. That which is born of the flesh is flesh, and that which is born of the Spirit is spirit. Do not marvel that I said to you, 'You must be born anew.' The wind blows where it wills, and you hear the sound of it, but you do not know whence it comes or whither it goes; so it is with every one who is born of the Spirit." Nicode'mus said to him, "How can this be?" Jesus answered him, "Are you a teacher of Israel, and yet you do not understand this? Truly, truly, I say to you, we speak of what we know, and bear witness to what we have seen; but you do not receive our testimony. If I have told you earthly things and you do not believe, how can you believe if I tell you heavenly things? No one has ascended into heaven but he who descended from heaven, the Son of man. And as Moses lifted up the serpent in the wilderness, so must the Son of man be lifted up, that whoever believes in him may have eternal life." For God so loved the world that he gave his only Son, that whoever believes in him should not perish but have eternal life. For God sent the Son into the world, not to condemn the world, but that the world might be saved through him.

Third Sunday in Lent

A Reading (Lesson) from the Book of Exodus [17:1-7]

All the congregation of the people of Israel moved on from the wilderness of Sin by stages, according to the commandment of the Lord, and camped at Reph'idim; but there was no water for the people to drink. Therefore the people found fault with Moses, and said, "Give us water to drink." And Moses said to them, "Why do you find fault with me? Why do you put the Lord to the proof?" But the people thirsted there for water, and the people murmured against Moses, and said, "Why did you bring us up out of Egypt, to kill us and our children and our cattle with thirst?" So Moses cried to the Lord, "What shall I do with this people? They are almost ready to stone me." And the Lord said to Moses, "Pass on before the people, taking with you some of the elders of Israel; and take in your hand the rod with which you struck the Nile, and go. Behold, I will stand before you there on the rock at Horeb; and you shall strike the rock, and water shall come out of it, that the people may drink." And Moses did so, in the sight of the elders of Israel. And he called the name of the place Massah and Mer'ibah, because of the faultfinding of the children of Israel, and because they put the Lord to the proof by saying, "Is the Lord among us or not?"

Psalm 95 [page 724] or *95:6-11* [page 725]

A Reading (Lesson) from the Letter of Paul to the Romans [5:1-11]

Since we are justified by faith, we have peace with God through our Lord Jesus Christ. Through him we have obtained access to this grace in which we stand, and we rejoice in our hope of sharing the glory of God. More than that, we rejoice in our sufferings, knowing that suffering produces endurance, and endurance produces character, and character produces hope, and hope does not disappoint us, because God's love has been poured into our hearts through the Holy Spirit which has been given to us. While we were still weak, at the right time Christ died for the ungodly. Why, one will hardly die for a righteous man—though perhaps for a good man one will dare even to die. But God shows his love for us in that while we were yet sinners Christ died for us. Since, therefore, we are now justified by his blood, much more shall we be saved by him from the wrath of God. For if while we were enemies we were reconciled to God by the death of his Son, much more, now that we are reconciled, shall we be saved by his life. Not only so, but we also rejoice in God through our Lord Jesus Christ, through whom we have now received our reconciliation.

✝ *The Holy Gospel of Our Lord Jesus Christ According to John* [4:5-26 (27-38) 39-42]

Jesus came to a city of Samar'ia, called Sy'char, near the field that Jacob gave to his son Joseph. Jacob's well was there, and so Jesus, wearied as he was with his journey, sat down beside the well. It was about the sixth hour. There came a woman of Samar'ia to draw water. Jesus said to her, "Give me a drink." For his disciples had gone away into the city to buy food. The Samaritan woman said to him, "How is it that you, a Jew, ask a drink of me, a woman of Samar'ia?" For Jews have no dealings with Samaritans. Jesus answered her, "If you knew the gift of God, and who it is that is saying to you, 'Give me a drink,' you would have asked him, and he would have given you living water." The woman said to him, "Sir, you have nothing to draw with, and the well is deep; where do you get that living water? Are you greater than our father Jacob, who gave us the well, and drank from it himself, and his sons, and his cattle?" Jesus said to her, "Every one who drinks of this water will thirst again, but whoever drinks of the water that I shall give him will never thirst; the water that I shall give him will become in him a spring of water welling up to eternal life." The woman said to him, "Sir, give me this water, that I may not thirst, nor come here to draw." Jesus said to her, "Go, call your husband, and come here." The woman answered him, "I have no husband." Jesus said to her, "You are right in saying, 'I have no husband'; for you have had five husbands, and he whom you now have is not your husband; this you said truly." The woman said to him, "Sir, I perceive that you are a prophet. Our fathers worshiped on this mountain; and you say that in Jerusalem is the place where men ought to worship." Jesus said to her, "Woman, believe me, the hour is coming when neither on this mountain nor in Jerusalem will you worship the Father. You worship what you do not know; we worship what we know, for salvation is from the Jews. But the hour is coming, and now is, when the true worshipers will worship the Father in spirit and truth, for such the Father seeks to worship him. God is spirit, and those who worship him must worship in spirit and truth." The woman said to him, "I know that Messiah is coming (he who is called Christ); when he comes, he will show us all things." Jesus said to her, "I who speak to you am he."

Just then his disciples came. They marveled that he was talking with a woman, but none said, "What do you wish?" or, "Why are you talking with her?" So the woman left her water jar, and went away into the city, and said to the people, "Come, see a man who told me all that I ever did. Can this be the Christ?" They went out of the city and were coming to him. Meanwhile the disciples besought him, saying, "Rabbi, eat." But he said to them, "I have food to eat of which you do not know." So the disciples said to one another, "Has any one brought him food?" Jesus said to them, "My food is to do the will of him who sent me, and to accomplish his work. Do you not say, 'There are yet four months, then comes the harvest'? I tell you, lift up your eyes, and see how the fields are already white for harvest. He who reaps receives wages, and gathers fruit for eternal life, so that sower and reaper may rejoice together. For here the saying holds true, 'One sows and another reaps.' I sent you to reap that for which you did not labor; others have labored, and you have entered into their labor."

[*The woman ran into the city and said to them, "Come, see a man who told me all that I ever did. Can this be the Christ?" So, many of the city were coming to him.*] Many Samaritans from the city believed in him because of the woman's testimony, "He told me all that I ever did." So when the Samaritans came to him, they asked him to stay with them; and he stayed there two days. And many more believed because of his word. They said to the woman, "It is no longer because of your words that we believe, for we have heard for ourselves, and we know that this is indeed the Savior of the world."

Fourth Sunday in Lent

A Reading (Lesson) from the First Book of Samuel [16:1-13]

The Lord said to Samuel, "How long will you grieve over Saul, seeing I have rejected him from being king over Israel? Fill your horn with oil, and go; I will send you to Jesse the Bethlehemite, for I have provided for myself a king among his sons." And Samuel said, "How can I go? If Saul hears it, he will kill me." And the Lord said, "Take a heifer with you, and say, 'I have come to sacrifice to the Lord.' And invite Jesse to the sacrifice, and I will show you what you shall do; and you shall anoint for me him whom I name to you." Samuel did what the Lord commanded, and came to Bethlehem. The elders of the city came to meet him trembling, and said, "Do you come peaceably?" And he said, "Peaceably; I have come to sacrifice to the Lord;

consecrate yourselves, and come with me to the sacrifice." And he consecrated Jesse and his sons, and invited them to the sacrifice. When they came, he looked on Eli'ab and thought,"Surely the Lord's anointed is before him." But the Lord said to Samuel,"Do not look on his appearance or on the height of his stature, because I have rejected him; for the Lord sees not as man sees; man looks on the outward appearance, but the Lord looks on the heart." Then Jesse called Abin'adab, and made him pass before Samuel. And he said,"Neither has the Lord chosen this one." Then Jesse made Shammah pass by. And he said,"Neither has the Lord chosen this one." And Jesse made seven of his sons pass before Samuel. And Samuel said to Jesse,"The Lord has not chosen these." And Samuel said to Jesse,"Are all your sons here?" And he said,"There remains yet the youngest, but behold, he is keeping the sheep." And Samuel said to Jesse,"Send and fetch him; for we will not sit down till he comes here." And he sent, and brought him in. Now he was ruddy, and had beautiful eyes, and was handsome. And the Lord said,"Arise, anoint him; for this is he." Then Samuel took the horn of oil, and anointed him in the midst of his brothers; and the Spirit of the Lord came mightily upon David from that day forward. And Samuel rose up, and went to Ramah.

Psalm 23 [page 612]

A Reading (Lesson) from the Letter of Paul to the Ephesians [5:(1-7)8-14]

Be imitators of God, as beloved children. And walk in love, as Christ loved us and gave himself up for us, a fragrant offering and sacrifice to God. But fornication and all impurity of covetousness must not even be named among you, as is fitting among saints. Let there be no filthiness, nor silly talk, nor levity, which are not fitting; but instead let there be thanksgiving. Be sure of this, that no fornicator or impure man, or one who is covetous (that is, an idolater), has any inheritance in the kingdom of Christ and of God. Let no one deceive you with empty words, for it is because of these things that the wrath of God comes upon the sons of disobedience. Therefore do not associate with them, for

Once you were darkness, but now you are light in the Lord; walk as children of light (for the fruit of light is found in all that is good and right and true), and try to learn what is pleasing to the Lord. Take no part in the unfruitful works of darkness, but instead expose them. For it is a shame even to speak of the things that they do in secret; but when anything is exposed by the light it becomes visible, for anything that becomes visible is light. Therefore it is said,"Awake, O sleeper, and arise from the dead, and Christ shall give you light."

✝ *The Holy Gospel of Our Lord Jesus Christ According to John* [9:1-13 (14-27) 28-38]

Jesus saw a man blind from his birth. And his disciples asked him,"Rabbi, who sinned, this man or his parents, that he was born blind?" Jesus answered,"It was not that this man sinned, or his parents, but that the works of God might be made manifest in him. We must work the works of him who sent me, while it is day; night comes, when no one can work. As long as I am in the world, I am the light of the world." As he said this, he spat on the ground and made clay of the spittle and anointed the man's eyes with the clay, saying to him,"Go wash in the pool of Silo'am" (which means Sent). So he went and washed and came back seeing. The neighbors and those who had seen him before as a beggar, said,"Is not this the man who used to sit and beg?" Some said,"It is he"; others said,"No, but he is like him." He said,"I am the man." They said to him, "Then how were your eyes opened?" He answered, "The man called Jesus made clay and anointed my eyes and said to me, 'Go to Silo'am and wash'; so I went and washed and received my sight." They said to him, "Where is he?" He said, "I do not know." They brought to the Pharisees the man who had formerly been blind.

Now it was a sabbath day when Jesus made the clay and opened his eyes. The Pharisees again asked him how he had received his sight. And he said to them, "He put clay on my eyes, and I washed, and I see." Some of the Pharisees said, "This man is not from God, for he does not keep the sabbath." But others said, "How can a man who is a sinner do such signs?" There was a division among them. So they again said to the blind man, "What do you say about him, since he has opened your eyes?" He said, "He is a prophet." The Jews did not believe that he had been blind and had received his sight, until they called the parents of the man who had received his sight, and asked them, "Is this your son, who you say was born blind? How then does he now see?" His parents answered, "We know that this is our son, and that he was born blind; but how he now sees we do not know, nor do we know who opened his eyes. Ask him; he is of age, he will speak for himself." His parents said this because they feared the Jews, for the Jews had already agreed that if any one should confess him to be Christ, he was to be put out of the synagogue. Therefore his parents said, "He is of age, ask him." So for the second time they called the man who had been blind, and said to him, "Give God the praise; we know that this man is a sinner." He answered, "Whether he is a sinner, I do not know; one thing I know, that though I was blind, now I see." They said to him, "What did he do to you? How did he open your eyes?" He answered them, "I have told you already, and you would not listen.

Why do you want to hear it again? Do you too want to become his disciples?"

[*Now it was a sabbath day when Jesus opened his eyes. There was a division among the Pharisees. They questioned the man a second time. He told them that the man who opened his eyes was a prophet. But they called him a sinner, and accused the man who was blind of being his disciple.*]

And they reviled him, saying, "You are his disciple, but we are disciples of Moses. We know that God has spoken to Moses, but as for this man, we do not know where he comes from." The man answered, "Why, this is a marvel! You do not know where he comes from, and yet he opened my eyes. We know that God does not listen to sinners, but if any one is a worshiper of God and does his will, God listens to him. Never since the world began has it been heard that any one opened the eyes of a man born blind. If this man were not from God, he could do nothing." They answered him, "You were born in utter sin, and would you teach us?" And they cast him out. Jesus heard that they had cast him out, and having found him he said, "Do you believe in the Son of man?" He answered, "And who is he, sir, that I may believe in him?" Jesus said to him, "You have seen him, and it is he who speaks to you." He said, "Lord, I believe"; and he worshiped him.

Fifth Sunday in Lent

A Reading (Lesson) from the Book of Ezekiel
[37:1-3 (4-10) 11-14]

The hand of the Lord was upon me, and he brought me out by the Spirit of the Lord, and set me down in the midst of the valley; it was full of bones. And he led me round among them; and behold, there were very many upon the valley; and lo, they were very dry. And he said to me, "Son of man, can these bones live?" And I answered, "O Lord God, thou knowest."

Again he said to me, "Prophesy to these bones, and say to them, O dry bones, hear the word of the Lord. Thus says the Lord God to these bones: Behold, I will cause breath to enter you, and you shall live. And I will lay sinews upon you, and will cause flesh to come upon you, and cover you with skin, and put breath in you, and you shall live; and you shall know that I am the Lord." So I prophesied as I was commanded; and as I prophesied, there was a noise, and behold, a rattling; and the bones came together, bone to its bone. And as I looked, there were sinews on them, and flesh had come upon them, and skin had covered them; but there was no breath in them. Then he said to me, "Prophesy to the breath, prophesy, son of man, and say to the breath, Thus says the Lord God: Come from the four winds, O breath, and breathe upon these slain, that they may live." So I prophesied as he commanded me, and the breath came into them, and they lived, and stood upon their feet, an exceedingly great host.

Then he said to me, "Son of man, these bones are the whole house of Israel. Behold, they say, 'Our bones are dried up, and our hope is lost; we are clean cut off.' Therefore prophesy, and say to them, Thus says the Lord God: Behold, I will open your graves, and raise you from your graves, O my people; and I will bring you home into the land of Israel. And you shall know that I am the Lord, when I open your graves, and raise you from your graves, O my people. And I will put my Spirit within you, and you shall live, and I will place you in your own land; then you shall know that I, the Lord, have spoken, and I have done it, says the Lord."

Psalm 130 [page 784]

A Reading (Lesson) from the letter of Paul to the Romans
[6:16-23]

Do you not know that if you yield yourselves to any one as
obedient slaves, you are slaves of the one whom you obey,
either of sin, which leads to death, or of obedience, which
leads to righteousness? But thanks be to God, that you
who were once slaves of sin have become obedient from
the heart to the standard of teaching to which you were
committed, and, having been set free from sin, have
become slaves of righteousness. I am speaking in human
terms, because of your natural limitations. For just as you
once yielded your members to impurity and to greater and
greater iniquity, so now yield your members to
righteousness for sanctification. When you were slaves of
sin, you were free in regard to righteousness. But then what
return did you get from the things of which you are now
ashamed? The end of those things is death. But now that
you have been set free from sin and have become slaves of
God, the return you get is sanctification and its end, eternal
life. For the wages of sin is death, but the free gift of God is
eternal life in Christ Jesus our Lord.

✝ *The Holy Gospel of Our Lord Jesus Chirst
According to John* [11: (1-16) 17-44]

Now a certain man was ill, Laz'arus of Bethany, the
village of Mary and her sister Martha. It was Mary who
anointed the Lord with ointment and wiped his feet with
her hair, whose brother Laz'arus was ill. So the sisters
sent to him, saying, "Lord, he whom you love is ill." But
when Jesus heard it he said, "This illness is not unto
death; it is for the glory of God, so that the Son of God
may be glorified by means of it." Now Jesus loved
Martha and her sister and Laz'arus. So when he heard
that he was ill, he stayed two days longer in the place
where he was. Then after this he said to the disciples,

"Let us go into Judea again." The disciples said to
him, "Rabbi, the Jews were but now seeking to stone you,
and are you going there again?" Jesus answered,
"Are there not twelve hours in the day? If any one walks
in the day, he does not stumble, because he sees the light
of this world. But if any one walks in the night, he
stumbles, because the light is not in him." Thus he
spoke, and then he said to them, "Our friend Laz'arus
has fallen asleep, but I go to awake him out of sleep."
The disciples said to him, "Lord, if he has fallen asleep,
he will recover." Now Jesus had spoken of his death, but
they thought he meant taking rest in sleep. Then Jesus
told them plainly, "Laz'arus is dead; and for your sake I
am glad that I was not there, so that you may believe.
But let us go to him." Thomas, called the Twin, said to
his fellow disciples, "Let us also go, that we may die
with him."

[*Laz'arus of Bethany, brother of Mary and Martha, was ill.
The sisters sent to Jesus to tell him. Jesus waited for two
days, and then he told his disciples, "Laz'arus is dead; let us
go to him."*]

When Jesus came to Bethany, he found that Laz'arus had
already been in the tomb four days. Bethany was near
Jerusalem, about two miles off, and many of the Jews had
come to Martha and Mary to console them concerning
their brother. When Martha heard that Jesus was coming,
she went and met him, while Mary sat in the house.
Martha said to Jesus, "Lord, if you had been here, my
brother would not have died. And even now I know that
whatever you ask from God, God will give you." Jesus said
to her, "Your brother will rise again." Martha said to
him, "I know that he will rise again in the resurrection at
the last day." Jesus said to her, "I am the resurrection and
the life; he who believes in me, though he die, yet shall he

live, and whoever lives and believes in me shall never die.
Do you believe this?" She said to him, "Yes, Lord; I believe
that you are the Christ, the Son of God, he who is coming
into the world." When she had said this, she went and
called her sister Mary, saying quietly, "The Teacher is here
and is calling for you." And when she heard it, she rose
quickly and went to him. Now Jesus had not yet come to
the village, but was still in the place where Martha had met
him. When the Jews who were with her in the house,
consoling her, saw Mary rise quickly and go out, they
followed her, supposing that she was going to the tomb to
weep there. Then Mary, when she came where Jesus was
and saw him, fell at his feet, saying to him, "Lord, if you
had been here, my brother would not have died." When
Jesus saw her weeping, and the Jews who came with her
also weeping, he was deeply moved in spirit and troubled;
and he said, "Where have you laid him?" They said to him,
"Lord, come and see." Jesus wept. So the Jews said, "See
how he loved him!" But some of them said, "Could not he
who opened the eyes of the blind man have kept this man
from dying?" Then Jesus, deeply moved again, came to the
tomb; it was a cave, and a stone lay upon it. Jesus
said, "Take away the stone." Martha, the sister of the dead
man, said to him, "Lord, by this time there will be an odor,
for he has been dead four days." Jesus said to her, "Did I
not tell you that if you would believe you would see the
glory of God?" So they took away the stone. And Jesus
lifted up his eyes and said, "Father, I thank thee that thou
hast heard me. I knew that thou hearest me always, but I
have said this on account of the people standing by, that
they may believe that thou didst send me." When he had
said this, he cried with a loud voice, "Laz'arus, come
out." The dead man came out, his hands and feet bound
with bandages, and his face wrapped with a cloth. Jesus
said to them, "Unbind him, and let him go."

The Sunday of the Passion: Palm Sunday

At the Liturgy of the Palms

✝ *The Holy Gospel of Our Lord Jesus Christ According to Matthew* [21:1-11]

When Jesus and his disciples drew near to Jerusalem and came to Beth'phage, to the Mount of Olives, then Jesus sent two disciples, saying to them, "Go into the village opposite you, and immediately you will find an ass tied, and a colt with her; untie them and bring them to me. If any one says anything to you, you shall say, 'The Lord has need of them,' and he will send them immediately." This took place to fulfill what was spoken by the prophet, saying, "Tell the daughter of Zion, Behold, your king is coming to you, humble, and mounted on an ass, and on a colt, the foal of an ass." The disciples went and did as Jesus had directed them; they brought the ass and the colt, and put their garments on them, and he sat thereon. Most of the crowd spread their garments on the road, and others cut branches from the trees and spread them on the road. And the crowds that went before him and that followed him shouted, "Hosanna to the Son of David! Blessed is he who comes in the name of the Lord! Hosanna in the highest!" And when he entered Jerusalem, all the city was stirred, saying, "Who is this?" And the crowds said, "This is the prophet Jesus from Nazareth of Galilee."

The Blessing over the Branches follows
[page 271 of the Prayer Book]

Processional Psalm 118:19-29 [page 762]

At the Liturgy of the Word

A Reading (Lesson) from the Book of Isaiah [45:21-25]

Thus says the Lord,"Declare and present your case; let them take counsel together! Who told this long ago? Who declared it of old? Was it not I, the Lord? And there is no other god besides me, a righteous God and a Savior; there is none besides me. Turn to me and be saved, all the ends of the earth! For I am God, and there is no other. By myself I have sworn, from my mouth has gone forth in righteousness a word that shall not return: 'To me every knee shall bow, every tongue shall swear.' Only in the Lord, it shall be said of me, are righteousness and strength; to him shall come and be ashamed, all who were incensed against him. In the Lord all the offspring of Israel shall triumph and glory."

or this

Isaiah 52:13 —53:12 [page 93 below]

Psalm 22:1-21 [page 610]   or   *22:1-11* [page 610]

A Reading (Lesson) from the letter of Paul to the Philippians [2:5-11]

Have this mind among yourselves, which is yours in Christ Jesus, who, though he was in the form of God, did not count equality with God a thing to be grasped, but emptied himself, taking the form of a servant, being born in the likeness of men. And being found in human form he humbled himself and became obedient unto death, even death on a cross. Therefore God has highly exalted him and bestowed on him the name which is above every name, that at the name of Jesus every knee should bow, in heaven and on earth and under the earth, and every tongue confess that Jesus Christ is Lord, to the glory of God the Father.

The Passion of Our Lord Jesus Christ
According to Matthew
[26:36—27:54(55-66)]   or   [27:1-54(55-66)]

The customary responses before and after the Gospel are omitted.

The shorter form of the Passion [Matthew 27:1-54(55-66)] begins on page 75.

The Passion may be read by one or more persons.

The congregation may be seated for the first part of the Passion. At the verse which mentions the arrival at Golgotha [Matthew 27:33], page 78, all stand.

Narrator Jesus went to a place called Gethsem'ane, and he said to his disciples,

Jesus Sit here, while I go yonder and pray.

Narrator And taking with him Peter and the two sons of Zeb'edee, he began to be sorrowful and troubled. Then he said to them,

Jesus My soul is very sorrowful, even to death; remain here, and watch with me.

Narrator And going a little farther he fell on his face and prayed,

Jesus My Father, if it be possible, let this cup pass from me; nevertheless, not as I will, but as thou wilt.

Narrator And he came to the disciples and found them sleeping; and he said to Peter,

Jesus So, could you not watch with me one hour? Watch and pray that you may not enter into temptation; the spirit indeed is willing, but the flesh is weak.

Narrator   Again, for the second time, he went away and prayed,

Jesus   My Father, if this cannot pass unless I drink it, thy will be done.

Narrator   And again he came and found them sleeping, for their eyes were heavy. So, leaving them again, he went away and prayed for the third time, saying the same words. Then he came to the disciples and said to them,

Jesus   Are you still sleeping and taking your rest? Behold, the hour is at hand, and the Son of man is betrayed into the hands of sinners. Rise, let us be going; see, my betrayer is at hand.

Narrator   While he was still speaking, Judas came, one of the twelve, and with him a great crowd with swords and clubs, from the chief priests and the elders of the people. Now the betrayer had given them a sign, saying,

Reader   The one I shall kiss is the man; seize him.

Narrator   And he came up to Jesus at once and said,

Reader   Hail, Master!

Narrator   And he kissed him. Jesus said to him,

Jesus   Friend, why are you here?

Narrator   Then they came up and laid hands on Jesus and seized him. And behold, one of those who were with Jesus stretched out his hand and drew his sword, and struck the slave of the high priest, and cut off his ear. Then Jesus said to him,

Jesus	Put your sword back into its place; for all who take the sword will perish by the sword. Do you think that I cannot appeal to my Father, and he will at once send me more than twelve legions of angels? But how then should the scriptures be fulfilled, that it must be so?
Narrator	At that hour Jesus said to the crowds,
Jesus	Have you come out as against a robber, with swords and clubs to capture me? Day after day I sat in the temple teaching, and you did not seize me. But all this has taken place, that the scriptures of the prophets might be fulfilled.
Narrator	Then all the disciples forsook him and fled. Then those who had seized Jesus led him to Ca'iaphas the high priest, where the scribes and the elders had gathered. But Peter followed him at a distance, as far as the courtyard of the high priest, and going inside he sat with the guards to see the end. Now the chief priests and the whole council sought false testimony against Jesus that they might put him to death, but they found none, though many false witnesses came forward. At last two came forward and said,
Reader(s)	This fellow said, "I am able to destroy the temple of God, and to build it in three days."
Narrator	And the high priest stood up and said,
Reader	Have you no answer to make? What is it that these men testify against you?
Narrator	But Jesus was silent. And the high priest said to him,
Reader	I adjure you by the living God, tell us if you are the Christ, the Son of God.

Narrator	Jesus said to him,
Jesus	You have said so. But I tell you, hereafter you will see the Son of man seated at the right hand of Power, and coming on the clouds of heaven.
Narrator	Then the high priest tore his robes, and said,
Reader	He has uttered blasphemy. Why do we still need witnesses? You have now heard his blasphemy. What is your judgment?
Narrator	They answered and said,
Reader(s)	He deserves death.
Narrator	Then they spat in his face, and struck him; and some slapped him, saying,
Reader(s)	Prophesy to us, you Christ! Who is it that struck you?
Narrator	Now Peter was sitting outside in the courtyard. And a maid came up to him, and said,
Reader	You also were with Jesus the Galilean.
Narrator	But he denied it before them all, saying,
Reader	I do not know what you mean.
Narrator	And when he went out to the porch, another maid saw him, and she said to the bystanders,
Reader	This man was with Jesus of Nazareth.
Narrator	And again he denied it with an oath,
Reader	I do not know the man.
Narrator	After a little while the bystanders came up and said to Peter,
Reader(s)	Certainly you are also one of them, for your accent betrays you.

Narrator	Then he began to invoke a curse on himself and to swear,
Reader	I do not know the man.
Narrator	And immediately the cock crowed. And Peter remembered the saying of Jesus, "Before the cock crows, you will deny me three times." And he went out and wept bitterly.

The shorter form of the Passion begins here
[Matthew 27:1-54 (55-66)]

Narrator	When morning came, all the chief priests and the elders of the people took counsel against Jesus to put him to death; and they bound him and led him away and delivered him to Pilate the governor. When Judas, his betrayer, saw that he was condemned, he repented and brought back the thirty pieces of silver to the chief priests and the elders, saying,
Reader	I have sinned in betraying innocent blood.
Narrator	And they said,
Reader(s)	What is that to us? See to it yourself.
Narrator	And throwing down the pieces of silver in the temple, he departed; and he went and hanged himself. But the chief priests, taking the pieces of silver, said,
Reader(s)	It is not lawful to put them into the treasury, since they are blood money.
Narrator	So they took counsel, and bought with them the potter's field, to bury strangers in. Therefore that field has been called the Field of Blood to this day. Then was fulfilled what had been spoken by

the prophet Jeremiah, saying, "And they took the thirty pieces of silver, the price of him on whom a price had been set by some of the sons of Israel, and they gave them for the potter's field, as the Lord directed me." Now Jesus stood before the governor; and the governor asked him,

Reader   Are you the King of the Jews?

Narrator Jesus said to him,

Jesus   You have said so.

Narrator But when he was accused by the chief priests and elders, he made no answer. Then Pilate said to him,

Reader   Do you not hear how many things they testify against you?

Narrator But he gave him no answer, not even to a single charge; so that the governor wondered greatly. Now at the feast the governor was accustomed to release for the crowd any one prisoner whom they wanted. And they had then a notorious prisoner, called Barab'bas. So when they had gathered, Pilate said to them,

Reader   Whom do you want me to release for you, Barab'bas or Jesus who is called Christ?

Narrator For he knew that it was out of envy that they had delivered him up. Besides, while he was sitting on the judgment seat, his wife sent word to him,

Reader   Have nothing to do with that righteous man, for I have suffered much over him today in a dream.

Narrator Now the chief priests and the elders persuaded the people to ask for Barab'bas and destroy Jesus. The governor again said to them,

Reader	Which of the two do you want me to release for you?
Narrator	And they all said,
Crowd	Barab'bas.
Narrator	Pilate said to them,
Reader	Then what shall I do with Jesus who is called Christ?
Narrator	They all answered,
Crowd	Let him be crucified.
Narrator	And Pilate said,
Reader	Why, what evil has he done?
Narrator	But they shouted all the more,
Crowd	Let him be crucified.
Narrator	So when Pilate saw that he was gaining nothing, but rather that a riot was beginning, he took water and washed his hands before the crowd, saying,
Reader	I am innocent of this man's blood; see to it yourselves.
Narrator	And all the people answered,
Crowd	His blood be on us and on our children!
Narrator	Then he released for them Barab'bas, and having scourged Jesus, delivered him to be crucified. Then the soldiers of the governor took Jesus into the praetorium, and they gathered the whole battalion before him. And they stripped him and put a scarlet robe upon him, and plaiting a crown of thorns they put it on his head, and put a reed

in his right hand. And kneeling before him they mocked him, saying,

Readers   Hail, King of the Jews!

Narrator   And they spat upon him, and took the reed and struck him on the head. And when they had mocked him, they stripped him of the robe, and put his own clothes on him, and led him away to crucify him. As they went out, they came upon a man of Cyre'ne, Simon by name; this man they compelled to carry his cross.

All stand.

Narrator   And when they came to a place called Gol'gotha (which means the place of a skull), they offered him wine to drink, mingled with gall; but when he tasted it, he would not drink it. And when they had crucified him, they divided his garments among them by casting lots; then they sat down and kept watch over him there. And over his head they put the charge against him, which read, "This is Jesus the King of the Jews." Then two robbers were crucified with him, one on the right and one on the left. And those who passed by derided him, wagging their heads and saying,

Crowd   You who would destroy the temple and build it in three days, save yourself! If you are the Son of God, come down from the cross.

Narrator   So also the chief priests, with the scribes and elders, mocked him, saying,

Crowd   He saved others; he cannot save himself. He is the King of Israel; let him come down now from the cross, and we will believe in him. He trusts in

God; let God deliver him now, if he desires him; for he said,"I am the Son of God."

Narrator And the robbers who were crucified with him also reviled him in the same way. Now from the sixth hour there was darkness over all the land until the ninth hour. And about the ninth hour Jesus cried with a loud voice, saying,

Jesus Eli, Eli, la'ma sabach-tha'ni?

Narrator That is: My God, my God, why hast thou forsaken me? And some of the bystanders hearing it said,

Crowd This man is calling Eli'jah.

Narrator And one of them at once ran and took a sponge, filled it with vinegar, and put it on a reed, and gave it to him to drink. But the others said,

Crowd Wait, let us see whether Eli'jah will come to save him.

Narrator And Jesus cried again with a loud voice and yielded up his spirit.

Silence may be kept.

Narrator And behold, the curtain of the temple was torn in two, from top to bottom; and the earth shook, and the rocks were split; the tombs also were opened, and many bodies of the saints who had fallen asleep were raised, and coming out of the tombs after his resurrection they went into the holy city and appeared to many. When the centurion and those who were with him, keeping watch over Jesus, saw the earthquake and what took place, they were filled with awe, and said,

Crowd Truly this was the Son of God!

The following passage may be added
[Matthew 27:55-66]

Narrator   There were also many women there, looking on from afar, who had followed Jesus from Galilee, ministering to him; among whom were Mary Mag'dalene, and Mary the mother of James and Joseph, and the mother of the sons of Zeb'edee. When it was evening, there came a rich man from Arimathe'a, named Joseph, who also was a disciple of Jesus. He went to Pilate and asked for the body of Jesus. Then Pilate ordered it to be given to him. And Joseph took the body, and wrapped it in a clean linen shroud, and laid it in his own new tomb, which he had hewn in the rock; and he rolled a great stone to the door of the tomb, and departed. Mary Mag'dalene and the other Mary were there, sitting opposite the sepulchre. Next day, that is, after the day of Preparation, the chief priests and the Pharisees gathered before Pilate and said,

Reader(s)   Sir, we remember how that impostor said, while he was still alive, "After three days I will rise again." Therefore order the sepulchre to be made secure until the third day, lest his disciples go and steal him away, and tell the people, "He has risen from the dead," and the last fraud will be worse than the first.

Narrator   Pilate said to them,

Reader   You have a guard of soldiers; go, make it as secure as you can.

Narrator   So they went and made the sepulchre secure by sealing the stone and setting a guard.

Monday in Holy Week

A Reading (Lesson) from the Book of Isaiah [42:1-9]

Behold my servant, whom I uphold, my chosen, in whom
my soul delights; I have put my Spirit upon him, he will
bring forth justice to the nations. He will not cry or lift up
his voice, or make it heard in the street; a bruised reed he
will not break, and a dimly burning wick he will not
quench; he will faithfully bring forth justice. He will not
fail or be discouraged till he has established justice in the
earth; and the coastlands wait for his law. Thus says God,
the Lord, who created the heavens and stretched them out,
who spread forth the earth and what comes from it, who
gives breath to the people upon it and spirit to those
who walk in it: "I am the Lord, I have called you in
righteousness, I have taken you by the hand and kept you;
I have given you as a covenant to the people, a light to the
nations, to open the eyes that are blind, to bring out the
prisoners from the dungeon, from the prison those who sit
in darkness. I am the Lord, that is my name; my glory I give
to no other, nor my praise to graven images. Behold, the
former things have come to pass, and new things I now
declare; before they spring forth I tell you of them."

Psalm 36:5-10 [page 632]

A Reading (Lesson) from the Letter to the Hebrews
[11:39—12:3]

All these, the patriarchs, prophets, and heroes of the old
covenant, though well attested by their faith, did not
receive what was promised, since God had forseen
something better for us, that apart from us they should not
be made perfect. Therefore, since we are surrounded by so
great a cloud of witnesses, let us also lay aside every
weight, and sin which clings so closely, and let us run with

perseverance the race that is set before us, looking to Jesus the pioneer and perfecter of our faith, who for the joy that was set before him endured the cross, despising the shame, and is seated at the right hand of the throne of God. Consider him who endured from sinners such hostility against himself, so that you may not grow weary or fainthearted.

✝ *The Holy Gospel of Our Lord Jesus Christ According to John* [12:1-11]

Six days before the Passover, Jesus came to Bethany, where Laz'arus was, whom Jesus had raised from the dead. There they made him a supper; Martha served, and Laz'arus was one of those at table with him. Mary took a pound of costly ointment of pure nard and anointed the feet of Jesus and wiped his feet with her hair; and the house was filled with the fragrance of the ointment. But Judas Iscariot, one of the disciples (he who was to betray him), said, "Why was this ointment not sold for three hundred denarii and given to the poor?" This he said, not that he cared for the poor but because he was a thief, and as he had the money box he used to take what was put into it. Jesus said, "Let her alone, let her keep it for the day of my burial. The poor you always have with you, but you do not always have me." When the great crowd of the Jews learned that he was there, they came, not only on account of Jesus but also to see Laz'arus, whom he had raised from the dead. So the chief priests planned to put Laz'arus also to death, because on account of him many of the Jews were going away and believing in Jesus.

or the following

✝ *The Holy Gospel of Our Lord Jesus Christ*
According to Mark [14:3-9]

While Jesus was at Bethany in the house of Simon the leper, as he sat at table, a woman came with an alabaster flask of ointment of pure nard, very costly, and she broke the flask and poured it over his head. But there were some who said to themselves indignantly, "Why was the ointment thus wasted? For this ointment might have been sold for more than three hundred denarii, and given to the poor." And they reproached her. But Jesus said, "Let her alone; why do you trouble her? She has done a beautiful thing to me. For you always have the poor with you, and whenever you will, you can do good to them; but you will not always have me. She has done what she could; she has anointed my body beforehand for burying. And truly, I say to you, wherever the gospel is preached in the whole world, what she has done will be told in memory of her."

Tuesday in Holy Week

A Reading (Lesson) from the Book of Isaiah [49:1-6]

Listen to me, O coastlands, and hearken, you peoples from afar. The Lord called me from the womb, from the body of my mother he named my name. He made my mouth like a sharp sword, in the shadow of his hand he hid me; he made me a polished arrow, in his quiver he hid me away. And he said to me, "You are my servant, Israel, in whom I will be glorified." But I said, "I have labored in vain, I have spent my strength for nothing and vanity; yet surely my right is with the Lord, and my recompense with my God." And now the Lord says, who formed me from the womb to be his servant, to bring Jacob back to him, and that Israel might be gathered to him, for I am honored in the eyes of the Lord, and my God has become my strength—he says:

"It is too light a thing that you should be my servant to raise up the tribes of Jacob and to restore the preserved of Israel; I will give you as a light to the nations, that my salvation may reach to the end of the earth."

Psalm 71:1-12 [page 683]

A Reading (Lesson) from the First Letter of Paul to the Corinthians [1:18-31]

The word of the cross is folly to those who are perishing, but to us who are being saved it is the power of God. For it is written, "I will destroy the wisdom of the wise, and the cleverness of the clever I will thwart." Where is the wise man? Where is the scribe? Where is the debater of this age? Has not God made foolish the wisdom of the world? For since, in the wisdom of God, the world did not know God through wisdom, it pleased God through the folly of what we preach to save those who believe. For Jews demand signs and Greeks seek wisdom, but we preach Christ crucified, a stumbling block to Jews and folly to Gentiles, but to those who are called, both Jews and Greeks, Christ the power of God and the wisdom of God. For the foolishness of God is wiser than men, and the weakness of God is stronger than men. For consider your call, brethren; not many of you were wise according to worldly standards, not many were powerful, not many were of noble birth; but God chose what is foolish in the world to shame the wise, God chose what is weak in the world to shame the strong, God chose what is low and despised in the world, even things that are not, to bring to nothing things that are, so that no human being might boast in the presence of God. He is the source of your life in Christ Jesus, whom God made our wisdom, our righteousness and sanctification and redemption; therefore, as it is written, "Let him who boasts, boast of the Lord."

✝ *The Holy Gospel of Our Lord Jesus Christ*
According to John [12:37-38,42-50]

Though Jesus had done so many signs before the people,
yet they did not believe in him; it was that the word spoken
by the prophet Isaiah might be fulfilled, "Lord, who has
believed our report, and to whom has the arm of the Lord
been revealed?" Nevertheless many even of the authorities
believed in him, but for fear of the Pharisees they did not
confess it, lest they should be put out of the synagogue: for
they loved the praise of men more than the praise of God.
And Jesus cried out and said, "He who believes in me,
believes not in me but in him who sent me. And he who
sees me sees him who sent me. I have come as light into the
world, that whoever believes in me may not remain in
darkness. If any one hears my sayings and does not keep
them I do not judge him; for I did not come to judge the
world but to save the world. He who rejects me and does
not receive my sayings has a judge; the word that I have
spoken will be his judge on the last day. For I have not
spoken on my own authority; the Father who sent me has
himself given me commandment what to say and what to
speak. And I know that his commandment is eternal life.
What I say, therefore, I say as the Father has bidden me."

or this

✝ *The Holy Gospel of Our Lord Jesus Christ*
According to Mark [11:15-19]

Jesus and those who followed came to Jerusalem. And
Jesus entered the temple and began to drive out those
who sold and those who bought in the temple, and he
overturned the tables of the money-changers and the seats
of those who sold pigeons; and he would not allow any
one to carry anything through the temple. And he taught,
and said to them, "Is it not written, 'My house shall be

called a house of prayer for all nations'? But you have
made it a den of robbers." And the chief priests and the
scribes heard it and sought a way to destroy him; for they
feared him, because all the multitude was astonished at his
teaching. And when evening came they went out of the city.

Wednesday in Holy Week

A Reading (Lesson) from the Book of Isaiah [50:4-9a]

The Lord God has given me the tongue of those who are
taught, that I may know how to sustain with a word him
that is weary. Morning by morning he wakens, he wakens
my ear to hear as those who are taught. The Lord God has
opened my ear, and I was not rebellious, I turned not
backward. I gave my back to the smiters, and my cheeks to
those who pulled out the beard; I hid not my face from
shame and spitting. For the Lord God helps me; therefore I
have not been confounded; therefore I have set my face like
a flint, and I know that I shall not be put to shame; he who
vindicates me is near. Who will contend with me? Let us
stand up together. Who is my adversary? Let him come
near to me. Behold, the Lord God helps me; who will
declare me guilty?

Psalm 69:7-15, 22-23 [page 679]

A Reading (Lesson) from the Letter to the Hebrews
[9:11-15, 24-28]

When Christ appeared as a high priest of the good things
that have come, then through the greater and more perfect
tent (not made with hands, that is, not of this creation) he
entered once for all into the Holy Place, taking not the
blood of goats and calves but his own blood, thus securing
an eternal redemption. For if the sprinkling of defiled

persons with the blood of goats and bulls and with the ashes of a heifer sanctifies for the purification of the flesh, how much more shall the blood of Christ, who through the eternal Spirit offered himself without blemish to God, purify your conscience from dead works to serve the living God. Therefore he is the mediator of a new covenant, so that those who are called may receive the promised eternal inheritance, since a death has occurred which redeems them from the transgressions under the first covenant. For Christ has entered, not into a sanctuary made with hands, a copy of the true one, but into heaven itself, now to appear in the presence of God on our behalf. Nor was it to offer himself repeatedly, as the high priest enters the Holy Place yearly with blood not his own; for then he would have had to suffer repeatedly since the foundation of the world. But as it is, he has appeared once for all at the end of the age to put away sin by the sacrifice of himself. And just as it is appointed for men to die once, and after that comes judgment, so Christ, having been offered once to bear the sins of many, will appear a second time, not to deal with sin but to save those who are eagerly waiting for him.

✝ *The Holy Gospel of Our Lord Jesus Christ*
According to John [13:21-35]

At supper with his friends, Jesus was troubled in spirit, and testified, "Truly, truly, I say to you, one of you will betray me." The disciples looked at one another, uncertain of whom he spoke. One of his disciples, whom Jesus loved, was lying close to the breast of Jesus; so Simon Peter beckoned to him and said, "Tell us who it is of whom he speaks." So lying thus, close to the breast of Jesus, he said to him, "Lord, who is it?" Jesus answered, "It is he to whom I shall give this morsel when I have dipped it." So when he had dipped the morsel, he gave it to Judas, the son of

Simon Iscariot. Then after the morsel, Satan entered into him. Jesus said to him, "What you are going to do, do quickly." Now no one at the table knew why he said this to him. Some thought that, because Judas had the money box, Jesus was telling him, "Buy what we need for the feast"; or, that he should give something to the poor. So, after receiving the morsel, he immediately went out; and it was night. When he had gone out, Jesus said, "Now is the Son of man glorified, and in him God is glorified; if God is glorified in him, God will also glorify him in himself, and glorify him at once. Little children, yet a little while I am with you. You will seek me; and as I said to the Jews so now I say to you, 'Where I am going you cannot come.' A new commandment I give to you, that you love one another; even as I have loved you, that you also love one another. By this all men will know that you are my disciples, if you have love for one another."

or this

✝ *The Holy Gospel of Our Lord Jesus Christ According to Matthew* [26:1-5, 14-25]

Jesus said to his disciples, "You know that after two days the Passover is coming, and the Son of man will be delivered up to be crucified." Then the chief priests and the elders of the people gathered in the palace of the high priest, who was called Ca'iaphas, and took counsel together in order to arrest Jesus by stealth and kill him. But they said, "Not during the feast, lest there be a tumult among the people." Then one of the twelve, who was called Judas Iscariot, went to the chief priests, and said, "What will you give me if I deliver him to you?" And they paid him thirty pieces of silver. And from that moment he sought an opportunity to betray him. Now on the first day of Unleavened Bread the disciples came to

Jesus, saying,"Where will you have us prepare for you to eat the passover?" He said,"Go into the city to a certain one, and say to him,'The Teacher says, My time is at hand; I will keep the passover at your house with my disciples.' " And the disciples did as Jesus had directed them, and they prepared the passover. When it was evening, he sat at table with the twelve disciples; and as they were eating, he said,"Truly, I say to you, one of you will betray me." And they were very sorrowful, and began to say to him one after another,"Is it I, Lord?" He answered,"He who has dipped his hand in the dish with me, will betray me. The Son of man goes as it is written of him, but woe to that man by whom the Son of man is betrayed! It would have been better for that man if he had not been born." Judas, who betrayed him, said,"Is it I, Master?" He said to him,"You have said so."

Maundy Thursday

A Reading (Lesson) from the Book of Exodus [12:1-14a]

The Lord said to Moses and Aaron in the land of Egypt,"This month shall be for you the beginning of months; it shall be the first month of the year for you. Tell all the congregation of Israel that on the tenth day of this month they shall take every man a lamb according to their fathers' houses, a lamb for a household; and if the household is too small for a lamb, then a man and his neighbor next to his house shall take according to the number of persons; according to what each can eat you shall make your count for the lamb. Your lamb shall be without blemish, a male a year old; you shall take it from the sheep or from the goats; and you shall keep it until the fourteenth day of this month, when the whole assembly of the congregation of Israel shall kill their lambs in the evening. Then they shall take some of the blood, and put it on the two doorposts and the lintel of the houses in which they eat them. They shall eat the flesh that night, roasted; with unleavened bread and bitter herbs they shall eat it. Do not eat any of it raw or boiled with water, but roasted, its head with its legs and its inner parts. And you shall let none of it remain until the morning, anything that remains until the morning you shall burn. In this manner you shall eat it: your loins girded, your sandals on your feet, and your staff in your hand; and you shall eat it in haste. It is the Lord's passover. For I will pass through the land of Egypt that night, and I will smite all the first-born in the land of Egypt, both man and beast; and on all the gods of Egypt I will execute judgments: I am the Lord. The blood shall be a sign for you, upon the houses where you are; and when I see the blood, I will pass over you, and no plague shall fall upon you to destroy you, when I smite the land of Egypt. This day shall be for you a memorial day, and you shall keep it as a feast to the Lord."

Psalm 78:14-20, 23-25 [page 696]

A Reading (Lesson) from the First Letter of Paul to the Corinthians [11:23-26 (27-32)]

I received from the Lord what I also delivered to you, that the Lord Jesus on the night when he was betrayed took bread, and when he had given thanks, he broke it, and said,"This is my body which is for you. Do this in remembrance of me." In the same way also the cup, after supper, saying,"This cup is the new covenant in my blood. Do this, as often as you drink it, in remembrance of me." For as often as you eat this bread and drink the cup, you proclaim the Lord's death until he comes.

Whoever, therefore, eats the bread or drinks the cup of the Lord in an unworthy manner will be guilty of profaning the body and blood of the Lord. Let a man examine himself, and so eat of the bread and drink of the cup. For any one who eats and drinks without discerning the body eats and drinks judgment upon himself. That is why many of you are weak and ill, and some have died. But if we judged ourselves truly, we should not be judged. But when we are judged by the Lord, we are chastened so that we may not be condemned along with the world.

✝ *The Holy Gospel of Our Lord Jesus Christ According to John* [13:1-15]

Now before the feast of the Passover, when Jesus knew that his hour had come to depart out of this world to the Father, having loved his own who were in the world, he loved them to the end. And during supper, when the devil had already put it into the heart of Judas Iscariot, Simon's son, to betray him, Jesus, knowing that the Father had given all things into his hands, and that he had come from God and was going to God, rose from supper, laid aside his garments, and girded himself with a towel. Then he poured water into a basin, and began to wash the disciples' feet, and to wipe them with the towel with which he was girded. He came to Simon Peter; and Peter said to him, "Lord, do you wash my feet?" Jesus answered him, "What I am doing you do not know now, but afterward you will understand." Peter said to him, "You shall never wash my feet." Jesus answered him, "If I do not wash you, you have no part in me." Simon Peter said to him, "Lord, not my feet only but also my hands and my head!" Jesus said to him, "He who has bathed does not need to wash, except for his feet, but he is clean all over; and you are clean, but not every one of you." For he knew who was to betray him; that was why he said, "You are not all clean." When he had washed their feet, and taken his garments, and resumed his place, he said to them, "Do you know what I have done to you? You call me Teacher and Lord; and you are right, for so I am. If I then, your Lord and Teacher, have washed your feet, you also ought to wash one another's feet. For I have given you an example, that you also should do as I have done to you."

or this

✝ *The Holy Gospel of Our Lord Jesus Christ*
According to Luke [22:14-30]

And when the hour came, Jesus sat at table, and the apostles with him. And he said to them, "I have earnestly desired to eat this passover with you before I suffer; for I tell you I shall not eat it until it is fulfilled in the kingdom of God." And he took a cup, and when he had given thanks he said, "Take this, and divide it among yourselves; for I tell you that from now on I shall not drink of the fruit of the vine until the kingdom of God comes." And he took bread, and when he had given thanks he broke it, and gave it to them, saying, "This is my body which is given for you. Do this in remembrance of me." And likewise the cup after supper, saying, "This cup which is poured out for you is the new covenant in my blood. But behold the hand of him who betrays me is with me on the table. For the Son of man goes as it has been determined; but woe to that man by whom he is betrayed!" And they began to question one another, which of them it was that would do this. A dispute also arose among them, which of them was to be regarded as the greatest. And he said to them, "The kings of the Gentiles exercise lordship over them; and those in authority over them are called benefactors. But not so with you; rather let the greatest among you become as the youngest, and the leader as one who serves. For which is the greater, one who sits at table, or one who serves? Is it not the one who sits at table? But I am among you as one who serves. You are those who have continued with me in my trials; and I assign to you, as my Father assigned to me, a kingdom, that you may eat and drink at my table in my kingdom, and sit on thrones judging the twelve tribes of Israel."

Good Friday

A Reading (Lesson) from the Book of Isaiah
[52:13—53:12]

Behold, my servant shall prosper, he shall be exalted and lifted up, and shall be very high. As many were astonished at him—his appearance was so marred, beyond human semblance, and his form beyond that of the sons of men— so shall he startle many nations; kings shall shut their mouths because of him; for that which has not been told them they shall see, and that which they have not heard they shall understand. Who has believed what we have heard? And to whom has the arm of the Lord been revealed? For he grew up before him like a young plant, and like a root out of dry ground; he had no form or comeliness that we should look at him, and no beauty that we should desire him. He was despised and rejected by men; a man of sorrows, and acquainted with grief; and as one from whom men hide their faces he was despised, and we esteemed him not. Surely he has borne our griefs and carried our sorrows; yet we esteemed him stricken, smitten by God, and afflicted. But he was wounded for our transgressions, he was bruised for our iniquities; upon him was the chastisement that made us whole, and with his stripes we are healed. All we like sheep have gone astray; we have turned every one to his own way; and the Lord has laid on him the iniquity of us all. He was oppressed, and he was afflicted, yet he opened not his mouth; like a lamb that is led to the slaughter, and like a sheep that before its shearers is dumb, so he opened not his mouth. By oppression and judgment he was taken away; and as for his generation, who considered that he was cut off out of the land of the living, stricken for the transgression of my people? And they made his grave with the wicked and with a rich man in his death, although he had done no violence, and there was no deceit in his mouth. Yet it was the will of the Lord to bruise him; he has put him to grief; when he makes himself an offering for sin, he shall see his offspring, he shall prolong his days; the will of the Lord shall prosper in his hand; he shall see the fruit of the travail of his soul and be satisfied; by his knowledge shall the righteous one, my servant, make many to be accounted righteous; and he shall bear their iniquities. Therefore I will divide him a portion with the great, and he shall divide the spoil with the strong; because he poured out his soul to death, and was numbered with the transgressors; yet he bore the sin of many, and made intercession for the transgressors.

or this

A Reading (Lesson) from the Book of Genesis [22:1-18]

God tested Abraham, and said to him, "Abraham!" And he said, "Here am I." He said, "Take your son, your only son Isaac, whom you love, and go to the land of Mori'ah, and offer him there as a burnt offering upon one of the mountains of which I shall tell you." So Abraham rose early in the morning, saddled his ass, and took two of his young men with him, and his son Isaac; and he cut the wood for the burnt offering, and arose and went to the place of which God had told him. On the third day Abraham lifted up his eyes and saw the place afar off. Then Abraham said to his young men, "Stay here with the ass; I and the lad will go yonder and worship, and come again to you." And Abraham took the wood of the burnt offering, and laid it on Isaac his son; and he took in his hand the fire and the knife. So they went both of them together. And Isaac said to his father Abraham, "My father!" And he said, "Here am I, my son." He said, "Behold, the fire and the wood; but where is the lamb for a burnt offering?" Abraham said, "God will provide himself the lamb for a burnt offering, my son." So they went both of them together. When they came to the place of which God had told him, Abraham built an altar there, and laid the wood in order, and bound Isaac his son, and laid him on the altar, upon the wood. Then Abraham put forth his hand, and took the knife to slay his son. But the angel of the Lord called to him from heaven and said, "Abraham, Abraham!" And he said, "Here am I." He said, "Do not lay your hand on the lad or do anything to him; for now I know that you fear God, seeing you have not withheld your son, your only son, from me." And Abraham lifted up his eyes and looked, and behold, behind him was a ram, caught in a thicket by his horns; and Abraham went and took the ram, and offered it up as a burnt offering instead of his son. So Abraham called the name of that place The Lord will provide; as it is said to this day, "On the mount of the Lord it shall be provided." And the angel of the Lord called to Abraham a second time from heaven, and said, "By myself I have sworn, says the Lord, because you have done this, and have not withheld your son, your only son, I will indeed bless you, and I will multiply your descendants as the stars of heaven and as the sand which is on the seashore. And your descendants shall possess the gate of their enemies, and by your descendants shall all the nations of the earth bless themselves, because you have obeyed my voice."

or this

A Reading (Lesson) from the Book of Wisdom [2:1, 12-24]

The ungodly reasoned unsoundly, saying to themselves, "Short and sorrowful is our life, and there is no remedy when a man comes to his end, and no one has been known to return from Hades. Let us lie in wait for the righteous man, because he is inconvenient to us and opposes our actions; he reproaches us for sins against the law, and accuses us of sins against our training. He professes to have knowledge of God, and calls himself a child of the Lord. He became to us a reproof of our thoughts; the very sight of him is a burden to us, because his manner of life is unlike that of others, and his ways are strange. We are considered by him as something base, and he avoids our ways as unclean; he calls the last end of the righteous happy, and boasts that God is his father. Let us see if his words are true, and let us test what will happen at the end of his life; for if the righteous man is God's son, he will help him, and will deliver him from the hand of his adversaries. Let us test him with insult and torture, that we may find out how gentle he is, and make trial of his forbearance. Let us condemn him to a shameful death, for, according to what he says, he will be protected." Thus they reasoned, but they were led astray, for their wickedness blinded them, and they did not know the secret purposes of God, nor hope for the wages of holiness, nor discern the prize for blameless souls; for God created man for incorruption, and made him in the image of his own eternity, but through the devil's envy death entered the world, and those who belong to his party experience it.

Psalm 22:1-21 [page 610]   or   *22:1-11* [page 610]   or

Psalm 40:1-14 [page 614]   or   *Psalm 69:1-23* [page 679]

A Reading (Lesson) from the Letter to the Hebrews [10:1-25]

Since the law has but a shadow of the good things to come instead of the true form of these realities, it can never, by the same sacrifices which are continually offered year after year, make perfect those who draw near. Otherwise, would they not have ceased to be offered? If the worshipers had once been cleansed, they would no longer have any consciousness of sin. But in these sacrifices there is a reminder of sin year after year. For it is impossible that the blood of bulls and goats should take away sins. Consequently, when Christ came into the world, he said, "Sacrifices and offerings thou hast not desired, but a body hast thou prepared for me; in burnt offerings and sin offerings thou hast taken no pleasure. Then I said, 'Lo, I have come to do thy will, O God,' as it is written of me in the roll of the book." When he said above, "Thou hast neither desired nor taken pleasure in sacrifices and offerings and burnt offerings and sin offerings" (these are offered according to the law), then he added, "Lo, I have to come to do thy will." He abolishes the first in order to establish the second. And by that will we have been sanctified through the offering of the body of Jesus Christ once for all. And every priest stands daily at his service, offering repeatedly the same sacrifices, which can never take away sins. But when Christ had offered for all time a single sacrifice for sins, he sat down at the right hand of God, then to wait until his enemies should be made a stool for his feet. For by a single offering he has perfected for all time those who are sanctified. And the Holy Spirit also bears witness to us; for after saying, "This is the covenant that I will make with them after those days, says the Lord: I will put my laws on their hearts, and write them on their minds," then he adds, "I will remember their sins and their misdeeds no more." Where there is forgiveness of these, there is no longer any offering for sin. Therefore, brethren, since we have confidence to enter the sanctuary by the blood of Jesus, by the new and living way which he opened for us through the curtain, that is, through his flesh, and since we have a great priest over the house of God, let us draw near with a true heart in full assurance of faith, with our hearts sprinkled clean from an evil conscience and our bodies washed with pure water. Let us hold fast the confession of our hope without wavering, for he who promised is faithful; and let us consider how to stir up one another to love and good works, not neglecting to meet together, as is the habit of some, but encouraging one another, and all the more as you see the Day drawing near.

The Passion of Our Lord Jesus Christ According to John
[18:1—19:37]   or   [19:1-37]

The customary responses before and after the Gospel are omitted.

The shorter form of the Passion begins on page 103.

The Passion may be read by one or more persons.

The congregation may be seated for the first part of the Passion. At the verse which mentions the arrival at Golgotha [John 19:17], page 105, all stand.

Narrator   Jesus went forth with his disciples across the Kidron valley, where there was a garden, which he and his disciples entered. Now Judas, who betrayed him, also knew the place; for Jesus often met there with his disciples. So Judas, procuring a band of soldiers and some officers from the chief priests and the Pharisees, went there with lanterns and torches and weapons. Then Jesus, knowing all that was to befall him, came forward and said to them,

Jesus   Whom do you seek?

Narrator   They answered him,

Reader(s)   Jesus of Nazareth.

Narrator   Jesus said to them,

Jesus   I am he.

Narrator   Judas, who betrayed him, was standing with them. When he said to them, "I am he," they drew back and fell to the ground. Again he asked them,

Jesus   Whom do you seek?

Narrator   And they said,

Reader(s)	Jesus of Nazareth.
Narrator	Jesus answered them,
Jesus	I told you that I am he; so, if you seek me, let these men go.
Narrator	This was to fulfill the word which he had spoken, "Of those whom thou gavest me I lost not one." Then Simon Peter, having a sword, drew it and struck the high priest's slave and cut off his right ear. The slave's name was Malchus. Jesus said to Peter,
Jesus	Put your sword into its sheath; shall I not drink the cup which the Father has given me?
Narrator	So the band of soldiers and their captain and the officers of the Jews seized Jesus and bound him. First they led him to Annas; for he was the father-in-law of Ca′iaphas, who was high priest that year. It was Ca′iaphas who had given counsel to the Jews that it was expedient that one man should die for the people. Simon Peter followed Jesus, and so did another disciple. As this disciple was known to the high priest, he entered the court of the high priest along with Jesus, while Peter stood outside at the door. So the other disciple, who was known to the high priest, went out and spoke to the maid who kept the door, and brought Peter in. The maid who kept the door said to Peter,
Reader	Are not you also one of this man's disciples?
Narrator	And he said,
Reader	I am not.
Narrator	Now the servants and officers had made a charcoal fire, because it was cold, and they were

standing and warming themselves; Peter also was with them, standing and warming himself. The high priest then questioned Jesus about his disciples and his teaching. Jesus answered him,

Jesus   I have spoken openly to the world; I have always taught in synagogues and in the temple, where all Jews come together; I have said nothing secretly. Why do you ask me? Ask those who have heard me, what I said to them; they know what I said.

Narrator   When he had said this, one of the officers standing by struck Jesus with his hand, saying,

Reader   Is that how you answer the high priest?

Narrator   Jesus answered him,

Jesus   If I have spoken wrongly, bear witness to the wrong; but if I have spoken rightly, why do you strike me?

Narrator   Annas then sent him bound to Ca'iaphas the high priest. Now Simon Peter was standing and warming himself. They said to him,

Reader(s)   Are not you also one of his disciples?

Narrator   He denied it and said,

Reader   I am not.

Narrator   One of the servants of the high priest, a kinsman of the man whose ear Peter had cut off, asked,

Reader   Did I not see you in the garden with him?

Narrator   Peter again denied it; and at once the cock crowed. Then they led Jesus from the house of Ca'iaphas to the praetorium. It was early. They themselves did not enter the praetorium, so that they might not be defiled, but might eat the passover. So Pilate went out to them and said,

Reader	What accusation do you bring against this man?
Narrator	They answered him,
Reader(s)	If this man were not an evildoer, we would not have handed him over.
Narrator	Pilate said to them,
Reader	Take him yourselves and judge him by your own law.
Narrator	The Jews said to him,
Reader(s)	It is not lawful for us to put any man to death.
Narrator	This was to fulfill the word which Jesus had spoken to show by what death he was to die. Pilate entered the praetorium again and called Jesus, and said to him,
Reader	Are you the King of the Jews?
Narrator	Jesus answered him,
Jesus	Do you say this of your own accord, or did others say it to you about me?
Narrator	Pilate answered,
Reader	Am I a Jew? Your own nation and the chief priests have handed you over to me; what have you done?
Narrator	Jesus answered him,
Jesus	My kingship is not of this world; if my kingship were of this world, my servants would fight, that I might not be handed over to the Jews; but my kingship is not from the world.
Narrator	Pilate said to him,
Reader	So you are a king?
Narrator	Jesus answered,

Jesus	You say that I am a king. For this I was born, and for this I have come into the world, to bear witness to the truth. Every one who is of the truth hears my voice.
Narrator	Pilate said to him,
Reader	What is truth?
Narrator	After he had said this, he went out to the Jews again, and told them,
Reader	I find no crime in him. But you have a custom that I should release one man for you at the Passover; will you have me release for you the King of the Jews?
Narrator	They cried out again,
Crowd	Not this man, but Barab'bas!
Narrator	Now Barab'bas was a robber.

The shorter form of the Passion begins here
[John 19:1-37]

Narrator	Pilate took Jesus and scourged him. And the soldiers plaited a crown of thorns, and put it on his head, and arrayed him in a purple robe; they came up to him, saying,
Reader(s)	Hail, King of the Jews!
Narrator	And struck him with their hands. Pilate went out again, and said to them,
Reader	See, I am bringing him out to you, that you may know that I find no crime in him.
Narrator	So Jesus came out, wearing the crown of thorns and the purple robe. Pilate said to them,
Reader	Behold the man!

Narrator	When the chief priests and the officers saw him, they cried out, saying,
Reader(s)	Crucify him, crucify him!
Narrator	Pilate said to them,
Reader	Take him yourselves and crucify him for I find no crime in him.
Narrator	The Jews answered him,
Reader(s)	We have a law, and by that law he ought to die, because he has made himself the Son of God.
Narrator	When Pilate heard these words, he was the more afraid; he entered the praetorium again and said to Jesus,
Reader	Where are you from?
Narrator	But Jesus gave no answer. Pilate therefore said to him,
Reader	You will not speak to me? Do you not know that I have power to release you, and power to crucify you?
Narrator	Jesus answered him,
Jesus	You would have no power over me unless it had been given you from above; therefore he who delivered me to you has the greater sin.
Narrator	Upon this Pilate sought to release him, but the Jews cried out,
Crowd	If you release this man, you are not Caesar's friend; every one who makes himself a king sets himself against Caesar.
Narrator	When Pilate heard these words, he brought Jesus out and sat down on the judgment seat at a place called the Pavement, and in Hebrew, Gab'batha.

Now it was the day of Preparation of the Passover; it was about the sixth hour. He said to the Jews,

Reader   Behold your King!

Narrator   They cried out,

Crowd   Away with him, away with him, crucify him!

Narrator   Pilate said to them,

Reader   Shall I crucify your King?

Narrator   The chief priests answered,

Reader(s)   We have no king but Caesar.

Narrator   Then he handed him over to them to be crucified.

All stand.

Narrator   So they took Jesus, and he went out, bearing his own cross, to the place of a skull, which is called in Hebrew Gol'gotha. There they crucified him, and with him two others, one on either side, and Jesus between them. Pilate also wrote a title and put it on the cross; it read, "Jesus of Nazareth, the King of the Jews." Many of the Jews read this title, for the place where Jesus was crucified was near the city; and it was written in Hebrew, in Latin, and in Greek. The chief priests of the Jews then said to Pilate,

Reader(s)   Do not write, "The King of the Jews," but, "This man said, I am King of the Jews."

Narrator   Pilate answered,

Reader   What I have written I have written.

Narrator   When the soldiers had crucified Jesus they took his garments and made four parts, one for each soldier; also his tunic. But the tunic was without seam, woven from top to bottom; so they said to one another,

Reader(s)   Let us not tear it, but cast lots for it to see whose it shall be.

Narrator   This was to fulfill the scripture, "They parted my garments among them, and for my clothing they cast lots." So the soldiers did this. But standing by the cross of Jesus were his mother, and his mother's sister, Mary the wife of Clopas, and Mary Mag'dalene. When Jesus saw his mother, and the disciple whom he loved standing near, he said to his mother,

Jesus   Woman, behold, your son!

Narrator   Then he said to the disciple,

Jesus   Behold, your mother!

Narrator   And from that hour the disciple took her to his own home. After this, Jesus, knowing that all was now finished, to fulfill the scripture said,

Jesus   I thirst.

Narrator   A bowl full of vinegar stood there; so they put a sponge full of the vinegar on hyssop and held it to his mouth. When Jesus had received the vinegar, he said,

Jesus   It is finished.

Narrator   And he bowed his head and gave up his spirit.

Silence may be kept.

Narrator   Since it was the day of Preparation, in order to prevent the bodies from remaining on the cross on the sabbath (for that sabbath was a high day), the Jews asked Pilate that their legs might be broken, and that they might be taken away. So the soldiers came and broke the legs of the first, and of the other who had been crucified with him; but when they came to Jesus and saw that he was already dead, they did not break his legs. But one of the soldiers pierced his side with a spear, and at once there came out blood and water. He who saw it has borne witness—his testimony is true, and he knows that he tells the truth—that you also may believe. For these things took place that the scripture might be fulfilled, "Not a bone of him shall be broken." And again another scripture says, "They shall look on him whom they have pierced."

Holy Saturday

A Reading (Lesson) from the Book of Job [14:1-14]

Man that is born of a woman is of few days, and full of trouble. He comes forth like a flower, and withers; he flees like a shadow, and continues not. And dost thou open thy eyes upon such a one and bring him into judgment with thee? Who can bring a clean thing out of an unclean? There is not one. Since his days are determined, and the number of his months is with thee, and thou hast appointed his bounds that he cannot pass, look away from him, and desist, that he may enjoy, like a hireling, his day. For there is hope for a tree, if it be cut down, that it will sprout again, and that its shoots will not cease. Though its root grow old in the earth, and its stump die in the ground, yet at the scent of water it will bud and put forth branches like a young plant. But man dies, and is laid low; man breathes his last, and where is he? As waters fail from a lake, and a river wastes away and dries up, so man lies down and rises not again; till the heavens are no more he will not awake, or be roused out of his sleep. Oh that thou wouldest hide me in Sheol, that thou wouldest conceal me until thy wrath be past, that thou wouldest appoint me a set time, and remember me! If a man die, shall he live again? All the days of my service I would wait, till my release should come.

Psalm 130 [page 784]   or   *Psalm 31:1-5* [page 622]

A Reading (Lesson) from the First Letter of Peter [4:1-8]

Since Christ suffered in the flesh, arm yourselves with the same thought, for whoever has suffered in the flesh has ceased from sin, so as to live for the rest of the time in the flesh no longer by human passions but by the will of God. Let the time that is past suffice for doing what the Gentiles like to do, living in licentiousness, passions, drunkenness, revels, carousing, and lawless idolatry. They are surprised that you do not now join them in the same wild profligacy, and they abuse you; but they will give account to him who is ready to judge the living and the dead. For this is why the gospel was preached even to the dead, that though judged in the flesh like men, they might live in the spirit like God. The end of all things is at hand; therefore keep sane and sober for your prayers. Above all hold unfailing your love for one another, since love covers a multitude of sins.

✝ *The Holy Gospel of Our Lord Jesus Christ According to Matthew* [27:57-66]

When it was evening, there came a rich man from Arimathe′a, named Joseph, who also was a disciple of Jesus. He went to Pilate and asked for the body of Jesus. Then Pilate ordered it to be given to him. And Joseph took the body, and wrapped it in a clean linen shroud, and laid it in his own new tomb, which he had hewn in the rock;

and he rolled a great stone to the door of the tomb, and departed. Mary Mag'dalene and the other Mary were there, sitting opposite the sepulchre. Next day, that is, after the day of Preparation, the chief priests and the Pharisees gathered before Pilate, and said, "Sir, we remember how that impostor said, while he was still alive, 'After three days I will rise again.' Therefore order the sepulchre to be made secure until the third day, lest his disciples go and steal him away, and tell the people, 'He has risen from the dead,' and the last fraud will be worse than the first." Pilate said to them, "You have a guard of soldiers; go, make it as secure as you can." So they went and made the sepulchre secure by sealing the stone and setting a guard.

or this

✝ *The Holy Gospel of Our Lord Jesus Christ According to John* [19:38-42]

Joseph of Arimathe'a, who was a disciple of Jesus, but secretly, for fear of the Jews, asked Pilate that he might take away the body of Jesus, and Pilate gave him leave. So he came and took away his body. Nicode'mus also, who had first come to him by night, came bringing a mixture of myrrh and aloes about a hundred pounds' weight. They took the body of Jesus, and bound it in linen cloths with the spices, as is the burial custom of the Jews. Now in the place where he was crucified there was a garden, and in the garden a new tomb where no one had ever been laid. So because of the Jewish day of Preparation, as the tomb was close at hand, they laid Jesus there.

The Great Vigil of Easter

At the Liturgy of the Word

At least two of the following Lessons are read, of which one is always the Lesson from Exodus. After each Lesson, the Psalm or Canticle listed, or some other suitable psalm, canticle, or hymn may be sung. A period of silence may be kept; and the Collect provided (pages 288-291 of the Prayer Book), or some other suitable Collect, may be said.

[The Story of Creation]

A Reading (Lesson) from the Book of Genesis [1:1 — 2:2]

In the beginning God created the heavens and the earth. The earth was without form and void, and darkness was upon the face of the deep; and the Spirit of God was moving over the face of the waters. And God said,"Let there be light"; and there was light. And God saw that the light was good; and God separated the light from the darkness. God called the light Day, and the darkness he called Night. And there was evening and there was morning, one day. And God said,"Let there be a firmament in the midst of the waters, and let it separate the waters from the waters." And God made the firmament and separated the waters which were under the firmament from the waters which were above the firmament. And it was so. And God called the firmament Heaven. And there was evening and there was morning, a second day. And God said,"Let the waters under the heavens be gathered together into one place, and let the dry land appear." And it was so. God called the dry land Earth, and the waters that were gathered together he called Seas. And God saw that it was good. And God said,"Let the earth put forth vegetation, plants yielding seed, and fruit trees bearing fruit in which is their seed, each according to its kind, upon the earth." And it was so. The earth brought forth vegetation, plants yielding seed according to their own kinds, and trees bearing fruit in which is their seed, each according to its kind. And God saw that it was good. And there was evening and there was morning, a third day. And God said,"Let there be lights in the firmament of the heavens to separate the day from the night; and let them be for signs and for seasons and for days and years, and let them be lights in the firmament of the heavens to give light upon the earth." And it was so. And God made the two great lights, the greater light to rule the day, and the lesser light to rule the night; he made the stars also. And God set them in the firmament of the heavens to give light upon the earth, to rule over the day, and over the night, and to separate the light from the darkness. And God saw that it was good. And there was evening and there was morning, a fourth day. And God said,"Let the waters bring forth swarms of living creatures, and let birds fly above the earth across the firmament of the heavens." So God created the great sea monsters and every living creature that moves, with which the waters swarm, according to their kinds, and every winged bird according to its kind. And God saw that it was good. And God blessed them, saying,"Be fruitful and multiply and fill the waters in the seas, and let birds multiply on the earth." And there was evening and there was morning, a fifth day. And God said,"Let the earth bring forth living creatures according to their kinds: cattle and creeping things and beasts of the earth according to their kinds." And it was so. And God made the beasts of the earth according to their kinds and the cattle according to their kinds, and everything that creeps upon the ground according to its kind. And God saw that it was good. Then

God said, "Let us make man in our image, after our likeness; and let them have dominion over the fish of the sea, and over the birds of the air, and over the cattle, and over all the earth, and over every creeping thing that creeps upon the earth." So God created man in his own image, in the image of God he created him; male and female he created them. And God blessed them, and God said to them, "Be fruitful and multiply, and fill the earth and subdue it; and have dominion over the fish of the sea and over the birds of the air and over every living thing that moves upon the earth." And God said, "Behold, I have given you every plant yielding seed which is upon the face of all the earth, and every tree with seed in its fruit; you shall have them for food. And to every beast of the earth, and to every bird of the air, and to everything that creeps on the earth, everything that has the breath of life, I have given every green plant for food." And it was so. And God saw everything that he had made, and behold, it was very good. And there was evening and there was morning, a sixth day. Thus the heavens and the earth were finished, and all the host of them. And on the seventh day God finished his work which he had done, and he rested on the seventh day from all his work which he had done.

Psalm 33:1-11 [page 626]   or   *Psalm 36:5-10* [page 632]

[The Flood]

A Reading (Lesson) from the Book of Genesis
[7:1-5, 11-18; 8:6-18; 9:8-13]

The Lord said to Noah, "Go into the ark, you and all your household, for I have seen that you are righteous before me in this generation. Take with you seven pairs of all clean animals, the male and his mate; and a pair of the animals that are not clean, the male and his mate; and seven pairs of the birds of the air also, male and female, to keep their kind alive upon the face of all the earth. For in seven days I will send rain upon the earth forty days and forty nights; and every living thing that I have made I will blot out from the face of the ground." And Noah did all that the Lord had commanded him. In the six hundredth year of Noah's life, in the second month, on the seventeenth day of the month, on that day all the fountains of the great deep burst forth, and the windows of the heavens were opened. And rain fell upon the earth forty days and forty nights. On the very same day Noah and his sons, Shem and Ham and Japheth, and Noah's wife and the three wives of his sons with them entered the ark, they and every beast according to its kind, and all the cattle according to their kinds, and every creeping thing that creeps on the earth according to its kind, and every bird according to its kind, every bird of every sort. They went into the ark with Noah, two and two of all flesh in which there was the breath of life. And they that entered, male and female of all flesh, went in as God had commanded him; and the Lord shut him in. The flood continued forty days upon the earth; and the waters increased, and bore up the ark, and it rose high above the earth. The waters prevailed and increased greatly upon the earth; and the ark floated on the face of the waters. At the end of forty days Noah opened the window of the ark which he had made, and sent forth a raven; and it went to and fro until the waters were dried up from the earth. Then he sent forth a dove from him, to see if the waters had subsided from the face of the ground; but the dove found no place to set her foot, and she returned to him to the ark, for the waters were still on the face of the whole earth. So he put forth his hand and took her and brought her into the ark with him. He waited another seven days, and again he sent forth the dove out of the ark; and the dove came back to him in the evening, and lo, in her mouth a freshly plucked olive leaf; so Noah knew that the waters had subsided from the earth. Then he waited another seven days, and sent forth the dove; and she did not return to him any more. In the six hundred and first year, in the first month, the first day of the month, the waters were dried from off the earth; and Noah removed the covering of the ark, and looked, and behold, the face of the ground was dry. In the second month, on the twenty-seventh day of the month, the earth was dry. Then God said to Noah, "Go forth from the ark, you and your wife, and your sons and your sons' wives with you. Bring forth with you every living thing that is with you of all flesh—birds and animals and every creeping thing that creeps on the earth—that they may breed abundantly on the earth, and be fruitful and multiply upon the earth." So Noah went forth, and his sons and his wife and his sons' wives with him. Then God said to Noah and to his sons with him, "Behold, I establish my covenant with you and your descendants after you, and with every living creature that is with you, the birds, the cattle, and every beast of the earth with you, as many as came out of the ark. I establish my covenant with you, that never again shall all flesh be cut off by the waters of a flood, and never again shall there be a flood to destroy the earth." And God said, "This is the sign of the covenant which I make between me and you and every living creature that is with you, for all future generations: I set my bow in the cloud, and it shall be a sign of the covenant between me and the earth."

Psalm 46 [page 649]

[Abraham's sacrifice of Issac]

A Reading (Lesson) from the Book of Genesis [22:1-18]

God tested Abraham, and said to him, "Abraham!" And he said, "Here am I." He said, "Take your son, your only son

Isaac, whom you love, and go to the land of Mori'ah, and offer him there as a burnt offering upon one of the mountains of which I shall tell you." So Abraham rose early in the morning, saddled his ass, and took two of his young men with him, and his son Isaac; and he cut the wood for the burnt offering, and arose and went to the place of which God had told him. On the third day Abraham lifted up his eyes and saw the place afar off. Then Abraham said to his young men, "Stay here with the ass; I and the lad will go yonder and worship, and come again to you." And Abraham took the wood of the burnt offering, and laid it on Isaac his son; and he took in his hand the fire and the knife. So they went both of them together. And Isaac said to his father Abraham, "My father!" And he said, "Here am I, my son." He said, "Behold, the fire and the wood; but where is the lamb for a burnt offering?" Abraham said, "God will provide himself the lamb for a burnt offering, my son." So they went both of them together. When they came to the place of which God had told him, Abraham built an altar there, and laid the wood in order, and bound Isaac his son, and laid him on the altar, upon the wood. Then Abraham put forth his hand, and took the knife to slay his son. But the angel of the Lord called to him from heaven, and said, "Abraham, Abraham!" And he said, "Here am I." He said, "Do not lay your hand on the lad or do anything to him; for now I know that you fear God, seeing you have not withheld your son, your only son, from me." And Abraham lifted up his eyes and looked, and behold, behind him was a ram, caught in a thicket by his horns; and Abraham went and took the ram, and offered it up as a burnt offering instead of his son. So Abraham called the name of that place The Lord will provide; as it is said to this day, "On the mount of the Lord it shall be provided." And the angel of the Lord called to Abraham a second time from heaven, and said, "By myself I have sworn, says the Lord, because you have done this, and have not withheld your son, your only son, I will indeed bless you, and I will multiply your descendants as the stars of heaven and as the sand which is on the seashore. And your descendants shall possess the gate of their enemies, and by your descendants shall all the nations of the earth bless themselves, because you have obeyed my voice."

Psalm 33:12-22 [page 626] or *Psalm 16* [page 599]

[Israel's deliverance at the Red Sea]

A Reading (Lesson) from the Book of Exodus
[14:10—15:1]

When Pharaoh drew near, the people of Israel lifted up their eyes, and behold, the Egyptians were marching after them; and they were in great fear. And the people of Israel cried out to the Lord; and they said to Moses,"Is it because there are no graves in Egypt that you have taken us away to die in the wilderness? What have you done to us, in bringing us out of Egypt? Is not this what we have said to you in Egypt,'Let us alone and let us serve the Egyptians'? For it would have been better for us to serve the Egyptians than die in the wilderness." And Moses said to the people, "Fear not, stand firm, and see the salvation of the Lord, which he will work for you today; for the Egyptians whom you see today, you shall never see again. The Lord will fight for you, and you have only to be still." The Lord said to Moses,"Why do you cry to me? Tell the people of Israel to go forward. Lift up your rod, and stretch out your hand over the sea and divide it, that the people of Israel may go on dry ground through the sea. And I will harden the hearts of the Egyptians so that they shall go in after them, and I will get glory over Pharaoh and all his host, his chariots, and his horsemen. And the Egyptians shall know that I am the Lord, when I have gotten glory over Pharaoh, his chariots, and his horsemen." Then the angel of God who went before the host of Israel moved and went behind them; and the pillar of cloud moved from before them and stood behind them, coming between the host of Egypt and the host of Israel. And there was the cloud and the darkness; and the night passed without one coming near the other all night. Then Moses stretched out his hand over the sea; and the Lord drove the sea back by a strong east wind all night, and made the sea dry land, and the waters were divided. And the people of Israel went into the midst of the sea on dry ground, the waters being a wall to them on their right hand and on their left. The Egyptians pursued, and went in after them into the midst of the sea, all Pharaoh's horses, his chariots, and his horsemen. And in the morning watch, the Lord in the pillar of fire and of cloud looked down upon the host of the Egyptians, and discomfited the host of the Egyptians, clogging their chariot wheels so that they drove heavily; and the Egyptians said,"Let us flee from before Israel; for the Lord fights for them against the Egyptians." Then the Lord said to Moses,"Stretch out your hand over the sea, that the water may come back upon the Egyptians, upon their chariots, and upon their horsemen." So Moses stretched forth his hand over the sea, and the sea returned to its wonted flow when the morning appeared; and the Egyptians fled into it, and the Lord routed the Egyptians in the midst of the sea. The waters returned and covered the chariots and the horsemen and all the host of Pharaoh that had followed them into the sea; not so much as one of them remained. But the people of Israel walked on dry ground through the sea, the waters being a wall to them on their right hand and on their left. Thus the Lord saved Israel that day from the hand of the Egyptians; and Israel saw the Egyptians dead upon the seashore. And Israel saw the great work which the Lord did against the Egyptians, and the people feared the Lord; and they believed in the Lord and in his servant Moses. Then Moses and the people of Israel sang this song to the Lord, saying, "I will sing to the Lord, for he has triumphed gloriously; the horse and his rider he has thrown into the sea."

Canticle 8, The Song of Moses [page 85]

[God's Presence in a renewed Israel]

A Reading (Lesson) from the Book of Isaiah [4:2-6]

In that day the branch of the Lord shall be beautiful and glorious, and the fruit of the land shall be the pride and glory of the survivors of Israel. And he who is left in Zion and remains in Jerusalem will be called holy, every one who has been recorded for life in Jerusalem, when the Lord shall have washed away the filth of the daughters of Zion, and cleansed the bloodstains of Jerusalem from its midst by a spirit of judgment and by a spirit of burning. Then the Lord will create over the whole site of Mount Zion and over her assemblies a cloud by day, and smoke and the shining of a flaming fire by night; for over all the glory there will be a canopy and a pavilion. It will be for a shade by day from the heat, and for a refuge and a shelter from the storm and rain.

Psalm 122 [page 779]

[Salvation offered freely to all]

A Reading (Lesson) from the Book of Isaiah [55:1-11]

Thus says the Lord: "Ho, every one who thirsts, come to the waters; and he who has no money, come, buy and eat! Come, buy wine and milk without money and without price. Why do you spend your money for that which is not bread, and your labor for that which does not satisfy? Hearken diligently to me, and eat what is good, and delight yourselves in fatness. Incline your ear, and come to me; hear, that your soul may live; and I will make with you an everlasting covenant, my steadfast, sure love for David. Behold, I made him a witness to the peoples, a leader and commander for the peoples. Behold, you shall call nations that you know not, and nations that knew you not shall run to you, because of the Lord your God, and of the Holy One of Israel, for he has glorified you. Seek the Lord while he may be found, call upon him while he is near; let the wicked forsake his way, and the unrighteous man his thoughts; let him return to the Lord, that he may have mercy on him, and to our God, for he will abundantly pardon. For my thoughts are not your thoughts, neither are your ways my ways, says the Lord. For as the heavens are higher than the earth, so are my ways higher than your ways and my thoughts than your thoughts. For as the rain and the snow come down from heaven, and return not thither but water the earth, making it bring forth and sprout, giving seed to the sower and bread to the eater, so shall my word be that goes forth from my mouth; it shall not return to me empty, but it shall accomplish that which I purpose, and prosper in the thing for which I sent it."

Canticle 9, The First Song of Isaiah [Page 86] or

Psalm 42:1-7 [page 643]

[A new heart and a new spirit]

A Reading (Lesson) from the Book of Ezekiel [36:24-28]

Thus says the Lord God: "I will take you from the nations, and gather you from all the countries, and bring you into your own land. I will sprinkle clean water upon you, and you shall be clean from all your uncleannesses, and from all your idols I will cleanse you. A new heart I will give you, and a new spirit I will put within you; and I will take out of your flesh the heart of stone and give you a heart of flesh. And I will put my spirit within you, and cause you to walk in my statutes and be careful to observe my ordinances. You shall dwell in the land which I gave to your fathers; and you shall be my people, and I will be your God."

Psalm 42:1-7 [page 643] or

Canticle 9, The First Song of Isaiah [page 86]

[The valley of dry bones]

A Reading (Lesson) from the Book of Ezekiel [37:1-14]

The hand of the Lord was upon me, and he brought me out by the Spirit of the Lord, and set me down in the midst of the valley; it was full of bones. And he led me round among them; and behold, there were very many upon the valley; and lo, they were very dry. And he said to me, "Son of man, can these bones live?" And I answered, "O Lord God, thou knowest." Again he said to me, "Prophesy to these bones, and say to them, O dry bones, hear the word of the Lord. Thus says the Lord God to these bones: Behold, I will cause breath to enter you, and you shall live. And I will lay sinews upon you, and will cause flesh to come upon you, and cover you with skin, and put breath in you, and you shall live; and you shall know that I am the Lord." So I prophesied as I was commanded; and as I prophesied there was a noise, and behold, a rattling; and the bones came together, bone to its bone. And as I looked, there were sinews on them, and flesh had come upon them, and skin had covered them; but there was no breath in them. Then he said to me, "Prophesy to the breath, prophesy, son of man, and say to the breath, Thus says the Lord God: Come from the four winds, O breath, and breathe upon these slain, that they may live." So I prophesied as he commanded me, and the breath came into them, and they lived, and stood upon their feet, an exceedingly great host. Then he said to me, "Son of man, these bones are the whole house of Israel. Behold, they say, 'Our bones are dried up, and our hope is lost; we are clean cut off.' Therefore prophesy, and say to them, Thus says the Lord God: Behold, I will open your graves, and raise you from your graves, O my people; and I will bring you home into the land of Israel. And you shall know that I am the Lord, when I open your graves, and raise you from your graves, O my people. And I will put my Spirit within you, and you shall live, and I will place you in your own land; then you shall know that I, the Lord, have spoken, and I have done it, says the Lord."

Psalm 30 [page 621] or *Psalm 143* [page 798]

[The gathering of God's people]

A Reading (Lesson) from the Book of Zephaniah
[3:12-20]

Thus says the Lord: "I will leave in the midst of you a people humble and lowly. They shall seek refuge in the name of the Lord, those who are left in Israel; they shall do no wrong and utter no lies, nor shall there be found in their mouth a deceitful tongue. For they shall pasture and lie down, and none shall make them afraid." Sing aloud, O daughter of Zion; shout, O Israel! Rejoice and exult with all your heart, O daughter of Jerusalem! The Lord has taken away the judgments against you, he has cast out your enemies. The King of Israel, the Lord, is in your midst; you shall fear evil no more. On that day it shall be said to Jerusalem: "Do not fear, O Zion; Let not your hands grow weak. The Lord, your God, is in your midst, a warrior who gives victory; he will rejoice over you with gladness, he will renew you in his love; he will exult over you with loud singing as on a day of festival. I will remove disaster from you, so that you will not bear reproach for it. Behold, at that time I will deal with all your oppressors. And I will save the lame, and gather the outcast, and I will change their shame into praise and renown in all the earth. At that time I will bring you home, at the time when I gather you together; yea, I will make you renowned and praised among all the peoples of the earth, when I restore your fortunes before your eyes," says the Lord.

Psalm 98 [page 727] or *Psalm 126* [page 782]

At the Eucharist

A Reading (Lesson) from the Letter of Paul to the Romans [6:3-11]

Do you not know that all of us who have been baptized into Christ Jesus were baptized into his death? We were buried therefore with him by baptism into death, so that as Christ was raised from the dead by the glory of the Father, we too might walk in newness of life. For if we have been united with him in a death like his, we shall certainly be united with him in a resurrection like his. We know that our old self was crucified with him so that the sinful body might be destroyed, and we might no longer be enslaved to sin. For he who has died is freed from sin. But if we have died with Christ, we believe that we shall also live with him. For we know that Christ being raised from the dead will never die again; death no longer has dominion over him. The death he died, he died to sin, once for all, but the life he lives, he lives to God. So you also must consider yourselves dead to sin and alive to God in Christ Jesus.

"Alleluia" may be sung and repeated.

Psalm 114 [page 756], *or some other suitable psalm or a hymn may be sung.*

✝ *The Holy Gospel of Our Lord Jesus Christ According to Matthew* [28:1-10]

After the sabbath, toward the dawn of the first day of the week, Mary Mag'dalene and the other Mary went to see the sepulchre. And behold, there was a great earthquake; for an angel of the Lord descended from heaven and came and rolled back the stone, and sat upon it. His appearance was like lightning, and his raiment white as snow. And for fear of him the guards trembled and became like dead men. But the angel said to the women, "Do not be afraid; for I know that you seek Jesus who was crucified. He is not here; for he has risen, as he said. Come, see the place where he lay. Then go quickly and tell his disciples that he has risen from the dead, and behold, he is going before you to Galilee; there you will see him. Lo, I have told you." So they departed quickly from the tomb with fear and great joy, and ran to tell his disciples. And behold, Jesus met them and said, "Hail!" And they came up and took hold of his feet and worshiped him. Then Jesus said to them, "Do not be afraid; go and tell my brethren to go to Galilee, and there they will see me."

Easter Day: Early Service

One of the Old Testament Lessons from the Vigil
[pages 110-122 above]

Psalm 114 [page 756]

The Epistle: Romans 6:3-11 [page 122 above]

The Holy Gospel: Matthew 28:1-10 [page 123 above]

Easter Day: Principal Service

A Reading (Lesson) from the Acts of the Apostles
[10:34-43]

Peter opened his mouth and said,"Truly I perceive that
God shows no partiality, but in every nation any one who
fears him and does what is right is acceptable to him. You
know the word which he sent to Israel, preaching good
news of peace by Jesus Christ (he is Lord of all), the word
which was proclaimed throughout all Judea, beginning
from Galilee after the baptism which John preached: how
God anointed Jesus of Nazareth with the Holy Spirit and
with power; how he went about doing good and healing all
that were oppressed by the devil, for God was with him.
And we are witnesses to all that he did both in the country
of the Jews and in Jerusalem. They put him to death by
hanging him on a tree; but God raised him on the third day
and made him manifest; not to all the people but to us who
were chosen by God as witnesses, who ate and drank with
him after he rose from the dead. And he commanded us to
preach to the people, and to testify that he is the one
ordained by God to be judge of the living and the dead. To
him all the prophets bear witness that every one who believes
in him receives forgiveness of sins through his name."

or the following

A Reading (Lesson) from the Book of Exodus
[14:10-14,21-25; 15:20-21]

When Pharaoh drew near, the people of Israel lifted up their eyes, and behold, the Egyptians were marching after them; and they were in great fear. And the people of Israel cried out to the Lord; and they said to Moses, "Is it because there are no graves in Egypt that you have taken us away to die in the wilderness? What have you done to us, in bringing us out of Egypt? Is not this what we said to you in Egypt, 'Let us alone and let us serve the Egyptians'? For it would have been better for us to serve the Egyptians than to die in the wilderness." And Moses said to the people, "Fear not, stand firm, and see the salvation of the Lord, which he will work for you today; for the Egyptians whom you see today, you shall never see again. The Lord will fight for you, and you have only to be still." Then Moses stretched out his hand over the sea; and the Lord drove the sea back by a strong east wind all night, and made the sea dry land, and the waters were divided. And the people of Israel went into the midst of the sea on dry ground, the waters being a wall to them on their right hand and on their left. The Egyptians pursued, and went in after them into the midst of the sea, all Pharaoh's horses, his chariots, and his horsemen. And in the morning watch the Lord in the pillar of fire and of cloud looked down upon the host of the Egyptians, and discomfited the host of the Egyptians, clogging their chariot wheels so that they drove heavily; and the Egyptians said, "Let us flee from before Israel; for the Lord fights for them against the Egyptians."

Then Miriam, the prophetess, the sister of Aaron, took a timbrel in her hand; and all the women went out after her with timbrels and dancing. And Miriam sang to them: "Sing to the Lord, for he has triumphed gloriously; the horse and his rider he has thrown into the sea."

Psalm 118:14-29 [page 761]   or

118:14-17, 22-24 [page 761]

*A Reading (Lesson) from the Letter of Paul
to the Colossians* [3:1-4]

Since you have been raised with Christ, seek the things that
are above, where Christ is, seated at the right hand of God.
Set your minds on things that are above, not on things that
are on earth. For you have died, and your life is hid with
Christ in God. When Christ who is our life appears, then
you also will appear with him in glory.

or this

Acts 10:34-43 [page 124 above]

✝ *The Holy Gospel of Our Lord Jesus Christ
According to John* [20:1-10 (11-18)]

On the first day of the week Mary Mag'dalene came to the
tomb early, while it was still dark, and saw that the stone
had been taken away from the tomb. So she ran, and went
to Simon Peter and the other disciple, the one whom Jesus
loved, and said to them, "They have taken the Lord out of
the tomb, and we do not know where they have laid him."
Peter then came out with the other disciple, and they
went toward the tomb. They both ran, but the other
disciple outran Peter and reached the tomb first; and
stooping to look in, he saw the linen cloths lying there, but
he did not go in. Then Simon Peter came, following him,
and went into the tomb; he saw the linen cloths lying, and
the napkin, which had been on his head, not lying with the
linen cloths but rolled up in a place by itself. Then the
other disciple, who reached the tomb first, also went in,
and he saw and believed; for as yet they did not know the
scripture, that he must rise from the dead. Then the
disciples went back to their homes.

But Mary stood weeping outside the tomb, and as she wept she stooped to look into the tomb; and she saw two angels in white, sitting where the body of Jesus had lain, one at the head and one at the feet. They said to her, "Woman, why are you weeping?" She said to them, "Because they have taken away my Lord, and I do not know where they have laid him." Saying this, she turned round and saw Jesus standing, but she did not know that it was Jesus. Jesus said to her, "Woman, why are you weeping? Whom do you seek?" Supposing him to be the gardener, she said to him, "Sir, if you have carried him away, tell me where you have laid him, and I will take him away." Jesus said to her, "Mary." She turned and said to him in Hebrew, "Rab-bo'ni!" (which means Teacher). Jesus said to her, "Do not hold me, for I have not yet ascended to the Father; but go to my brethren and say to them, I am ascending to my Father and your Father, to my God and your God." Mary Mag'dalene went and said to the disciples, "I have seen the Lord"; and she told them that he had said these things to her.

or this

✝ *The Holy Gospel of Our Lord Jesus Christ According to Matthew* [28:1-10]

After the sabbath, toward the dawn of the first day of the week, Mary Mag'dalene and the other Mary went to see the sepulchre. And behold, there was a great earthquake; for an angel of the Lord descended from heaven and came and rolled back the stone, and sat upon it. His appearance was like lightning, and his raiment white as snow. And for fear of him the guards trembled and became like dead men. But the angel said to the women, "Do not be afraid; for I know that you seek Jesus who was crucified. He is not here; for he has risen, as he said. Come, see the place where he lay. Then go quickly and tell his disciples that he has risen from the dead, and behold, he is going before you to Galilee; there you will see him. Lo, I have told you." So they departed quickly from the tomb with fear and great joy, and ran to tell his disciples. And behold, Jesus met them and said, "Hail!" And they came up and took hold of his feet and worshiped him. Then Jesus said to them, "Do not be afraid; go and tell my brethren to go to Galilee, and there they will see me."

Easter Day: Evening Service

A Reading (Lesson) from the Acts of the Apostles
[5:29a,30-32]

Peter and the apostles said to the high priest and the council, "The God of our fathers raised Jesus whom you killed by hanging him on a tree. God exalted him at his right hand as Leader and Savior, to give repentance to Israel and forgiveness of sins, and we are witnesses to these things, and so is the Holy Spirit whom God has given to those who obey him."

or this

A Reading (Lesson) from the Book of Daniel [12:1-3]

The Lord spoke to Daniel in a vision and said, "At that time shall arise Michael, the great prince who has charge of your people. And there shall be a time of trouble, such as never has been since there was a nation till that time; but at that time your people shall be delivered, every one whose name shall be found written in the book. And many of those who sleep in the dust of the earth shall awake, some to everlasting life, and some to shame and everlasting contempt. And those who are wise shall shine like the brightness of the firmament; and those who turn many to righteousness, like the stars for ever and ever."

Psalm 114 [page 756] or *Psalm 136* [page 789] or

Psalm 118:14-17, 22-24 [page 761]

A Reading (Lesson) from the First Letter of Paul to the Corinthians [5:6b-8]

Do you not know that a little leaven leavens the whole lump? Cleanse out the old leaven that you may be a new lump, as you really are unleavened. For Christ, our paschal lamb, has been sacrificed. Let us, therefore, celebrate the festival, not with the old leaven, the leaven of malice and evil, but with the unleavened bread of sincerity and truth.

or this

Acts 5:29a,30-32 [page 128 above]

✝ *The Holy Gospel of Our Lord Jesus Christ According to Luke* [24:13-35]

That very day, the first day of the week, two of the disciples were going to a village named Emma'us, about seven miles from Jerusalem, and talking with each other about all these things that had happened. While they were talking and discussing together, Jesus himself drew near and went with them. But their eyes were kept from recognizing him. And he said to them, "What is this conversation which you are holding with each other as you walk?" And they stood still, looking sad. Then one of them, named Cle'opas, answered him, "Are you the only visitor to Jerusalem who does not know the things that have happened there in these days?" And he said to them, "What things?" And they said to him, "Concerning Jesus of Nazareth, who was a prophet mighty in deed and word before God and all the people, and how our chief priests and rulers delivered him up to be condemned to death, and crucified him. But we had hoped that he was the one to redeem Israel. Yes, and besides all this, it is now the third day since this happened. Moreover, some women of our company amazed us. They were at the tomb early in the morning and did not find his body; and they came back saying that they had even seen a vision of angels, who said that he was alive. Some of those who were with us went to the tomb, and found it just as the women had said; but him they did not see." And he said to them, "O foolish men, and slow of heart to believe all that the prophets have spoken! Was it not necessary that the Christ should suffer these things and enter into his glory?" And beginning with Moses and all the prophets, he interpreted to them in all the scriptures the things concerning himself. So they drew near to the village to which they were going. He appeared to be going further, but they constrained him, saying, "Stay with us, for it is toward evening and the day is now far spent." So he went in to stay with them. When he was at table with them, he took the bread and blessed, and broke it, and gave it to them. And their eyes were opened and they recognized him; and he vanished out of their sight. They said to each other, "Did not our hearts burn within us while he talked to us on the road, while he opened to us the scriptures?" And they rose that same hour and returned to Jerusalem; and they found the eleven gathered together and those who were with them, who said, "The Lord has risen indeed, and has appeared to Simon!" Then they told what had happened on the road, and how he was known to them in the breaking of the bread.

Monday in Easter Week

A Reading (Lesson) from the Acts of the Apostles
[2:14,22b-32]

Peter, standing with the eleven, lifted up his voice and addressed the multitude, "Men of Judea and all who dwell in Jerusalem, let this be known to you, and give ear to my words: Jesus of Nazareth, a man attested to you by God with mighty works and wonders and signs which God did through him in your midst, as you yourselves know—this Jesus, delivered up according to the definite plan and foreknowledge of God, you crucified and killed by the hands of lawless men. But God raised him up, having loosed the pangs of death, because it was not possible for him to be held by it. For David says concerning him, 'I saw the Lord always before me, for he is at my right hand that I may not be shaken; therefore my heart was glad, and my tongue rejoiced; moreover my flesh will dwell in hope. For thou wilt not abandon my soul to Hades, nor let thy Holy One see corruption. Thou hast made known to me the ways of life; thou wilt make me full of gladness with thy presence.' Brethren, I may say to you confidently of the patriarch David that he both died and was buried, and his tomb is with us to this day. Being therefore a prophet, and knowing that God had sworn with an oath to him that he would set one of his descendants upon his throne, he foresaw and spoke of the resurrection of the Christ, that he was not abandoned to Hades, nor did his flesh see corruption. This Jesus God raised up, and of that we all are witnesses."

Psalm 16:8-11 [page 600]   or   *Psalm 118:19-24* [page 762]

✝ *The Holy Gospel of Our Lord Jesus Christ*
According to Matthew [28:9-15]

Behold, Jesus met Mary Mag'dalene and the other Mary
and said, "Hail!" And they came up and took hold of his
feet and worshiped him. Then Jesus said to them, "Do not
be afraid; go and tell my brethren to go to Galilee, and
there they will see me." While they were going, behold,
some of the guard went into the city and told the chief
priests all that had taken place. And when they had
assembled with the elders and taken counsel, they gave a
sum of money to the soldiers and said, "Tell people, 'His
disciples came by night and stole him away while we were
asleep.' And if this comes to the governor's ears, we will
satisfy him and keep you out of trouble." So they took the
money and did as they were directed; and this story has
been spread among the Jews to this day.

Tuesday in Easter Week

A Reading (Lesson) from the Acts of the Apostles
[2:36-41]

Peter said to the multitude, "Let all the house of Israel
therefore know assuredly that God has made him both
Lord and Christ, this Jesus whom you crucified." Now
when they heard this they were cut to the heart, and said to
Peter and the rest of the apostles, "Brethren, what shall we
do?" And Peter said to them, "Repent, and be baptized
every one of you in the name of Jesus Christ for the
forgiveness of your sins; and you shall receive the gift of
the Holy Spirit. For the promise is to you and to your
children and to all that are far off, every one whom the
Lord our God calls to him." And he testified with many
other words and exhorted them, saying, "Save yourselves
from this crooked generation." So those who received his

word were baptized, and there were added that day about three thousand souls.

Psalm 33:18-22 [page 627]   or

Psalm 118:19-24 [page 762]

✝ *The Holy Gospel of Our Lord Jesus Christ According to John* [20:11-18]

Mary Mag'dalene stood weeping outside the tomb, and as she wept she stooped to look into the tomb; and she saw two angels in white, sitting where the body of Jesus had lain, one at the head and one at the feet. They said to her, "Woman, why are you weeping?" She said to them, "Because they have taken away my Lord, and I do not know where they have laid him." Saying this, she turned round and saw Jesus standing, but she did not know that it was Jesus. Jesus said to her, "Woman, why are you weeping? Whom do you seek?" Supposing him to be the gardener, she said to him, "Sir, if you have carried him away, tell me where you have laid him, and I will take him away." Jesus said to her, "Mary." She turned and said to him in Hebrew, "Rab-bo'ni!" (which means Teacher). Jesus said to her, "Do not hold me, for I have not yet ascended to the Father; but go to my brethren and say to them, I am ascending to my Father and your Father, to my God and your God." Mary Mag'dalene went and said to the disciples, "I have seen the Lord"; and she told them that he had said these things to her.

Wednesday in Easter Week

A Reading (Lesson) from the Acts of the Apostles [3:1-10]

Now Peter and John were going up to the temple at the hour of prayer, the ninth hour. And a man lame from birth was being carried, whom they laid daily at that gate of the temple which is called Beautiful to ask alms of those who entered the temple. Seeing Peter and John about to go into the temple, he asked for alms. And Peter directed his gaze at him, with John, and said, "Look at us." And he fixed his attention upon them, expecting to receive something from them. But Peter said, "I have no silver and gold, but I give you what I have; in the name of Jesus Christ of Nazareth, walk." And he took him by the right hand and raised him up; and immediately his feet and ankles were made strong. And leaping up he stood and walked and entered the temple with them, walking and leaping and praising God. And all the people saw him walking and praising God, and recognized him as the one who sat for alms at the Beautiful Gate of the temple; and they were filled with wonder and amazement at what had happened to him.

Psalm 105:1-8 [page 738]   or   *Psalm 118:19-24* [page 762]

✝ *The Holy Gospel of Our Lord Jesus Christ*
According to Luke [24:13-35] [page 129 above]

Thursday in Easter Week

A Reading (Lesson) from the Acts of the Apostles
[3:11-26]

While the lame man whom Peter and John had healed clung to them, all the people ran together to them in the portico called Solomon's, astounded. And when Peter saw it he addressed the people, "Men of Israel, why do you wonder at this, or why do you stare at us, as though by our own power or piety we had made him walk? The God of Abraham and of Isaac and of Jacob, the God of our fathers, glorified his servant Jesus, whom you delivered up and denied in the presence of Pilate, when he had decided to release him. But you denied the Holy and Righteous One, and asked for a murderer to be granted to you, and killed the Author of life, whom God raised from the dead. To this we are witnesses. And his name, by faith in his name, has made this man strong whom you see and know; and the faith which is through Jesus has given the man this perfect health in the presence of you all. And now, brethren, I know that you acted in ignorance, as did also your rulers. But what God foretold by the mouth of all the prophets, that his Christ should suffer, he thus fulfilled. Repent therefore, and turn again, that your sins may be blotted out, that times of refreshing may come from the presence of the Lord, and that he may send the Christ appointed for you, Jesus, whom heaven must receive until the time for establishing all that God spoke by the mouth of his holy prophets from of old. Moses said, 'The Lord God will raise up for you a prophet from your brethren as he raised me up. You shall listen to him in whatever he tells you. And it shall be that every soul that does not listen to that prophet shall be destroyed from the people.' And all the prophets who have spoken, from Samuel and those who came afterwards, also proclaimed these days. You are the sons of the prophets and of the covenant which God gave to your fathers, saying to Abraham, 'And in your posterity shall all the families of the earth be blessed.' God, having raised up his servant, sent him to you first, to bless you in turning every one of you from your wickedness."

Psalm 8 [page 592]   or   *Psalm 114* [page 756]   or

Psalm 118:19-24 [page 762]

✝ *The Holy Gospel of Our Lord Jesus Christ According to Luke* [24:36b-48]

While the disciples were telling how they had seen Jesus risen from the dead, Jesus himself stood among them. But they were startled and frightened, and supposed that they saw a ghost. And he said to them, "Why are you troubled, and why do questionings rise in your hearts? See my hands and my feet, that it is I myself; handle me, and see; for a spirit has not flesh and bones as you see that I have." And while they still disbelieved for joy, and wondered, he said to them, "Have you anything here to eat?" They gave him a piece of broiled fish, and he took it and ate it before them. Then he said to them, "These are my words which I spoke to you, while I was still with you, that everything written about me in the law of Moses and the prophets and the psalms must be fulfilled." Then he opened their minds to understand the scriptures, and said to them, "Thus it is written, that the Christ should suffer and on the third day rise from the dead, and that repentance and forgiveness of sins should be preached in his name to all nations, beginning from Jerusalem. You are witnesses of these things."

Friday in Easter Week

A Reading (Lesson) from the Acts of the Apostles [4:1-12]

As Peter and John were speaking to the people, the priests and the captain of the temple and the Sad'ducees came upon them, annoyed because they were teaching the people and proclaiming in Jesus the resurrection from the dead. And they arrested them and put them in custody until the morrow, for it was already evening. But many of those who heard the word believed; and the number of the men came to about five thousand. On the morrow their rulers and elders and scribes were gathered together in Jerusalem, with Annas the high priest and Ca'iaphas and John and Alexander, and all who were of the high-priestly family. And when they had set them in the midst, they inquired, "By what power or by what name did you do this?"

Then Peter, filled with the Holy Spirit, said to them, "Rulers of the people and elders, if we are being examined today concerning a good deed done to a cripple, by what means this man has been healed, be it known to you all, and to all the people of Israel, that by the name of Jesus Christ of Nazareth, whom you crucified, whom God raised from the dead, by him this man is standing before you well. This is the stone which was rejected by you builders, but which has become the head of the corner. And there is salvation in no one else, for there is no other name under heaven given among men by which we must be saved."

Psalm 116:1-8 [page 759]   or   *Psalm 118:19-24* [page 762]

✝ *The Holy Gospel of Our Lord Jesus Christ According to John* [21:1-14]

After this Jesus revealed himself again to the disciples by the Sea of Tibe'ri-as; and he revealed himself in this way. Simon Peter, Thomas called the Twin, Nathan'a-el of Cana in Galilee, the sons of Zeb'edee, and two others of his disciples were together. Simon Peter said to them, "I am going fishing." They said to him, "We will go with you." They went out and got into the boat; but that night they caught nothing. Just as day was breaking, Jesus stood on the beach; yet the disciples did not know that it was Jesus. Jesus said to them, "Children, have you any fish?" They answered him, "No." He said to them, "Cast the net on the right side of the boat, and you will find some." So they cast it, and now they were not able to haul it in, for the quantity of fish. That disciple whom Jesus loved said to Peter, "It is the Lord!" When Simon Peter heard that it was the Lord, he put on his clothes, for he was stripped for work, and sprang into the sea. But the other disciples came in the boat, dragging the net full of fish, for they were not far from the land, but about a hundred yards off. When they got out on land, they saw a charcoal fire there, with fish lying on it, and bread. Jesus said to them, "Bring some of the fish that you have just caught." So Simon Peter went aboard and hauled the net ashore, full of large fish, a hundred and fifty-three of them; and although there were so many, the net was not torn. Jesus said to them, "Come and have breakfast." Now none of the disciples dared ask him, "Who are you?" They knew it was the Lord. Jesus came and took the bread and gave it to them, and so with the fish. This was now the third time that Jesus was revealed to the disciples after he was raised from the dead.

Saturday in Easter Week

A Reading (Lesson) from the Acts of the Apostles [4:13-21]

Now when the rulers and elders and scribes saw the boldness of Peter and John, and perceived that they were uneducated, common men, they wondered; and they recognized that they had been with Jesus. But seeing the man that had been healed standing beside them, they had nothing to say in opposition. But when they had commanded them to go aside out of the council, they conferred with one another, saying, "What shall we do with these men? For that a notable sign has been performed through them is manifest to all the inhabitants of Jerusalem, and we cannot deny it. But in order that it may spread no further among the people, let us warn them to speak no more to any one in this name." So they called them and charged them not to speak or teach at all in the name of Jesus. But Peter and John answered them, "Whether it is right in the sight of God to listen to you rather than to God, you must judge; for we cannot but speak of what we have seen and heard." And when they had further threatened them, they let them go, finding no way to punish them, because of the people; for all men praised God for what had happened.

Psalm 118:14-18 [page 761] or *118:19-24* [page 762]

✝ *The Holy Gospel of Our Lord Jesus Christ*
According to Mark [16:9-15, 20]

Now when Jesus rose early on the first day of the week, he appeared first to Mary Mag'dalene, from whom he had cast out seven demons. She went out and told those who had been with him, as they mourned and wept. But when they heard that he was alive and had been seen by her, they would not believe it. After this he appeared in another form to two of them as they were walking into the country. And they went back and told the rest, but they did not believe them. Afterward he appeared to the eleven themselves as they sat at table; and he upbraided them for their unbelief and hardness of heart, because they had not believed those who saw him after he had risen. And he said to them, "Go into all the world and preach the gospel to the whole creation." And they went forth and preached everywhere, while the Lord worked with them and confirmed the message by the signs that attended it.

Second Sunday of Easter

A Reading (Lesson) from the Acts of the Apostles
[2:14a,22-32]

Peter, standing with the eleven, lifed up his voice and addressed the multitude, "Men of Israel, hear these words: Jesus of Nazareth, a man attested to you by God with mighty works and wonders and signs which God did through him in your midst, as you yourselves know—

this Jesus, delivered up according to the definite plan and foreknowledge of God, you crucified and killed by the hands of lawless men. But God raised him up, having loosed the pangs of death, because it was not possible for him to be held by it. For David says concerning him, 'I saw the Lord always before me, for he is at my right hand that I may not be shaken; therefore my heart was glad, and my tongue rejoiced; moreover my flesh will dwell in hope. For thou wilt not abandon my soul to Hades, nor let thy Holy One see corruption. Thou hast made known to me the ways of life; thou wilt make me full of gladness with thy presence.' Brethren, I may say to you confidently of the patriarch David that he both died and was buried, and his tomb is with us to this day. Being therefore a prophet, and knowing that God had sworn with an oath to him that he would set one of his descendants upon his throne, he foresaw and spoke of the resurrection of the Christ, that he was not abandoned to Hades, nor did his flesh see corruption. This Jesus God raised up, and of that we all are witnesses."

or this

A Reading (Lesson) from the Book of Genesis
[8:6-16; 9:8-16]

At the end of the flood Noah opened the window of the ark which he had made, and sent forth a raven; and it went to and fro until the waters were dried up from the earth. Then he sent forth a dove from him, to see if the waters had subsided from the face of the ground; but the dove found no place to set her foot, and she returned to him to the ark, for the waters were still on the face of the whole earth. So he put forth his hand and took her and brought her into the ark with him. He waited another seven days, and again he sent forth the dove out of the ark; and the dove came back to him in the evening, and lo, in her mouth a freshly plucked olive leaf; so Noah knew that the waters had subsided from the earth. Then he waited another seven days, and set forth the dove; and she did not return to him any more. In the six hundred and first year, in the first month, the first day of the month, the waters were dried from off the earth; and Noah removed the covering of the ark, and looked, and behold, the face of the ground was dry. In the second month, on the twenty-seventh day of the month, the earth was dry. Then God said to Noah, "Go forth from the ark, you and your wife, and your sons and your sons' wives with you." Then God said to Noah and to his sons with him, "Behold, I establish my convenant with you and your descendants after you, and with every living creature that is with you, the birds, the cattle, and every beast of the earth with you, as many as came out of the ark. I establish my covenant with you, that never again shall all flesh be cut off by the waters of a flood, and never again shall there be a flood to destroy the earth." And God said, "This is the sign of the covenant which I make between me and you and every living creature that is with you, for all future generations: I set my bow in the cloud, and it shall be a sign of the covenant between me and the earth. When I bring clouds over the earth and the bow is seen in the clouds, I will remember my covenant which is between me and you and every living creature of all flesh; and the waters shall never again become a flood to destroy all flesh. When the bow is in the clouds, I will look upon it and remember the everlasting covenant between God and every living creature of all flesh that is upon the earth."

Psalm 111 [page 754] or *Psalm 118:19-24* [page 762]

A Reading (Lesson) from the First Letter of Peter [1:3-9]

Blessed be the God and Father of our Lord Jesus Christ! By his great mercy we have been born anew to a living hope through the resurrection of Jesus Christ from the dead, and to an inheritance which is imperishable, undefiled, and unfading, kept in heaven for you, who by God's power are guarded through faith for a salvation ready to be revealed in the last time. In this you rejoice, though now for a little while you may have to suffer various trials, so that the genuineness of your faith, more precious than gold which though perishable is tested by fire, may redound to praise and glory and honor at the revelation of Jesus Christ. Without having seen him you love him; though you do not now see him you believe in him and rejoice with unutterable and exalted joy. As the outcome of your faith you obtain the salvation of your souls.

or this

Acts 2:14a,22-32 [page 139 above]

✝ *The Holy Gospel of Our Lord Jesus Christ*
According to John [20:19-31]

On the evening of the first day of the week, the doors being shut where the disciples were, for fear of the Jews, Jesus came and stood among them and said to them, "Peace be with you." When he had said this, he showed them his hands and his side. Then the disciples were glad when they saw the Lord. Jesus said to them again, "Peace be with you. As the Father has sent me, even so I send you." And when he had said this, he breathed on them, and said to them, "Receive the Holy Spirit. If you forgive the sins of any, they are forgiven; if you retain the sins of any, they are retained." Now Thomas, one of the twelve, called the Twin, was not with them when Jesus came. So the other disciples told him, "We have seen the Lord." But he said to them, "Unless I see in his hands the print of the nails, and place my finger in the mark of the nails, and place my hand in his side, I will not believe." Eight days later, his disciples were again in the house, and Thomas was with them. The doors were shut, but Jesus came and stood among them, and said, "Peace be with you." Then he said to Thomas, "Put your finger here, and see my hands; and put out your hand, and place it in my side; do not be faithless, but believing." Thomas answered him, "My Lord and my God!" Jesus said to him, "Have you believed because you have seen me? Blessed are those who have not seen and yet believe." Now Jesus did many other signs in the presence of the disciples, which are not written in this book; but these are written that you may believe that Jesus is the Christ, the Son of God, and that believing you may have life in his name.

Third Sunday of Easter

A Reading (Lesson) from the Acts of the Apostles
[2:14a, 36-47]

Peter, standing with the eleven, lifted up his voice and addressed the multitude, "Let all the house of Israel therefore know assuredly that God has made him both Lord and Christ, this Jesus whom you crucified." Now when they heard this they were cut to the heart, and said to Peter and the rest of the apostles, "Brethren, what shall we do?" And Peter said to them, "Repent, and be baptized every one of you in the name of Jesus Christ for the forgiveness of your sins; and you shall receive the gift of the Holy Spirit. For the promise is to you and to your children and to all that are far off, every one whom the Lord our God calls to him." And he testified with many other words and exhorted them, saying, "Save yourselves from this crooked generation." So those who received his word were baptized, and there were added that day about three thousand souls. And they devoted themselves to the apostles' teaching and fellowship, to the breaking of bread and the prayers. And fear came upon every soul; and many wonders and signs were done through the apostles. And all who believed were together and had all things in common; and they sold their possessions and goods and distributed them to all, as any had need. And day by day, attending the temple together and breaking bread in their homes, they partook of food with glad and generous hearts, praising God and having favor with all the people. And the Lord added to their number day by day those who were being saved.

or this

A Reading (Lesson) from the Book of Isaiah [43:1-12]

Now thus says the Lord, he who created you, O Jacob, he who formed you, O Israel: "Fear not, for I have redeemed you; I have called you by name, you are mine. When you pass through the waters I will be with you; and through the rivers, they shall not overwhelm you; when you walk through fire you shall not be burned, and the flame shall not consume you. For I am the Lord your God, the Holy One of Israel, your Savior. I give Egypt as your ransom, Ethiopia and Seba in exchange for you. Because you are precious in my eyes, and honored, and I love you, I give men in return for you, peoples in exchange for your life. Fear not, for I am with you; I will bring your offspring from the east, and from the west I will gather you; I will say to the north, Give up, and to the south, Do not withhold; bring my sons from afar and my daughters from the end of the earth, every one who is called by my name, whom I created for my glory, whom I formed and made." Bring forth the people who are blind, yet have eyes, who are deaf, yet have ears! Let all the nations gather together, and let the peoples assemble. Who among them can declare this, and show us the former things? Let them bring their witnesses to justify them, and let them hear and say, It is true. "You are my witnesses," says the Lord, "and my servant whom I have chosen, that you may know and believe me and understand that I am He. Before me no god was formed, nor shall there be any after me. I, I am the Lord, and besides me there is no savior. I declared and saved and proclaimed, when there was no strange god among you; and you are my witnesses," says the Lord.

Psalm 116 [page 759]   or   *116:10-17* [page 759]

A Reading (Lesson) from the First Letter of Peter [1:17-23]

If you invoke as Father him who judges each one impartially according to his deeds, conduct yourselves with fear throughout the time of your exile. You know that you were ransomed from the futile ways inherited from your fathers, not with perishable things such as silver or gold, but with the precious blood of Christ, like that of a lamb without blemish or spot. He was destined before the foundation of the world but was made manifest at the end of the times for your sake. Through him you have confidence in God, who raised him from the dead and gave him glory, so that your faith and hope are in God. Having purified your souls by your obedience to the truth for a sincere love of the brethren, love one another earnestly from the heart. You have been born anew, not of perishable seed but of imperishable, through the living and abiding word of God.

or this

Acts 2:14a, 36-47 [page 143 above]

✝ *The Holy Gospel of Our Lord Jesus Christ*
According to Luke [24:13-35]

That very day, the first day of the week, two of the disciples
were going to a village named Emma'us, about seven miles
from Jerusalem, and talking with each other about all these
things that had happened. While they were talking and
discussing together, Jesus himself drew near and went with
them. But their eyes were kept from recognizing him. And
he said to them,"What is this conversation which you are
holding with each other as you walk?" And they stood still,
looking sad. Then one of them, named Cle'opas, answered
him,"Are you the only visitor to Jerusalem who does not
know the things that have happened there in these days?"
And he said to them,"What things?" And they said to
him,"Concerning Jesus of Nazareth, who was a prophet
mighty in deed and word before God and all the people,
and how our chief priests and rulers delivered him up to be
condemned to death, and crucified him. But we had hoped
that he was the one to redeem Israel. Yes, and besides all
this, it is now the third day since this happened. Moreover,
some women of our company amazed us. They were at the
tomb early in the morning and did not find his body; and
they came back saying that they had even seen a vision of
angels, who said that he was alive. Some of those who were
with us went to the tomb, and found it just as the women
had said; but him they did not see." And he said to
them,"O foolish men, and slow of heart to believe all that
the prophets have spoken! Was it not necessary that the
Christ should suffer these things and enter into his glory?"
And beginning with Moses and all the prophets, he
interpreted to them in all the scriptures the things
concerning himself. So they drew near to the village to
which they were going. He appeared to be going further,
but they constrained him, saying,"Stay with us, for it is
toward evening and the day is now far spent." So he went

in to stay with them. When he was at table with them, he took the bread and blessed, and broke it, and gave it to them. And their eyes were opened and they recognized him; and he vanished out of their sight. They said to each other, "Did not our hearts burn within us while he talked to us on the road, while he opened to us the scriptures?" And they rose that same hour and returned to Jerusalem; and they found the eleven gathered together and those who were with them, who said, "The Lord has risen indeed, and has appeared to Simon!" Then they told what had happened on the road, and how he was known to them in the breaking of the bread.

Fourth Sunday of Easter

A Reading (Lesson) from the Acts of the Apostles
[6:1-9; 7:2a, 51-60]

Now in the days when the disciples were increasing in number, the Hellenists murmured against the Hebrews because their widows were neglected in the daily distribution. And the twelve summoned the body of the disciples and said, "It is not right that we should give up preaching the word of God to serve tables. Therefore, brethren, pick out from among you seven men of good repute, full of the Spirit and of wisdom, whom we may appoint to this duty. But we will devote ourselves to prayer and to the ministry of the word." And what they said pleased the whole multitude, and they chose Stephen, a man full of faith and of the Holy Spirit, and Philip, and Proch'orus, and Nica'nor, and Timon, and Par'menas, and Nicola'us, a proselyte of Antioch. These they set before the apostles, and they prayed and laid their hands upon them. And the word of God increased; and the number of the disciples multiplied greatly in Jerusalem, and a great many of the priests were obedient to the faith. And Stephen, full of grace and power, did great wonders and signs among the people. Then some of those who belonged to the synagogue of the Freedmen (as it was called), and of the Cyre'nians, and of the Alexandrians, and of those from Cili'cia and Asia, arose and disputed with Stephen. (And they brought him before the council.) And Stephen said,"You stiff-necked people, uncircumcised in heart and ears, you always resist the Holy Spirit. As your fathers did, so do you. Which of the prophets did not your fathers persecute? And they killed those who announced beforehand the coming of the Righteous One, whom you have now betrayed and murdered, you who received the law as delivered by angels and did not keep it." Now when they heard these things they were enraged, and they ground their teeth against him. But he, full of the Holy Spirit, gazed into heaven and saw the glory of God, and Jesus standing at the right hand of God; and he said, "Behold, I see the heavens opened, and the Son of man standing at the right hand of God." But they cried out with a loud voice and stopped their ears and rushed together upon him. Then they cast him out of the city and stoned him; and the witnesses laid down their garments at the feet of a young man named Saul. And as they were stoning Stephen, he prayed,"Lord Jesus, receive my spirit." And he knelt down and cried with a loud voice,"Lord, do not hold this sin against them." And when he had said this, he fell asleep.

or this

A Reading (Lesson) from the Book of Nehemiah [9:6-15]

Ezra said: "Thou art the Lord, thou alone; thou hast made heaven, the heaven of heavens, with all their host, the earth and all that is on it, the seas and all that is in them; and thou preservest all of them; and the host of heaven worships thee. Thou art the Lord, the God who didst choose Abram and bring him forth out of Ur of the Chalde'ans and give him the name Abraham; and thou didst find his heart faithful before thee, and didst make with him the covenant to give to his descendants the land of the Canaanite, the Hittite, the Amorite, the Per'izzite, the Jeb'usite, and the Gir'gashite; and thou hast fulfilled thy promise, for thou art righteous. And thou didst see the affliction of our fathers in Egypt and hear their cry at the Red Sea, and didst perform signs and wonders against Pharaoh and all his servants and all the people of his land, for thou knewest that they acted insolently against our fathers; and thou didst get thee a name, as it is to this day. And thou didst divide the sea before them, so that they went through the midst of the sea on dry land; and thou didst cast their pursuers into the depths, as a stone into mighty waters. By a pillar of cloud thou didst lead them in the day, and by a pillar of fire in the night to light for them the way in which they should go. Thou didst come down upon Mount Sinai, and speak with them from heaven and give them right ordinances and true laws, good statutes and commandments, and thou didst make known to them thy holy sabbath and command them commandments and statutes and a law by Moses thy servant. Thou didst give them bread from heaven for their hunger and bring forth water for them from the rock for their thirst, and thou didst tell them to go in and possess the land which thou hadst sworn to give them."

Psalm 23 [page 612]

A Reading (Lesson) from the First Letter of Peter [2:19-25]

One is approved if, mindful of God, he endures pain while suffering unjustly. For what credit is it, if when you do wrong and are beaten for it you take it patiently? But if when you do right and suffer for it you take it patiently, you have God's approval. For to this you have been called, because Christ also suffered for you, leaving you an example, that you should follow in his steps. He committed no sin; no guile was found on his lips. When he was reviled, he did not revile in return; when he suffered, he did not threaten; but he trusted to him who judges justly. He himself bore our sins in his body on the tree, that we might die to sin and live to righteousness. By his wounds you have been healed. For you were straying like sheep, but have now returned to the Shepherd and Guardian of your souls.

or this

Acts 6:1-9; 7:2a, 51-60 [page 147 above]

✝ *The Holy Gospel of Our Lord Jesus Christ According to John* [10:1-10]

Jesus said,"Truly, truly, I say to you, he who does not enter the sheepfold by the door but climbs in by another way, that man is a thief and a robber; but he who enters by the door is the shepherd of the sheep. To him the gatekeeper opens; the sheep hear his voice, and he calls his own sheep by name and leads them out. When he has brought out all his own, he goes before them, and the sheep follow him, for they know his voice. A stranger they will not follow, but they will flee from him, for they do not know the voice of strangers." This figure Jesus used with them, but they did not understand what he was saying to them. So Jesus again said to them,"Truly, truly, I say to you, I am the door of the sheep. All who came before me are thieves and robbers; but the sheep did not heed them. I am the door; if any one enters by me, he will be saved, and will go in and out and find pasture. The thief comes only to steal and kill and destroy; I came that they may have life, and have it abundantly."

Fifth Sunday of Easter

A Reading (Lesson) from the Acts of the Apostles [17:1-15]

When Paul and Silas had passed through Amphip′olis and Apollo′nia, they came to Thessaloni′ca, where there was a synagogue of the Jews. And Paul went in, as was his custom, and for three weeks he argued with them from the scriptures, explaining and proving that it was necessary for the Christ to suffer and to rise from the dead, and saying, "This Jesus, whom I proclaim to you, is the Christ." And some of them were persuaded, and joined Paul and Silas; as did a great many of the devout Greeks and not a few of the leading women. But the Jews were jealous, and taking some wicked fellows of the rabble, they gathered a crowd, set the city in an uproar, and attacked the house of Jason, seeking to bring them out to the people. And when they could not find them, they dragged Jason and some of the brethren before the city authorities, crying, "These men who have turned the world upside down have come here also, and Jason has received them; and they are all acting against the decrees of Caesar, saying that there is another king, Jesus." And the people and the city authorities were disturbed when they heard this. And when they had taken security from Jason and the rest, they let them go. The brethren immediately sent Paul and Silas away by night to Beroe′a; and when they arrived they went into the Jewish synagogue. Now these Jews were more noble than those in Thessaloni′ca, for they received the word with all eagerness, examining the scriptures daily to see if these things were so. Many of them therefore believed, with not a few Greek women of high standing as well as men. But when the Jews of Thessaloni′ca learned that the word of God was proclaimed by Paul at Beroe′a also, they came there too, stirring up and inciting the crowds. Then the brethren immediately sent Paul off on his way to the sea, but Silas and Timothy remained there. Those who conducted Paul brought him as far as Athens; and receiving a command for Silas and Timothy to come to him as soon as possible, they departed.

or this

A Reading (Lesson) from the Book of Deuteronomy [6:20-25]

Moses said: "When your son asks you in time to come, 'What is the meaning of the testimonies and the statutes and the ordinances which the Lord our God has commanded you?' then you shall say to your son, 'We were Pharaoh's slaves in Egypt; and the Lord brought us out of Egypt with a mighty hand; and the Lord showed signs and wonders, great and grievous, against Egypt and against Pharaoh and all his household, before our eyes; and he brought us out from there, that he might bring us in and give us the land which he swore to give to our fathers. And the Lord commanded us to do all these statutes, to fear the Lord our God, for our good always, that he might preserve us alive, as at this day. And it will be righteousness for us, if we are careful to do all this commandment before the Lord our God, as he has commanded us.' "

Psalm 66:1-11 [page 673]   or   *66:1-8* [page 673]

A Reading (Lesson) from the First Letter of Peter [2:1-10]

Put away all malice and all guile and insincerity and envy and all slander. Like newborn babes, long for the pure spiritual milk, that by it you may grow up to salvation; for you have tasted the kindness of the Lord. Come to him, to that living stone, rejected by men but in God's sight chosen and precious; and like living stones be yourselves built into a spiritual house, to be a holy priesthood, to offer spiritual sacrifices acceptable to God through Jesus Christ. For it stands in scripture: "Behold, I am laying in Zion a stone, a cornerstone chosen and precious, and he who believes in him will not be put to shame." To you therefore who believe, he is precious, but for those who do not believe, "The very stone which the builders rejected has become the head of the corner," and "A stone that will make men stumble, a rock that will make them fall"; for they stumble because they disobey the word, as they were destined to do. But you are a chosen race, a royal priesthood, a holy nation, God's own people, that you may declare the wonderful deeds of him who called you out of darkness into his marvelous light. Once you were no people but now you are God's people; once you had not received mercy but now you have received mercy.

or this

Acts 17:1-15 [page 151 above]

✝ *The Holy Gospel of Our Lord Jesus Christ According to John* [14:1-14]

Jesus said, "Let not your hearts be troubled; believe in God, believe also in me. In my Father's house are many rooms; if it were not so, would I have told you that I go to prepare a place for you? And when I go and prepare a place for you, I will come again and will take you to myself, that where I am you may be also. And you know the way where I am going." Thomas said to him, "Lord, we do not know where you are going; how can we know the way?" Jesus said to him, "I am the way, and the truth, and the life; no one comes to the Father, but by me. If you had known me, you would have known my Father also; henceforth you know him and have seen him." Philip said to him, "Lord, show us the Father, and we shall be satisfied." Jesus said to him,

"Have I been with you so long, and yet you do not know me, Philip? He who has seen me has seen the Father; how can you say, 'Show us the Father'? Do you not believe that I am in the Father and the Father in me? The words that I say to you I do not speak on my own authority; but the Father who dwells in me does his works. Believe me that I am in the Father and the Father in me; or else believe me for the sake of the works themselves. Truly, truly, I say to you, he who believes in me will also do the works that I do; and greater works than these will he do, because I go to the Father. Whatever you ask in my name, I will do it, that the Father may be glorified in the Son; if you ask anything in my name, I will do it."

Sixth Sunday of Easter

A Reading (Lesson) from the Acts of the Apostles
[17:22-31]

Paul, standing in the middle of the Are-op'agus, said: "Men of Athens, I perceive that in every way you are very religious. For as I passed along, and observed the objects of your worship, I found also an altar with this inscription, 'To an unknown god.' What therefore you worship as unknown, this I proclaim to you. The God who made the world and everything in it, being Lord of heaven and earth, does not live in shrines made by man, nor is he served by human hands, as though he needed anything, since he himself gives to all men life and breath and everything. And he made from one every nation of men to live on all the face of the earth, having determined allotted periods and the boundaries of their habitation, that they should seek God, in the hope that they might feel after him and find him. Yet he is not far from each one of us, for 'In him we live and move and have our being'; as even some of your poets have said, 'For we are indeed his offspring.'

Being then God's offspring, we ought not to think that the Deity is like gold, or silver, or stone, a representation by the art and imagination of man. The times of ignorance God overlooked, but now he commands all men everywhere to repent, because he has fixed a day on which he will judge the world in righteousness by a man whom he has appointed, and of this he has given assurance to all men by raising him from the dead."

or this

A Reading (Lesson) from the Book of Isaiah [41:17-20]

Thus says the Lord your God: "When the poor and needy seek water, and there is none, and their tongue is parched with thirst, I the Lord will answer them, I the God of Israel will not forsake them. I will open rivers on the bare heights, and fountains in the midst of the valleys; I will make the wilderness a pool of water, and the dry land springs of water. I will put in the wilderness the cedar, the acacia, the myrtle, and the olive; I will set in the desert the cypress, the plane and the pine together; that men may see and know, may consider and understand together, that the hand of the Lord has done this, the Holy One of Israel has created it."

Psalm 148 [page 805]   or   *148:7-14* [page 806]

A Reading (Lesson) from the First Letter of Peter [3:8-18]

All of you, beloved, have unity of spirit, sympathy, love of the brethren, a tender heart and a humble mind. Do not return evil for evil or reviling for reviling; but on the contrary bless, for to this you have been called, that you may obtain a blessing. For "He that would love life and see good days, let him keep his tongue from evil and his lips from speaking guile; let him turn away from evil and do right; let him seek peace and pursue it. For the eyes of the Lord are upon the righteous, and his ears are open to their prayer. But the face of the Lord is against those that do evil." Now who is there to harm you if you are zealous for what is right? But even if you do suffer for righteousness' sake, you will be blessed. Have no fear of them, nor be troubled, but in your hearts reverence Christ as Lord. Always be prepared to make a defense to any one who calls you to account for the hope that is in you, yet do it with gentleness and reverence; and keep your conscience clear, so that, when you are abused, those who revile your good behavior in Christ may be put to shame. For it is better to suffer for doing right, if that should be God's will, than for doing wrong. For Christ also died for sins once for all, the righteous for the unrighteous, that he might bring us to God, being put to death in the flesh but made alive in the spirit.

or this

Acts 17:22-31 [page 154 above]

✝ *The Holy Gospel of Our Lord Jesus Christ According to John* [15:1-8]

Jesus said, "I am the true vine, and my Father is the vinedresser. Every branch of mine that bears no fruit, he takes away, and every branch that does bear fruit he prunes, that it may bear more fruit. You are already made clean by the word which I have spoken to you. Abide in me, and I in you. As the branch cannot bear fruit by itself, unless it abides in the vine, neither can you, unless you abide in me. I am the vine, you are the branches. He who abides in me, and I in him, he it is that bears much fruit, for apart from me you can do nothing. If a man does not abide in me, he is cast forth as a branch and withers; and the branches are gathered, thrown into the fire and burned. If you abide in me, and my words abide in you, ask whatever you will, and it shall be done for you. By this my Father is glorified, that you bear much fruit, and so prove to be my disciples.

Ascension Day

A Reading (Lesson) from the Acts of the Apostles [1:1-11]

In the first book, O The-oph'ilus, I have dealt with all that Jesus began to do and teach, until the day when he was taken up, after he had given commandment through the Holy Spirit to the apostles whom he had chosen. To them he presented himself alive after his passion by many proofs, appearing to them during forty days, and speaking of the kingdom of God. And while staying with them he charged them not to depart from Jerusalem, but to wait for the promise of the Father, which, he said, "you heard from me, for John baptized with water, but before many days you shall be baptized with the Holy Spirit." So when they had come together, they asked him, "Lord, will you at this time restore the kingdom to Israel?" He said to them, "It is not for you to know times or seasons which the Father has fixed by his own authority. But you shall receive power when the Holy Spirit has come upon you; and you shall be my witnesses in Jerusalem and in all Judea and Samar'ia and to the end of the earth." And when he had said this, as they were looking on, he was lifted up, and a cloud took him out of their sight. And while they were gazing into heaven as he went, behold, two men stood by them in white robes, and said, "Men of Galilee, why do you stand looking into heaven? This Jesus, who was taken up from you into heaven, will come in the same way as you saw him go into heaven."

or the following

A Reading (Lesson) from the Book of Daniel [7:9-14]

Daniel had a dream and visions, and he wrote down the
dream and said, "As I looked, thrones were placed and one
that was ancient of days took his seat; his raiment was
white as snow, and the hair of his head like pure wool; his
throne was fiery flames, its wheels were burning fire. A
stream of fire issued and came forth from before him; a
thousand thousands served him, and ten thousand times
ten thousand stood before him; the court sat in judgment,
and the books were opened. I looked then because of the
sound of the great words which the horn was speaking.
And as I looked, the beast was slain, and its body
destroyed and given over to be burned with fire. As for the
rest of the beasts, their dominion was taken away, but their
lives were prolonged for a season and a time. I saw in the
night visions, and behold, with the clouds of heaven there
came one like a son of man, and he came to the Ancient of
Days and was presented before him. And to him was given
dominion and glory and kingdom, that all peoples,
nations, and languages should serve him; his dominion is
an everlasting dominion, which shall not pass away, and
his kingdom one that shall not be destroyed."

Psalm 47 [page 650] or *Psalm 110:1-5* [page 753]

*A Reading (Lesson) from the Letter of Paul
to the Ephesians* [1:15-23]

Because I have heard of your faith in the Lord Jesus and
your love toward all the saints, I do not cease to give
thanks for you, remembering you in my prayers, that the
God of our Lord Jesus Christ, the Father of glory, may give
you a spirit of wisdom and of revelation in the knowledge
of him, having the eyes of your hearts enlightened, that you
may know what is the hope to which he has called you,
what are the riches of his glorious inheritance in the saints,

and what is the immeasurable greatness of his power in us who believe, according to the working of his great might which he accomplished in Christ when he raised him from the dead and made him sit at his right hand in the heavenly places, far above all rule and authority and power and dominion, and above every name that is named, not only in this age but also in that which is to come; and he has put all things under his feet and has made him the head over all things for the church, which is his body, the fullness of him who fills all in all.

or this

Acts 1:1-11 [page 157 above]

✝ *The Holy Gospel of Our Lord Jesus Christ According to Luke* [24:49-53]

Jesus said to his disciples, "Behold, I send the promise of my Father upon you; but stay in the city, until you are clothed with power from on high." Then he led them out as far as Bethany, and lifting up his hands he blessed them. While he blessed them, he parted from them, and was carried up into heaven. And they returned to Jerusalem with great joy, and were continually in the temple blessing God.

or this

✝ *The Holy Gospel of Our Lord Jesus Christ According to Mark* [16:9-15, 19-20]

Now when Jesus rose early on the first day of the week, he appeared first to Mary Mag'dalene, from whom he had cast out seven demons. She went out and told those who had been with him, as they mourned and wept. But when they heard that he was alive and had been seen by her, they would not believe it. After this he appeared in another form to two of them, as they were walking into the country. And they went back and told the rest, but they did not believe them. Afterward he appeared to the eleven themselves as they sat at table; and he upbraided them for their unbelief and hardness of heart, because they had not believed those who saw him after he had risen. And he said to them, "Go into all the world and preach the gospel to the whole creation." So then the Lord Jesus, after he had spoken to them, was taken up into heaven, and sat down at the right hand of God. And they went forth and preached everywhere, while the Lord worked with them and confirmed the message by the signs that attended it.

Seventh Sunday of Easter

A Reading (Lesson) from the Acts of the Apostles
[1:(1-7) 8-14]

In the first book, O The-oph'ilus, I have dealt with all that Jesus began to do and teach, until the day when he was taken up, after he had given commandment through the Holy Spirit to the apostles whom he had chosen. To them he presented himself alive after his passion by many proofs, appearing to them during forty days, and speaking of the kingdom of God. And while staying with them he charged them not to depart from Jerusalem, but to wait for the promise of the Father, which, he said, "you heard from me, for John baptized with water, but before many days you shall be baptized with the Holy Spirit." So when they had come together, they asked him, "Lord, will you at this time restore the kingdom to Israel?" He said to them, "It is not for you to know times or seasons which the Father has fixed by his own authority. But

[Jesus said to the apostles,] "You shall receive power when the Holy Spirit has come upon you; and you shall be my witnesses in Jerusalem and in all Judea and Samar'ia and to

the end of the earth." And when he had said this, as they were looking on, he was lifted up, and a cloud took him out of their sight. And while they were gazing into heaven as he went, behold, two men stood by them in white robes, and said, "Men of Galilee, why do you stand looking into heaven? This Jesus, who was taken up from you into heaven, will come in the same way as you saw him go into heaven." Then they returned to Jerusalem from the mount called Olivet, which is near Jerusalem, a sabbath day's journey away; and when they had entered, they went up to the upper room, where they were staying, Peter and John and James and Andrew, Philip and Thomas, Bartholomew and Matthew, James the son of Alphaeus and Simon the Zealot and Judas the son of James. All these with one accord devoted themselves to prayer, together with the women and Mary the mother of Jesus, and with his brothers.

or this

A Reading (Lesson) from the Book of Ezekiel [39:21-29]

Thus says the Lord God: "I will set my glory among the nations; and all the nations shall see my judgment which I have executed, and my hand which I have laid on them. The house of Israel shall know that I am the Lord their God, from that day forward. And the nations shall know that the house of Israel went into captivity for their iniquity, because they dealt so treacherously with me that I hid my face from them and gave them into the hand of their adversaries, and they all fell by the sword. I dealt with them according to their uncleanness and their transgressions, and hid my face from them. Therefore thus says the Lord God: Now I will restore the fortunes of Jacob, and have mercy upon the whole house of Israel; and I will be jealous for my holy name. They shall forget their shame, and all the treachery they have practiced against me, when they dwell securely in their land with none to make them afraid, when I have brought them back from the peoples and gathered them from their enemies' lands, and through them have vindicated my holiness in the sight of many nations. Then they shall know that I am the Lord their God because I sent them into exile among the nations, and then gathered them into their own land. I will leave none of them remaining among the nations any more; and I will not hide my face any more from them, when I pour out my Spirit upon the house of Israel, says the Lord God."

Psalm 68:1-20 [page 676]   or   *Psalm 47* [page 650]

A Reading (Lesson) from the First Letter of Peter [4:12-19]

Beloved, do not be surprised at the fiery ordeal which comes upon you to prove you, as though something strange were happening to you. But rejoice and be glad when his glory is revealed. If you are reproached for the name of Christ, you are blessed, because the spirit of glory and of God rests upon you. But let none of you suffer as a murderer, or a thief, or a wrongdoer, or a mischiefmaker; yet if one suffers as a Christian, let him not be ashamed, but under that name let him glorify God. For the time has come for judgment to begin with the household of God; and if it begins with us, what will be the end of those who do not obey the gospel of God? And "If the righteous man is scarcely saved, where will the impious and sinner appear?" Therefore let those who suffer according to God's will do right and entrust their souls to a faithful Creator.

or this

Acts 1:(1-7) 8-14 [page 160 above]

✝ *The Holy Gospel of our Lord Jesus Christ*
According to John [17:1-11]

Jesus lifted up his eyes to heaven and said,"Father, the hour has come; glorify thy Son that the Son may glorify thee, since thou hast given him power over all flesh, to give eternal life to all whom thou hast given him. And this is eternal life, that they know thee the only true God, and Jesus Christ whom thou hast sent. I glorified thee on earth, having accomplished the work which thou gavest me to do; and now, Father, glorify thou me in thy own presence with the glory which I had with thee before the world was made. I have manifested thy name to the men whom thou gavest me out of the world; thine they were, and thou gavest them to me, and they kept thy word. Now they know that everything that thou hast given me is from thee; for I have given them the words which thou gavest me, and they have received them and know in truth that I came from thee; and they have believed that thou didst send me. I am praying for them; I am not praying for the world but for those whom thou hast given me, for they are thine; all mine are thine, and thine are mine, and I am glorified in them. And now I am no more in the world, but they are in the world, and I am coming to thee. Holy Father, keep them in thy name, which thou hast given me, that they may be one, even as we are one."

Day of Pentecost: Vigil or Early Service

A Reading (Lesson) from the Book of Genesis [11:1-9]

Now the whole earth had one language and few words. And as men migrated from the east, they found a plain in the land of Shinar and settled there. And they said to one another,"Come, let us make bricks, and burn them thoroughly." And they had brick for stone, and bitumen for mortar. Then they said,"Come, let us build ourselves a city, and a tower with its top in the heavens, and let us make a name for ourselves, lest we be scattered abroad upon the face of the whole earth." And the Lord came down to see the city and the tower, which the sons of men had built. And the Lord said,"Behold, they are one people, and they have all one language; and this is only the beginning of what they will do; and nothing that they propose to do will now be impossible for them. Come, let us go down, and there confuse their language, that they may not understand one another's speech." So the Lord scattered them abroad from there over the face of all the earth, and they left off building the city. Therefore its name was called Babel, because there the Lord confused the language of all the earth; and from there the Lord scattered them abroad over the face of all the earth.

Psalm 33:12-22 [page 626]

or this

A Reading (Lesson) from the Book of Exodus
[19:1-9a, 16-20a; 20:18-20]

On the third new moon after the people of Israel had gone forth out of the land of Egypt, on that day they came into the wilderness of Sinai. And when they set out from Reph'idim and came into the wilderness of Sinai, they encamped in the wilderness; and there Israel encamped before the mountain. And Moses went up to God, and the Lord called to him out of the mountain, saying,"Thus you shall say to the house of Jacob, and tell the people of Israel: You have seen what I did to the Egyptians, and how I bore you on eagles' wings and brought you to myself. Now therefore, if you will obey my voice and keep my covenant, you shall be my own possession among all peoples; for all the earth is mine, and you shall be to me a kingdom of priests and a holy nation. These are the words which you shall speak to the children of Israel." So Moses came and called the elders of the people, and set before them all these words which the Lord had commanded him. And all the people answered together and said, "All that the Lord has spoken we will do." And Moses reported the words of the people to the Lord. And the Lord said to Moses, "Lo, I am coming to you in a thick cloud, that the people may hear when I speak with you, and may also believe you for ever." On the morning of the third day there were thunders and lightnings, and a thick cloud upon the mountain, and a very loud trumpet blast, so that all the people who were in the camp trembled. Then Moses brought the people out of the camp to meet God; and they took their stand at the foot of the mountain. And Mount Sinai was wrapped in smoke, because the Lord descended upon it in fire; and the smoke of it went up like the smoke of a kiln, and the whole mountain quaked greatly. And as the sound of the trumpet grew louder and louder, Moses spoke, and God answered him in thunder. And the Lord came down upon Mount Sinai, to the top of the moutain. Now when all the people perceived the thunderings and the lightnings and the sound of the trumpet and the mountain smoking, the people were afraid and trembled; and they stood afar off, and said to Moses, "You speak to us, and we will hear; but let not God speak to us, lest we die." And Moses said to the people, "Do not fear; for God has come to prove you, and that the fear of him may be before your eyes, that you may not sin."

Canticle 2 or 13, A Song of Praise [page 49 or 90]

or the following

A Reading (Lesson) from the Book of Ezekiel [37:1-14]

The hand of the Lord was upon me, and he brought me out by the Spirit of the Lord, and set me down in the midst of the valley; it was full of bones. And he led me round among them; and behold, there were very many upon the valley; and lo, they were very dry. And he said to me,"Son of man, can these bones live?" And I answered,"O Lord God, thou knowest." Again he said to me,"Prophesy to these bones, and say to them, O dry bones, hear the word of the Lord. Thus says the Lord God to these bones: Behold, I will cause breath to enter you, and you shall live. And I will lay sinews upon you, and will cause flesh to come upon you, and cover you with skin, and put breath in you, and you shall live; and you shall know that I am the Lord." So I prophesied as I was commanded; and as I prophesied, there was a noise and behold, a rattling; and the bones came together, bone to its bone. And as I looked, there were sinews on them, and flesh had come upon them, and skin had covered them; but there was no breath in them. Then he said to me,"Prophesy to the breath, prophesy, son of man, and say to the breath, Thus says the Lord God: Come from the four winds, O breath, and breathe upon these slain, that they may live." So I prophesied as he commanded me, and the breath came into them, and they lived, and stood upon their feet, an exceedingly great host. Then he said to me,"Son of man, these bones are the whole house of Israel. Behold, they say,'Our bones are dried up, and our hope is lost; we are clean cut off.' Therefore prophesy, and say to them, Thus says the Lord God: Behold, I will open your graves and raise you from your graves, O my people; and I will bring you home into the land of Israel. And you shall know that I am the Lord, when I open your graves, and raise you from your graves, O my people. And I will put my Spirit within you, and you shall live, and I will place you in your own land; then you shall know that I, the Lord, have spoken, and I have done it, says the Lord."

Psalm 130 [page 784]

or this

A Reading (Lesson) from the Book of Joel [2:28-32]

The Lord said to his people,"It shall come to pass afterward, that I will pour out my spirit on all flesh; your sons and daughters shall prophesy, your old men shall dream dreams, and your young men shall see visions. Even upon the menservants and maidservants in those days, I will pour out my spirit. And I will give portents in the heavens and on the earth, blood and fire and columns of smoke. The sun shall be turned to darkness, and the moon to blood, before the great and terrible day of the Lord comes. And it shall come to pass that all who call upon the name of the Lord shall be delivered; for in Mount Zion and in Jerusalem there shall be those who escape, as the Lord has said, and among the survivors shall be those whom the Lord calls."

Canticle 9, The First Song of Isaiah [page 86]

or this

Acts 2:1-11 [page 169 below]

Psalm 104:25-32 [page 736]

or the following

*A Reading (Lesson) from the Letter of Paul
to the Romans* [8:14-17, 22-27]

All who are led by the Spirit of God are sons of God. For
you did not receive the spirit of slavery to fall back into
fear, but you have received the spirit of sonship. When we
cry,"Abba! Father!" it is the Spirit himself bearing witness
with our spirit that we are children of God, and if children,
then heirs, heirs of God and fellow heirs with Christ,
provided we suffer with him in order that we may also be
glorified with him. We know that the whole creation has
been groaning in travail together until now; and not only
the creation, but we ourselves, who have the first fruits of
the Spirit, groan inwardly as we wait for adoption as sons,
the redemption of our bodies. For in this hope we were
saved. Now hope that is seen is not hope. For who hopes
for what he sees? But if we hope for what we do not see, we
wait for it with patience. Likewise the Spirit helps us in our
weakness; for we do not know how to pray as we ought,
but the Spirit himself intercedes for us with sighs too deep
for words. And he who searches the hearts of men knows
what is in the mind of the Spirit, because the Spirit
intercedes for the saints according to the will of God.

✝ *The Holy Gospel of Our Lord Jesus Christ
According to John* [7:37-39a]

On the last day of the feast, the great day, Jesus stood up
and proclaimed,"If any one thirst, let him come to me and
drink. He who believes in me, as the scripture has said,
'Out of his heart shall flow rivers of living water.'" Now
this he said about the Spirit, which those who believed
in him were to receive.

Day of Pentecost: Principal Service

A Reading (Lesson) from the Acts of the Apostles [2:1-11]

When the day of Pentecost had come, the disciples were all together in one place. And suddenly a sound came from heaven like the rush of a mighty wind, and it filled all the house where they were sitting. And there appeared to them tongues as of fire, distributed and resting on each one of them. And they were all filled with the Holy Spirit and began to speak in other tongues, as the Spirit gave them utterance. Now there were dwelling in Jerusalem Jews, devout men from every nation under heaven. And at this sound the multitude came together, and they were bewildered, because each one heard them speaking in his own language. And they were amazed and wondered, saying, "Are not all these who are speaking Galileans? And how is it that we hear, each of us in his own native language? Par'thians and Medes and Elamites and residents of Mesopota'mia, Judea and Cappado'cia, Pontus and Asia, Phryg'ia and Pamphyl'ia, Egypt and the parts of Libya belonging to Cyre'ne, and visitors from Rome, both Jews and proselytes, Cretans and Arabians, we hear them telling in our own tongues the mighty works of God."

or this

A Reading (Lesson) from the Book of Ezekiel [11:17-20]

Say this, "Thus says the Lord God: 'I will gather you from the peoples, and assemble you out of the countries where you have been scattered, and I will give you the land of Israel.' And when they come there, they will remove from it all its detestable things and all its abominations. And I will give them one heart, and put a new spirit within them; I will take the stony heart out of their flesh and give them a heart of flesh, that they may walk in my statutes and keep my ordinances and obey them; and they shall be my people, and I will be their God."

Psalm 104:25-37 [page 736]   or   *104:25-32* [page 736]   or

Psalm 33:12-15, 18-22 [page 626]

A Reading (Lesson) From the First Letter of Paul to the Corinthians [12:4-13]

Now there are varieties of gifts, but the same Spirit; and there are varieties of service, but the same Lord; and there are varieties of working, but it is the same God who inspires them all in every one. To each is given the manifestation of the Spirit for the common good. To one is given through the Spirit the utterance of wisdom, and to another the utterance of knowledge according to the same Spirit, to another faith by the same Spirit, to another gifts of healing by the one Spirit, to another the working of miracles, to another prophecy, to another the ability to distinguish between spirits, to another various kinds of tongues, to another the interpretation of tongues. All these are inspired by one and the same Spirit, who apportions to each one individually as he wills. For just as the body is one and has many members, and all the members of the body, though many, are one body, so it is with Christ. For by one Spirit we were all baptized into one body—Jews or Greeks, slaves or free—and all were made to drink of one Spirit.

or this

Acts 2:1-11 [page 169 above]

✝ *The Holy Gospel of Our Lord Jesus Christ*
According to John [20:19-23]

On the evening of that day, the first day of the week, the doors being shut where the disciples were, for fear of the Jews, Jesus came and stood among them and said to them, "Peace be with you." When he had said this, he showed them his hands and his side. Then the disciples were glad when they saw the Lord. Jesus said to them again, "Peace be with you. As the Father has sent me, even so I send you." And when he had said this, he breathed on them, and said to them, "Receive the Holy Spirit. If you forgive the sins of any, they are forgiven; if you retain the sins of any, they are retained."

or this

✝ *The Holy Gospel of Our Lord Jesus Christ*
According to John [14:8-17]

Philip said to Jesus, "Lord, show us the Father, and we shall be satisfied." Jesus said to him, "Have I been with you so long, and yet you do not know me, Philip? He who has seen me has seen the Father; how can you say, 'Show us the Father'? Do you not believe that I am in the Father and the Father in me? The words that I say to you I do not speak on my own authority; but the Father who dwells in me does his works. Believe me that I am in the Father and the Father in me; or else believe me for the sake of the works themselves. Truly, truly, I say to you, he who believes in me will also do the works that I do; and greater works than these will he do, because I go to the Father. Whatever you ask in my name, I will do it, that the Father may be glorified in the Son; if you ask anything in my name, I will do it. If you love me, you will keep my commandments. And I will pray the Father, and he will give you another Counselor, to be with you for ever, even the Spirit of truth, whom the world cannot receive, because it neither sees him nor knows him; you know him, for he dwells with you, and will be in you."

Trinity Sunday

A Reading (Lesson) from the Book of Genesis [1:1 — 2:3]

In the beginning God created the heavens and the earth. The earth was without form and void, and darkness was upon the face of the deep; and the Spirit of God was moving over the face of the waters. And God said,"Let there be light"; and there was light. And God saw that the light was good; and God separated the light from the darkness. God called the light Day, and the darkness he called Night. And there was evening and there was morning, one day. And God said,"Let there be a firmament in the midst of the waters, and let it separate the waters from the waters." And God made the firmament and separated the waters which were under the firmament from the waters which were above the firmament. And it was so. And God called the firmament Heaven. And there was evening and there was morning, a second day. And God said,"Let the waters under the heavens be gathered together into one place, and let the dry land appear." And it was so. God called the dry land Earth, and the waters that were gathered together he called Seas. And God saw that it was good. And God said,"Let the earth put forth vegetation, plants yielding seed, and fruit trees bearing fruit in which is their seed, each according to its kind, upon the earth." And it was so. The earth brought forth vegetation, plants yielding seed according to their own kinds, and trees bearing fruit in which is their seed, each according to its kind. And God saw that it was good. And there was evening and there was morning, a third day. And God said,"Let there be lights in the firmament of the heavens to separate the day from the night; and let them be for signs and for seasons and for days and years, and let them be lights in the firmament of the heavens to give light upon the earth." And it was so. And God made the two great lights, the greater light to rule the day, and the lesser light to rule the night; he made the stars also. And God set them in the firmament of the heavens to give light upon the earth, to rule over the day and over the night, and to separate the light from the darkness. And God saw that it was good. And there was evening and there was morning, a fourth day. And God said,"Let the waters bring forth swarms of living creatures, and let birds fly above the earth across the firmament of the heavens." So God created the great sea monsters and every living creature that moves, with which the waters swarm, according to their kinds, and every winged bird according to its kind. And God saw that it was good. And God blessed them, saying,"Be fruitful and multiply and fill the waters in the seas, and let birds multiply on the earth." And there was evening and there was morning, a fifth day. And God said,"Let the earth bring forth living creatures according to their kinds: cattle and creeping things and beasts of the earth according to their kinds." And it was so. And God made the beasts of the earth according to their kinds and the cattle according to their kinds, and everything that creeps upon the ground according to its kind. And God saw that it was good. Then God said,"Let us make man in our image, after our likeness; and let them have dominion over the fish of the sea, and over the birds of the air, and over the cattle, and over all the earth, and over every creeping thing that creeps upon the earth." So God created man in his own image, in the image of God he created him; male and female he created them. And God blessed them, and God said to them,"Be fruitful and multiply, and fill the earth and subdue it; and have dominion over the fish of the sea and over the birds of the air and over every living thing that moves upon the earth." And God said, "Behold, I have given you every plant yielding seed which is upon the face of all the earth, and every tree with seed in its fruit; you shall have them for food. And to every beast of the earth, and to every bird of the air, and to everything that creeps on the earth, everything that has the breath of life, I have given every green plant for food." And it was so. And God saw everything that he had made, and behold, it was very good. And there was evening and there was morning, a sixth day. Thus the heavens and the earth were finished, and all the host of them. And on the seventh day God finished his work which he had done, and he rested on the seventh day from all his work which he had done. So God blessed the seventh day and hallowed it, because on it God rested from all his work which he had done in creation.

Psalm 150 [page 807]   or

Benedictus es, Canticle 2 or 13 [page 49 or 90]

A Reading (Lesson) from the Second Letter of Paul to the Corinthians [13:(5-10) 11-14]

Examine yourselves, to see whether you are holding to your faith. Test yourselves. Do you not realize that Jesus Christ is in you? —unless indeed you fail to meet the test! I hope you will find out that we have not failed. But we pray God that you may not do wrong—not that we may appear to have met the test, but that you may do what is right, though we may seem to have failed. For we cannot do anything against the truth, but only for the truth. For we are glad when we are weak and you are strong. What we pray for is your improvement. I write this while I am away from you, in order that when I come I may not have to be severe in my use of the authority which the Lord has given me for building up and not for tearing down.

Finally, brethren, farewell. Mend your ways, heed my appeal, agree with one another, live in peace, and the God of love and peace will be with you. Greet one another with a holy kiss. All the saints greet you. The grace of the Lord Jesus Christ and the love of God and the fellowship of the Holy Spirit be with you all.

✝ *The Holy Gospel of Our Lord Jesus Christ*
According to Matthew [28:16-20]

The eleven disciples went to Galilee, to the mountain to which Jesus had directed them. And when they saw him they worshiped him; but some doubted. And Jesus came and said to them, "All authority in heaven and on earth has been given to me. Go therefore and make disciples of all nations, baptizing them in the name of the Father and of the Son and of the Holy Spirit, teaching them to observe all that I have commanded you; and lo, I am with you always, to the close of the age."

Proper 1   *The Sunday closest to May 11*

Same as on the Sixth Sunday after the Epiphany, pages 38-40

Proper 2   *The Sunday closest to May 18*

Same as on the Seventh Sunday after theEpiphany, pages 40-42

Proper 3   *The Sunday closest to May 25*

Same as on the Eighth Sunday after the Epiphany, pages 42-45

Proper 4 *The Sunday closest to June 1*

A Reading (Lesson) from the Book of Deuteronomy
[11:18-21, 26-28]

Moses said to the people, "You shall lay up these words of mine in your heart and in your soul; and you shall bind them as a sign upon your hand, and they shall be as frontlets between your eyes. And you shall teach them to your children, talking of them when you are sitting in your house, and when you are walking by the way, and when you lie down, and when you rise. And you shall write them upon the doorposts of your house and upon your gates, that your days and the days of your children may be multiplied in the land which the Lord swore to your fathers to give them, as long as the heavens are above the earth. Behold, I set before you this day a blessing and a curse: the blessing, if you obey the commandments of the Lord your God, which I command you this day, and the curse, if you do not obey the commandments of the Lord your God, but turn aside from the way which I command you this day, to go after other gods which you have not known."

Psalm 31 [page 622]   or   *31:1-5, 19-24* [page 622]

A Reading (Lesson) from the Letter of Paul to the Romans
[3:21-25a, 28]

Now the righteousness of God has been manifested apart from law, although the law and the prophets bear witness to it, the righteousness of God through faith in Jesus Christ for all who believe. For there is no distinction; since all have sinned and fall short of the glory of God, they are justified by his grace as a gift, through the redemption which is in Christ Jesus, whom God put forward as an expiation by his blood, to be received by faith. For we hold that a man is justified by faith apart from works of law.

✝ *The Holy Gospel Of Our Lord Jesus Christ*
According to Matthew [7:21-27]

Jesus said, "Not every one who says to me, 'Lord, Lord,' shall enter the kingdom of heaven, but he who does the will of my Father who is in heaven. On that day many will say to me, 'Lord, Lord, did we not prophesy in your name, and cast out demons in your name, and do many mighty works in your name?' And then will I declare to them, 'I never knew you; depart from me, you evildoers.' Every one then who hears these words of mine and does them will be like a wise man who built his house upon the rock; and the rain fell, and the floods came, and the winds blew and beat upon that house, but it did not fall, because it had been founded on the rock. And every one who hears these words of mine and does not do them will be like a foolish man who built his house upon the sand; and the rain fell, and the floods came, and the winds blew and beat against that house, and it fell; and great was the fall of it."

Proper 5 *The Sunday closest to June 8*

A Reading (Lesson) from the Book of Hosea [5:15 — 6:6]

Thus says the Lord: "I will return again to my place, until they acknowledge their guilt and seek my face, and in their distress they seek me, saying, 'Come, let us return to the Lord; for he has torn, that he may heal us; he has stricken, and he will bind us up. After two days he will revive us; on the third day he will raise us up, that we may live before him. Let us know, let us press on to know the Lord; his going forth is sure as the dawn; he will come to us as the showers, as the spring rains that water the earth.' What shall I do with you, O E'phraim? What shall I do with you, O Judah? Your love is like a morning cloud, like the dew that goes early away. Therefore I have hewn them by the prophets, I have slain them by the words of my mouth, and my judgment goes forth as the light. For I desire steadfast love and not sacrifice, the knowledge of God, rather than burnt offerings."

Psalm 50 [page 654]   or   *50:7-15* [page 654]

A Reading (Lesson) from the Letter of Paul to the Romans [4:13-18]

The promise to Abraham and his descendants, that they should inherit the world, did not come through the law but through the righteousness of faith. If it is the adherents of the law who are to be the heirs, faith is null and the promise is void. For the law brings wrath, but where there is no law there is no transgression. That is why it depends on faith, in order that the promise may rest on grace and be guaranteed to all his descendants—not only to the adherents of the law but also to those who share the faith of Abraham, for he is the father of us all, as it is written, "I have made you the father of many nations"—in the presence of the God in whom he believed, who gives life to the dead and calls into existence the things that do not exist. In hope he believed against hope, that he should become the father of many nations; as he had been told, "So shall your descendants be."

✝ *The Holy Gospel of our Lord Jesus Christ According to Matthew* [9:9-13]

Jesus saw a man called Matthew sitting at the tax office; and he said to him, "Follow me." And he rose and followed him. And as he sat at table in the house, behold, many tax collectors and sinners came and sat down with Jesus and his disciples. And when the Pharisees saw this, they said to his disciples,"Why does your teacher eat with tax collectors and sinners?"But when he heard it, he said,"Those who are well have no need for a physician, but those who are sick. Go and learn what this means,'I desire mercy, and not sacrifice.'For I came not to call the righteous, but sinners."

Proper 6 *The Sunday closest to June 15*

A Reading (Lesson) from the Book of Exodus [19:2-8a]

When the people of Israel set out from Reph'idim and came into the wilderness of Sinai, they encamped in the wilderness; and there Israel encamped before the mountain. And Moses went up to God, and the Lord called to him out of the mountain, saying,"Thus you shall say to the house of Jacob, and tell the people of Israel: You have seen what I did to the Egyptians, and how I bore you on eagles' wings and brought you to myself. Now therefore, if you will obey my voice and keep my covenant, you shall be my own possession among all peoples; for all the earth is mine, and you shall be to me a kingdom of priests and a holy nation. These are the words which you shall speak to the children of Israel." So Moses came and called the elders of the people, and set before them all these words which the Lord had commanded him. And all the people answered together and said,"All that the Lord has spoken we will do."

Psalm 100 [page 729]

A Reading (Lesson) from the Letter of Paul to the Romans [5:6-11]

While we were still weak, at the right time Christ died for the ungodly. Why, one will hardly die for a righteous man—though perhaps for a good man one will dare even to die. But God shows his love for us in that while we were yet sinners Christ died for us. Since, therefore, we are now justified by his blood, much more shall we be saved by him from the wrath of God. For if while we were enemies we were reconciled to God by the death of his Son, much more, now that we are reconciled, shall we be saved by his life. Not only so, but we also rejoice in God through our Lord Jesus Christ, through whom we have now received our reconciliation.

✝ *The Holy Gospel of Our Lord Jesus Christ*
According to Matthew [9:35 — 10:8 (9-15)]

Jesus went about all the cities and villages, teaching in their synagogues and preaching the gospel of the kingdom, and healing every disease and every infirmity. When he saw the crowds, he had compassion for them, because they were harassed and helpless, like sheep without a shepherd. Then he said to his disciples,"The harvest is plentiful, but the laborers are few; pray therefore the Lord of the harvest to send out laborers into his harvest." And he called to him his twelve disciples and gave them authority over unclean spirits, to cast them out, and to heal every disease and every infirmity. The names of the twelve apostles are these: first, Simon, who is called Peter, and Andrew his brother; James the son of Zeb'edee, and John his brother; Philip and Bartholomew; Thomas and Matthew the tax collector; James the son of Alphaeus, and Thaddaeus; Simon the Cananaean, and Judas Iscariot, who betrayed him. These twelve Jesus sent out, charging them,"Go nowhere among the Gentiles, and enter no town of the Samaritans, but go rather to the lost sheep of the house of Israel. And preach as you go, saying,'The kingdom of heaven is at hand.' Heal the sick, raise the dead, cleanse lepers, cast out demons. You received without paying, give without pay."

"Take no gold, nor silver, nor copper in your belts, no bag for your journey, nor two tunics, nor sandals, nor a staff; for the laborer deserves his food. And whatever town or village you enter, find out who is worthy in it, and stay with him until you depart. As you enter the house, salute it. And if the house is worthy, let your peace come upon it; but if it is not worthy, let your peace return to you. And if any one will not receive you or listen to your words, shake off the dust from your feet as you leave that house or town. Truly, I say to you, it shall be more tolerable on the day of judgment for the land of Sodom and Gomor'rah than for that town."

Proper 7 *The Sunday closest to June 22*

A Reading (Lesson) from the Book of Jeremiah [20:7-13]

O Lord, thou hast deceived me, and I was deceived; thou art stronger than I, and thou hast prevailed. I have become a laughingstock all the day; every one mocks me. For whenever I speak, I cry out, I shout, "Violence and destruction!" For the word of the Lord has become for me a reproach and derision all day long. If I say, "I will not mention him, or speak any more in his name," there is in my heart as it were a burning fire shut up in my bones, and I am weary with holding it in, and I cannot. For I hear many whispering. Terror is on every side! "Denounce him! Let us denounce him!" say all my familiar friends, watching for my fall. "Perhaps he will be deceived, then we can overcome him, and take our revenge on him." But the Lord is with me as a dread warrior; therefore my persecutors will stumble, they will not overcome me. They will be greatly shamed, for they will not succeed. Their eternal dishonor will never be forgotten. O Lord of hosts, who triest the righteous, who seest the heart and the mind, let me see thy vengeance upon them, for to thee have I committed my cause. Sing to the Lord; praise the Lord! For he has delivered the life of the needy from the hand of evildoers.

Psalm 69:1-18 [page 679]   or   *69:7-10, 16-18* [page 679]

A Reading (Lesson) from the Letter of Paul to the Romans
[5:15b-19]

For if many died through one man's trespass, much more
have the grace of God and the free gift in the grace of that
one man Jesus Christ abounded for many. And the free gift
is not like the effect of that one man's sin. For the judgment
following one trespass brought condemnation, but the free
gift following many trespasses brings justification. If,
because of one man's trespass, death reigned through that
one man, much more will those who receive the abundance
of grace and the free gift of righteousness reign in life
through the one man Jesus Christ. Then as one man's
trespass led to condemnation for all men, so one man's act
of righteousness leads to acquittal and life for all men. For
as by one man's disobedience many were made sinners, so
by one man's obedience many will be made righteous.

✝ *The Holy Gospel of Our Lord Jesus Christ
According to Matthew* [10:(16-23) 24-33]

Jesus said to the twelve apostles, "Behold, I send you out
as sheep in the midst of wolves; so be wise as serpents
and innocent as doves. Beware of men; for they will
deliver you up to councils, and flog you in their
synagogues, and you will be dragged before governors
and kings for my sake, to bear testimony before them
and the Gentiles. When they deliver you up, do not be
anxious how you are to speak or what you are to say;
for what you are to say will be given to you in that hour;
for it is not you who speak, but the Spirit of your Father
speaking through you. Brother will deliver up brother to
death, and the father his child, and children will rise
against parents and have them put to death; and you
will be hated by all for my name's sake. But he who
endures to the end will be saved. When they persecute

you in one town, flee to the next; for truly, I say to you, you will not have gone through all the towns of Israel, before the Son of man comes."

[*Jesus said to the twelve apostles,*] "A disciple is not above his teacher, nor a servant above his master; it is enough for the disciple to be like his teacher, and the servant like his master. If they have called the master of the house Be-el'zebul, how much more will they malign those of his household. So have no fear of them; for nothing is covered that will not be revealed, or hidden that will not be known. What I tell you in the dark, utter in the light; and what you hear whispered, proclaim upon the housetops. And do not fear those who kill the body but cannot kill the soul; rather fear him who can destroy both soul and body in hell. Are not two sparrows sold for a penny? And not one of them will fall to the ground without your Father's will. But even the hairs of your head are all numbered. Fear not, therefore; you are of more value than many sparrows. So every one who acknowledges me before men, I also will acknowledge before my Father who is in heaven; but whoever denies me before men, I also will deny before my Father who is in heaven."

Proper 8 *The Sunday closest to June 29*

A Reading (Lesson) from the Book of Isaiah [2:10-17]

Enter into the rock, and hide in the dust from before the terror of the Lord, and from the glory of his majesty. The haughty looks of man shall be brought low, and the pride of men shall be humbled; and the Lord alone will be exalted in that day. For the Lord of hosts has a day against all that is proud and lofty, against all that is lifted up and high; against all the cedars of Lebanon, lofty and lifted up; and against all the oaks of Bashan; against all the high mountains, and against all the lofty hills; against every high tower, and against every fortified wall; against all the ships of Tarshish, and against all the beautiful craft. And the haughtiness of man shall be humbled, and the pride of men shall be brought low; and the Lord alone will be exalted in that day.

Psalm 89:1-18 [page 713] or *89:1-4, 15-18* [page 713]

A Reading (Lesson) from the Letter of Paul to the Romans [6:3-11]

Do you not know that all of us who have been baptized into Christ Jesus were baptized into his death? We were buried therefore with him by baptism into death, so that as Christ was raised from the dead by the glory of the Father, we too might walk in newness of life. For if we have been united with him in a death like his, we shall certainly be united with him in a resurrection like his. We know that our old self was crucified with him so that the sinful body might be destroyed, and we might no longer be enslaved to sin. For he who has died is freed from sin. But if we have died with Christ, we believe that we shall also live with him. For we know that Christ being raised from the dead will never die again; death no longer has dominion over him. The death he died he died to sin, once for all, but the life he lives he lives to God. So you also must consider yourselves dead to sin and alive to God in Christ Jesus.

✝ *The Holy Gospel of Our Lord Jesus Christ According to Matthew* [10:34-42]

Jesus said, "Do not think that I have come to bring peace on earth; I have not come to bring peace, but a sword. For I have come to set a man against his father, and a daughter against her mother, and a daughter-in-law against her mother-in-law; and a man's foes will be those of his own household. He who loves father or mother more than me is not worthy of me; and he who loves son or daughter more than me is not worthy of me; and he who does not take his cross and follow me is not worthy of me. He who finds his life will lose it, and he who loses his life for my sake will find it. He who receives you receives me, and he who receives me receives him who sent me. He who receives a prophet because he is a prophet shall receive a prophet's reward, and he who receives a righteous man because he is a righteous man shall receive a righteous man's reward. And whoever gives to one of these little ones even a cup of cold water because he is a disciple, truly, I say to you, he shall not lose his reward."

Proper 9 *The Sunday closest to July 6*

A Reading (Lesson) from the Book of Zechariah [9:9-12]

Rejoice greatly, O daughter of Zion! Shout aloud, O daughter of Jerusalem! Lo, your king comes to you; triumphant and victorious is he, humble and riding on an ass, on a colt the foal of an ass. I will cut off the chariot from E′phraim and the war horse from Jerusalem; and the battle bow shall be cut off, and he shall command peace to the nations; his dominion shall be from sea to sea, and from the River to the ends of the earth. As for you also, because of the blood of my covenant with you, I will set your captives free from the waterless pit. Return to your stronghold, O prisoners of hope; today I declare that I will restore to you double.

Psalm 145 [page 801]   or   *145:8-14* [page 802]

A Reading (Lesson) from the Letter of Paul to the Romans
[7:21—8:6]

I find it to be a law that when I want to do right, evil lies
close at hand. For I delight in the law of God, in my inmost
self, but I see in my members another law at war with the
law of my mind and making me captive to the law of sin
which dwells in my members. Wretched man that I am!
Who will deliver me from this body of death? Thanks be to
God through Jesus Christ our Lord! So then, I of myself
serve the law of God with my mind, but with my flesh
I serve the law of sin. There is therefore now no
condemnation for those who are in Christ Jesus. For the
law of the Spirit of life in Christ Jesus has set me free from
the law of sin and death. For God has done what the law,
weakened by the flesh, could not do: sending his own Son
in the likeness of sinful flesh and for sin, he condemned sin
in the flesh, in order that the just requirement of the law
might be fulfilled in us, who walk not according to the flesh
but according to the Spirit. For those who live according to
the flesh set their minds on the things of the flesh, but those
who live according to the Spirit set their minds on the
things of the Spirit. To set the mind on the flesh is death,
but to set the mind on the Spirit is life and peace.

✝ *The Holy Gospel of Our Lord Jesus Christ*
According to Matthew [11:25-30]

Jesus said, "I thank thee, Father, Lord of heaven and earth,
that thou hast hidden these things from the wise and
understanding and revealed them to babes; yea, Father, for
such was thy gracious will. All things have been delivered
to me by my Father; and no one knows the Son except the
Father, and no one knows the Father except the Son and
any one to whom the Son chooses to reveal him. Come to
me, all who labor and are heavy laden, and I will give you
rest. Take my yoke upon you, and learn from me; for I am

gentle and lowly in heart, and you will find rest for your souls. For my yoke is easy, and my burden is light."

Proper 10   *The Sunday closest to July 13*

A Reading (Lesson) from the Book of Isaiah
[55:1-5, 10-13]

Thus says the Lord: "Ho, every one who thirsts, come to the waters; and he who has no money, come, buy and eat! Come, buy wine and milk without money and without price. Why do you spend your money for that which is not bread, and your labor for that which does not satisfy? Hearken diligently to me, and eat what is good, and delight yourselves in fatness. Incline your ear, and come to me; hear, that your soul may live; and I will make with you an everlasting covenant, my steadfast, sure love for David. Behold, I made him a witness to the peoples, a leader and commander for the peoples. Behold, you shall call nations that you know not, and nations that knew you not shall run to you, because of the Lord your God, and of the Holy One of Israel, for he has glorified you. For as the rain and the snow come down from heaven, and return not thither but water the earth, making it bring forth and sprout, giving seed to the sower and bread to the eater, so shall my word be that goes forth from my mouth; it shall not return to me empty, but it shall accomplish that which I purpose, and prosper in the thing for which I sent it. For you shall go out in joy, and be led forth in peace; the mountains and the hills before you shall break forth into singing, and all the trees of the field shall clap their hands. Instead of the thorn shall come up the cypress; instead of the brier shall come up the myrtle; and it shall be to the Lord for a memorial, for an everlasting sign which shall not be cut off."

Psalm 65 [page 672]   or   *65:9-14* [page 673]

A Reading (Lesson) from the Letter of Paul to the Romans
[8:9-17]

You are not in the flesh, you are in the Spirit, if in fact the Spirit of God dwells in you. Any one who does not have the Spirit of Christ does not belong to him. But if Christ is in you, although your bodies are dead because of sin, your spirits are alive because of righteousness. If the Spirit of him who raised Jesus from the dead dwells in you, he who raised Christ Jesus from the dead will give life to your mortal bodies also through his Spirit which dwells in you. So then, brethren, we are debtors, not to the flesh, to live according to the flesh—for if you live according to the flesh you will die, but if by the Spirit you put to death the deeds of the body you will live. For all who are led by the Spirit of God are sons of God. For you did not receive the spirit of slavery to fall back into fear, but you have received the spirit of sonship. When we cry, "Abba! Father!" it is the Spirit himself bearing witness with our spirit that we are children of God, and if children, then heirs, heirs of God and fellow heirs with Christ, provided we suffer with him in order that we may also be glorified with him.

✝ *The Holy Gospel of Our Lord Jesus Christ According to Matthew* [13:1-9, 18-23]

Jesus went out of the house and sat beside the sea. And great crowds gathered about him, so that he got into a boat and sat there; and the whole crowd stood on the beach. And he told them many things in parables, saying, "A sower went out to sow. And as he sowed, some seeds fell along the path, and the birds came and devoured them. Other seeds fell on rocky ground, where they had not much soil, and immediately they sprang up, since they had no depth of soil, but when the sun rose they were scorched; and since they had no root they withered away. Other seeds fell upon thorns, and the thorns grew up and choked them. Other seeds fell on good soil and brought forth grain, some a hundredfold, some sixty, some thirty. He who has ears, let him hear. Hear then the parable of the sower. When any one hears the word of the kingdom and does not understand it, the evil one comes and snatches away what is sown in his heart; this is what was sown along the path. As for what was sown on rocky ground, this is he who hears the word and immediately receives it with joy; yet he has no root in himself, but endures for a while, and when tribulation or persecution arises on account of the word, immediately he falls away. As for what was sown among thorns, this is he who hears the word, but the cares of the world and the delight in riches choke the word, and it proves unfruitful. As for what was sown on good soil, this is he who hears the word and understands it; he indeed bears fruit, and yields, in one case a hundredfold, in another sixty, and in another thirty."

Proper 11 *The Sunday closest to July 20*

A Reading (Lesson) from the Book of Wisdom
[12:13, 16-19]

There is no god besides thee, whose care is for all men, to whom thou shouldst prove that thou hast not judged unjustly; for thy strength is the source of righteousness, and thy sovereignty over all causes thee to spare all. For thou dost show thy strength when men doubt the completeness of thy power, and dost rebuke any insolence among those who know it. Thou who art sovereign in strength dost judge with mildness, and with great forbearance thou dost govern us; for thou hast power to act whenever thou dost choose. Through such works thou hast taught thy people that the righteous man must be kind, and thou hast filled thy sons with good hope, because thou givest repentance for sins.

Psalm 86 [page 709]   or   *86:11-17* [page 710]

A Reading (Lesson) from the Letter of Paul to the Romans [8:18-25]

I consider that the sufferings of this present time are not worth comparing with the glory that is to be revealed to us. For the creation waits with eager longing for the revealing of the sons of God; for the creation was subjected to futility, not of its own will but by the will of him who subjected it in hope; because the creation itself will be set free from its bondage to decay and obtain the glorious liberty of the children of God. We know that the whole creation has been groaning in travail together until now; and not only the creation, but we ourselves, who have the first fruits of the Spirit, groan inwardly as we wait for adoption as sons, the redemption of our bodies. For in this hope we were saved. Now hope that is seen is not hope. For who hopes for what he sees? But if we hope for what we do not see, we wait for it with patience.

✝ *The Holy Gospel of Our Lord Jesus Christ According to Matthew* [13:24-30, 36-43]

Another parable Jesus put before the crowds saying, "The kingdom of heaven may be compared to a man who sowed good seed in his field; but while men were sleeping, his enemy came and sowed weeds among the wheat, and went away. So when the plants came up and bore grain, then the weeds appeared also. And the servants of the householder came and said to him, 'Sir, did you not sow good seed in your field? How then has it weeds?' He said to them, 'An enemy has done this.' The servants said to him, 'Then do you want us to go and gather them?' But he said, 'No; lest in gathering the weeds you root up the wheat along with them. Let both grow together until the harvest; and at harvest time I will tell the reapers, Gather the weeds first and bind them in bundles to be burned, but gather the wheat into my barn.'" Then he left the crowds and went into the house. And his disciples came to him, saying, "Explain to us the parable of the weeds of the field." He answered, "He who sows the good seed is the Son of man; the field is the world, and the good seed means the sons of the kingdom; the weeds are the sons of the evil one, and the enemy who sowed them is the devil; the harvest is the close of the age, and the reapers are angels. Just as the weeds are gathered and burned with fire, so will it be at the close of the age. The Son of man will send his angels, and they will gather out of his kingdom all causes of sin and all evildoers, and throw them into the furnace of fire; there men will weep and gnash their teeth. Then the righteous will shine like the sun in the kingdom of their Father. He who has ears, let him hear."

Proper 12   *The Sunday closest to July 27*

A Reading (Lesson) from the First Book of the Kings
[3:5-12]

At Gibeon the Lord appeared to Solomon in a dream by night; and God said, "Ask what I shall give you." And Solomon said, "Thou hast shown great and steadfast love to thy servant David my father, because he walked before thee in faithfulness, in righteousness, and in uprightness of heart toward thee; and thou hast kept for him this great and steadfast love, and hast given him a son to sit on his throne this day. And now, O Lord my God, thou hast made thy servant king in place of David my father, although I am but a little child; I do not know how to go out or come in.

And thy servant is in the midst of thy people whom thou hast chosen, a great people, that cannot be numbered or counted for multitude. Give thy servant therefore an understanding mind to govern thy people, that I may discern between good and evil; for who is able to govern this thy great people?" It pleased the Lord that Solomon had asked this. And God said to him, "Because you have asked this, and have not asked for yourself long life or riches or the life of your enemies, but have asked for yourself understanding to discern what is right, behold, I now do according to your word. Behold, I give you a wise and discerning mind, so that none like you has been before you and none like you shall arise after you."

Psalm 119:121-136 [page 773]   or

119:129-136 [page 774]

A Reading (Lesson) from the Letter of Paul to the Romans [8:26-34]

The Spirit helps us in our weakness; for we do not know how to pray as we ought, but the Spirit himself intercedes for us with sighs too deep for words. And he who searches the hearts of men knows what is the mind of the Spirit, because the Spirit intercedes for the saints according to the will of God. We know that in everything God works for good with those who love him, who are called according to his purpose. For those whom he foreknew he also predestined to be conformed to the image of his Son, in order that he might be the first-born among many brethren. And those whom he predestined he also called; and those whom he called he also justified; and those whom he justified he also glorified. What then shall we say to this? If God is for us, who is against us? He who did not spare his own Son but gave him up for us all, will he not also give us all things with him? Who shall bring any charge against God's elect? It is God who justifies; who is to condemn? Is it Christ Jesus, who died, yes, who was raised from the dead, who is at the right hand of God, who indeed intercedes for us?

✝ *The Holy Gospel of Our Lord Jesus Christ*
According to Matthew [13:31-33, 44-49a]

Another parable Jesus put before the crowds, saying,"The kingdom of heaven is like a grain of mustard seed which a man took and sowed in his field; it is the smallest of all seeds, but when it has grown it is the greatest of shrubs and becomes a tree, so that the birds of the air come and make nests in its branches." He told them another parable. "The kingdom of heaven is like leaven which a woman took and hid in three measures of flour, till it was all leavened. The kingdom of heaven is like treasure hidden in a field, which a man found and covered up; then in his joy he goes and sells all that he has and buys that field. Again, the kingdom of heaven is like a merchant in search of fine pearls, who, on finding one pearl of great value, went and sold all that he had and bought it. Again, the kingdom of heaven is like a net which was thrown into the sea and gathered fish of every kind; when it was full, men drew it ashore and sat down and sorted the good into vessels but threw away the bad. So it will be at the close of the age."

Proper 13 *The Sunday closest to August 3*

A Reading (Lesson) from the Book of Nehemiah [9:16-20]

Ezra blessed the Lord, and said,"Our fathers acted presumptuously and stiffened their neck and did not obey thy commandments; they refused to obey, and were not mindful of the wonders which thou didst perform among them; but they stiffened their neck and appointed a leader to return to their bondage in Egypt. But thou art a God ready to forgive, gracious and merciful, slow to anger and abounding in steadfast love, and didst not forsake them. Even when they had made for themselves a molten calf and said,'This is your God who brought you up out of Egypt,' and had committed great blasphemies, thou in thy great mercies didst not forsake them in the wilderness; the pillar of cloud which led them in the way did not depart from them by day, nor the pillar of fire by night which lighted for them the way by which they should go. Thou gavest thy good Spirit to instruct them, and didst not withhold thy manna from their mouth, and gavest them water for their thirst."

Psalm 78:1-29 [page 694]   or   *78:14-20, 23-25* [page 696]

A Reading (Lesson) from the Letter of Paul to the Romans [8:35-39]

Who shall separate us from the love of Christ? Shall tribulation, or distress, or persecution, or famine, or nakedness, or peril, or sword? As it is written,"For thy sake we are being killed all the day long; we are regarded as sheep to be slaughtered." No, in all these things we are more than conquerors through him who loved us. For I am sure that neither death, nor life, nor angels, nor principalities, nor things present, nor things to come, nor powers, nor height, nor depth, nor anything else in all creation, will be able to separate us from the love of God in Christ Jesus our Lord.

✝ *The Holy Gospel of Our Lord Jesus Christ According to Matthew* [14:13-21]

Jesus withdrew in a boat to a lonely place apart. But when the crowds heard it, they followed him on foot from the towns. As he went ashore he saw a great throng; and he had compassion on them, and healed their sick. When it was evening, the disciples came to him and said,"This is a lonely place, and the day is now over; send the crowds away to go into the villages and buy food for themselves." Jesus said,"They need not go away; you give them something to eat." They said to him,"We have only five loaves here and two fish." And he said,"Bring them here to me." Then he ordered the crowds to sit down on the grass; and taking the five loaves and the two fish he looked up to heaven, and blessed, and broke and gave the loaves to the disciples, and the disciples gave them to the crowds. And they all ate and were satisfied. And they took up twelve baskets full of the broken pieces left over. And those who ate were about five thousand men, besides women and children.

Proper 14 *The Sunday closest to August 10*

A Reading (Lesson) from the Book of Jonah [2:1-9]

Jonah prayed to the Lord his God from the belly of the fish, saying,"I called the Lord, out of my distress, and he answered me; out of the belly of Sheol I cried, and thou didst hear my voice. For thou didst cast me into the deep, into the heart of the seas, and the flood was round about me; all thy waves and thy billows passed over me. Then I said,'I am cast out from thy presence; how shall I again look upon thy holy temple?' The waters closed in over me, the deep was round about me; weeds were wrapped about my head at the roots of the mountains. I went down to the land whose bars closed upon me for ever; yet thou didst bring up my life from the Pit, O Lord my God. When my soul fainted within me, I remembered the Lord; and my prayer came to thee, into thy holy temple. Those who pay regard to vain idols forsake their true loyalty. But I with the voice of thanksgiving will sacrifice to thee; what I have vowed I will pay. Deliverance belongs to the Lord!"

Psalm 29 [page 620]

A Reading (Lesson) from the Letter of Paul to the Romans [9:1-5]

I am speaking the truth in Christ, I am not lying; my conscience bears me witness in the Holy Spirit, that I have great sorrow and unceasing anguish in my heart. For I could wish that I myself were accursed and cut off from Christ for the sake of my brethren, my kinsmen by race. They are Israelites, and to them belong the sonship, the glory, the covenants, the giving of the law, the worship, and the promises; to them belong the patriarchs, and of their race, according to the flesh, is the Christ. God who is over all be blessed for ever. Amen.

✝ *The Holy Gospel of Our Lord Jesus Christ According to Matthew* [14:22-33]

Jesus made the disciples get into the boat and go before him to the other side, while he dismissed the crowds. And after he had dismissed the crowds, he went up on the mountain by himself to pray. When evening came, he was there alone, but the boat by this time was many furlongs distant from the land, beaten by the waves; for the wind was against them. And in the fourth watch of the night he came to them, walking on the sea. But when the disciples saw him walking on the sea, they were terrified, saying, "It is a ghost!" And they cried out for fear. But immediately he spoke to them, saying, "Take heart, it is I; have no fear." And Peter answered him, "Lord, if it is you, bid me come to you on the water." He said, "Come." So Peter got out of the boat and walked on the water and came to Jesus; but when he saw the wind, he was afraid, and beginning to sink he cried out,"Lord, save me." Jesus immediately reached out his hand and caught him, saying to him,"O man of little faith, why did you doubt?" And when they got into the boat, the wind ceased. And those in the boat worshiped him, saying,"Truly you are the Son of God."

Proper 15   *The Sunday closest to August 17*

A Reading (Lesson) from the Book of Isaiah
[56:1 (2-5) 6-7]

Thus says the Lord: "Keep justice, and do righteousness, for soon my salvation will come, and my deliverance be revealed.

"Blessed is the man who does this, and the son of man who holds it fast, who keeps the sabbath, not profaning it, and keeps his hand from doing any evil." Let not the foreigner who has joined himself to the Lord say,"The Lord will surely separate me from his people"; and let not the eunuch say,"Behold, I am a dry tree." For thus says the Lord: "To the eunuchs who keep my sabbaths, who choose the things that please me and hold fast my covenant, I will give in my house and within my walls a monument and a name better than sons and daughters; I will give them an everlasting name which shall not be cut off."

"And the foreigners who join themselves to the Lord, to minister to him, to love the name of the Lord, and to be his servants, every one who keeps the sabbath, and does not profane it, and holds fast my covenant—these I will bring to my holy mountain, and make them joyful in my house of prayer; their burnt offerings and their sacrifices will be accepted on my altar; for my house shall be called a house of prayer for all peoples."

Psalm 67 [page 675]

A Reading (Lesson) from the Letter of Paul to the Romans [11:13-15, 29-32]

Now I am speaking to you Gentiles. Inasmuch then as I am an apostle to the Gentiles, I magnify my ministry in order to make my fellow Jews jealous, and thus save some of them. For if their rejection means the reconciliation of the world, what will their acceptance mean but life from the dead? For the gifts and the call of God are irrevocable. Just as you were once disobedient to God but now have received mercy because of their disobedience, so they have now been disobedient in order that by the mercy shown to you they also may receive mercy. For God has consigned all men to disobedience, that he may have mercy upon all.

✝ *The Holy Gospel of Our Lord Jesus Christ According to Matthew* [15:21-28]

Jesus withdrew to the district of Tyre and Sidon. And behold, a Canaanite woman from that region came out and cried, "Have mercy on me, O Lord, Son of David; my daughter is severely possessed by a demon." But he did not answer her a word. And his disciples came and begged him, saying, "Send her away, for she is crying after us." He answered, "I was sent only to the lost sheep of the house of Israel." But she came and knelt before him, saying, "Lord, help me." And he answered, "It is not fair to take the children's bread and throw it to the dogs." She said, "Yes, Lord, yet even the dogs eat the crumbs that fall from their masters' table." Then Jesus answered her, "O woman, great is your faith! Be it done for you as you desire." And her daughter was healed instantly.

Proper 16   *The Sunday closest to August 24*

A Reading (Lesson) from the Book of Isaiah [51:1-6]

Thus says the Lord: "Hearken to me, you who pursue deliverance, you who seek the Lord; look to the rock from which you were hewn, and to the quarry from which you were digged. Look to Abraham your father and to Sarah who bore you; for when he was but one I called him, and I blessed him and made him many. For the Lord will comfort Zion; he will comfort all her waste places, and will make her wilderness like Eden, her desert like the garden of the Lord; joy and gladness will be found in her, thanksgiving and the voice of song. Listen to me, my people, and give ear to me, my nation; for a law will go forth from me, and my justice for a light to the peoples. My deliverance draws near speedily, my salvation has gone forth, and my arms will rule the peoples; the coastlands wait for me, and for my arm they hope. Lift up your eyes to the heavens, and look at the earth beneath; for the heavens will vanish like smoke, the earth will wear out like a garment, and they who dwell in it will die like gnats; but my salvation will be for ever, and my deliverance will never be ended."

Psalm 138 [page 793]

A Reading (Lesson) from the Letter of Paul to the Romans [11:33-36]

O the depth of the riches and wisdom and knowledge of God! How unsearchable are his judgments and how inscrutable his ways! "For who has known the mind of the Lord, or who has been his counselor? Or who has given a gift to him that he might be repaid?" For from him and through him and to him are all things. To him be glory for ever. Amen.

✝ *The Holy Gospel of Our Lord Jesus Christ*
According to Matthew [16:13-20]

When Jesus came into the district of Caesare'a Philippi, he asked his disciples, "Who do men say that the Son of man is?" And they said, "Some say John the Baptist, others say Eli'jah, and others Jeremiah or one of the prophets." He said to them, "But who do you say that I am?" Simon Peter replied, "You are the Christ, the Son of the living God." And Jesus answered him, "Blessed are you, Simon Bar-Jona! For flesh and blood has not revealed this to you, but my Father who is in heaven. And I tell you, you are Peter, and on this rock I will build my church, and the powers of death shall not prevail against it. I will give you the keys of the kingdom of heaven, and whatever you bind on earth shall be bound in heaven, and whatever you loose on earth shall be loosed in heaven." Then he strictly charged the disciples to tell no one that he was the Christ.

Proper 17 *The Sunday closest to August 31*

A Reading (Lesson) from the Book of Jeremiah [15:15-21]

O Lord, thou knowest; remember me and visit me, and take vengeance for me on my persecutors. In thy forbearance take me not away; know that for thy sake I bear reproach. Thy words were found, and I ate them, and thy words became to me a joy and the delight of my heart; for I am called by thy name, O Lord, God of hosts. I did not sit in the company of merrymakers, nor did I rejoice; I sat alone, because thy hand was upon me, for thou hadst filled me with indignation. Why is my pain unceasing, my wound incurable, refusing to be healed? Wilt thou be to me like a deceitful brook, like waters that fail? Therefore thus says the Lord: "If you return, I will restore you, and you shall stand before me. If you utter what is precious, and not what is worthless, you shall be as my mouth. They shall turn to you, but you shall not turn to them. And I will make you to this people a fortified wall of bronze; they will fight against you, but they shall not prevail over you, for I am with you to save you and deliver you, says the Lord. I will deliver you out of the hand of the wicked, and redeem you from the grasp of the ruthless."

Psalm 26 [page 616] or *26:1-8* [page 616]

A Reading (Lesson) from the Letter of Paul to the Romans [12:1-8]

I appeal to you therefore, brethren, by the mercies of God, to present your bodies as a living sacrifice, holy and acceptable to God, which is your spiritual worship. Do not be conformed to this world but be transformed by the renewal of your mind, that you may prove what is the will of God, what is good and acceptable and perfect. For by the grace given to me I bid every one among you not to think of himself more highly than he ought to think, but to think with sober judgment, each according to the measure of faith which God has assigned him. For as in one body we have many members, and all the members do not have the same function, so we, though many, are one body in Christ, and individually members one of another. Having gifts that differ according to the grace given to us, let us use them: if prophecy, in proportion to our faith; if service, in our serving; he who teaches, in his teaching; he who exhorts, in his exhortation; he who contributes, in liberality; he who gives aid, with zeal; he who does acts of mercy, with cheerfulness.

✝ *The Holy Gospel of Our Lord Jesus Christ*
According to Matthew [16:21-27]

Jesus began to show his disciples that he must go to
Jerusalem and suffer many things from the elders and chief
priests and scribes, and be killed, and on the third day be
raised. And Peter took him and began to rebuke him,
saying, "God forbid, Lord! This shall never happen to
you." But he turned and said to Peter, "Get behind me,
Satan! You are a hindrance to me; for you are not on the
side of God, but of men." Then Jesus told his disciples, "If
any man would come after me, let him deny himself and
take up his cross and follow me. For whoever would save
his life will lose it, and whoever loses his life for my sake
will find it. For what will it profit a man, if he gains the
whole world and forfeits his life? Or what shall a man give
in return for his life? For the Son of man is to come with his
angels in the glory of his Father, and then he will repay
every man for what he has done."

Proper 18   *The Sunday closest to September 7*

A Reading (Lesson) from the Book of Ezekiel
[33:(1-6) 7-11]

> The word of the Lord came to me: "Son of man, speak
> to your people and say to them, If I bring the sword
> upon a land, and the people of the land take a man from
> among them, and make him their watchman; and if he
> sees the sword coming upon the land and blows the
> trumpet and warns the people; then if any one who
> hears the sound of the trumpet does not take warning,
> and the sword comes and takes him away, his blood
> shall be upon his own head. He heard the sound of the
> trumpet, and did not take warning; his blood shall be
> upon himself. But if he had taken warning, he would

have saved his life. But if the watchman sees the sword coming and does not blow the trumpet, so that the people are not warned, and the sword comes, and takes any one of them; that man is taken away in his iniquity, but his blood I will require at the watchman's hand."

[*The word of the Lord came to me:*] "You, son of man, I have made a watchman for the house of Israel; whenever you hear a word from my mouth, you shall give them warning from me. If I say to the wicked, O wicked man, you shall surely die, and you do not speak to warn the wicked to turn from his way, that wicked man shall die in his iniquity, but his blood I will require at your hand. But if you warn the wicked to turn from his way, and he does not turn from his way; he shall die in his iniquity, but you will have saved your life. And you, son of man, say to the house of Israel, Thus have you said: 'Our transgressions and our sins are upon us, and we waste away because of them; how then can we live?' Say to them, As I live, says the Lord God, I have no pleasure in the death of the wicked, but that the wicked turn from his way and live; turn back, turn back from your evil ways; for why will you die, O house of Israel?"

Psalm 119:33-48 [page 766]   or   *119:33-40* [page 766]

A Reading (Lesson) from the Letter of Paul to the Romans [12:9-21]

Let love be genuine; hate what is evil, hold fast to what is good; love one another with brotherly affection; outdo one another in showing honor. Never flag in zeal, be aglow with the Spirit, serve the Lord. Rejoice in your hope, be patient in tribulation, be constant in prayer. Contribute to the needs of the saints, practice hospitality. Bless those who persecute you; bless and do not curse them. Rejoice with those who rejoice, weep with those who weep. Live in harmony with one another; do not be haughty, but associate with the lowly; never be conceited. Repay no one evil for evil, but take thought for what is noble in the sight of all. If possible, so far as it depends upon you, live peaceably with all. Beloved, never avenge yourselves, but leave it to the wrath of God; for it is written,"Vengeance is mine, I will repay, says the Lord." No,"if your enemy is hungry, feed him; if he is thirsty, give him drink; for by so doing you will heap burning coals upon his head." Do not be overcome by evil, but overcome evil with good.

✠ The Holy Gospel of Our Lord Jesus Christ
  According to Matthew [18:15-20]

Jesus said,"If your brother sins against you, go and tell him his fault, between you and him alone. If he listens to you, you have gained your brother. But if he does not listen, take one or two others along with you, that every word may be confirmed by the evidence of two or three witnesses. If he refuses to listen to them, tell it to the church; and if he refuses to listen even to the church, let him be to you a Gentile and a tax collector. Truly, I say to you, whatever you bind on earth shall be bound in heaven, and whatever you loose on earth shall be loosed in heaven. Again I say to you, if two of you agree on earth about anything they ask, it will be done for them by my Father in heaven. For where two or three are gathered in my name, there am I in the midst of them."

Proper 19   *The Sunday closest to September 14*

A Reading (Lesson) from the Book of Ecclesiasticus
[27:30—28:7]

Anger and wrath, these are abominations, and the sinful man will possess them. He that takes vengeance will suffer vengeance from the Lord, and he will firmly establish his sins. Forgive your neighbor the wrong he has done, and then your sins will be pardoned when you pray. Does a man harbor anger against another, and yet seek for healing from the Lord? Does he have no mercy toward a man like himself, and yet pray for his own sins? If he himself, being flesh, maintains wrath, who will make expiation for his sins? Remember the end of your life, and cease from enmity, remember destruction and death, and be true to the commandments. Remember the commandments, and do not be angry with your neighbor; remember the covenant of the Most High, and overlook ignorance.

Psalm 103 [page 733] or *103:8-13* [page 733]

A Reading (Lesson) from the Letter of Paul to the Romans
[14:5-12]

One man esteems one day as better than another, while another man esteems all days alike. Let every one be fully convinced in his own mind. He who observes the day, observes it in honor of the Lord. He also who eats, eats in honor of the Lord, since he gives thanks to God; while he who abstains, abstains in honor of the Lord and gives thanks to God. None of us lives to himself, and none of us dies to himself. If we live, we live to the Lord, and if we die, we die to the Lord; so then, whether we live or whether we die, we are the Lord's. For to this end Christ died and lived again, that he might be Lord both of the dead and of the living. Why do you pass judgment on your brother? Or you, why do you despise your brother? For we shall all stand before the judgment seat of God; for it is written, "As I live, says the Lord, every knee shall bow to me, and every tongue shall give praise to God." So each of us shall give account of himself to God.

✝ *The Holy Gospel of Our Lord Jesus Christ*
According to Matthew [18:21-35]

Peter came up and said to Jesus,"Lord, how often shall my brother sin against me, and I forgive him? As many as seven times?" Jesus said to him,"I do not say to you seven times, but seventy times seven. Therefore the kingdom of heaven may be compared to a king who wished to settle accounts with his servants. When he began the reckoning, one was brought to him who owed him ten thousand talents; and as he could not pay, his lord ordered him to be sold, with his wife and children and all that he had, and payment to be made. So the servant fell on his knees, imploring him,'Lord, have patience with me, and I will pay you everything.' And out of pity for him the lord of that servant released him and forgave him the debt. But that same servant, as he went out, came upon one of his fellow servants who owed him a hundred denarii; and seizing him by the throat he said,'Pay what you owe.' So his fellow servant fell down and besought him,'Have patience with me, and I will pay you.' He refused and went and put him in prison till be should pay the debt. When his fellow servants saw what had taken place, they were greatly distressed, and they went and reported to their lord all that had taken place. Then his lord summoned him and said to him,'You wicked servant! I forgave you all that debt because you besought me; and should not you have had mercy on your fellow servant, as I had mercy on you?' And in anger his lord delivered him to the jailers, till he should pay all his debt. So also my heavenly Father will do to every one of you, if you do not forgive your brother from your heart."

Proper 20   *The Sunday closest to September 21*

A Reading (Lesson) from the Book of Jonah [3:10—4:11]

When God saw what the people of Nin'eveh did, how they turned from their evil way, God repented of the evil which he had said he would do to them; and he did not do it. But it displeased Jonah exceedingly, and he was angry. And he prayed to the Lord and said, "I pray thee, Lord, is not this what I said when I was yet in my country? That is why I made haste to flee to Tarshish; for I knew that thou art a gracious God and merciful, slow to anger, and abounding in steadfast love, and repentest of evil. Therefore now, O Lord, take my life from me, I beseech thee, for it is better for me to die than to live." And the Lord said, "Do you do well to be angry?" Then Jonah went out of the city and sat to the east of the city, and made a booth for himself there. He sat under it in the shade, till he should see what would become of the city. And the Lord God appointed a plant, and made it come up over Jonah, that it might be a shade over his head, to save him from his discomfort. So Jonah was exceedingly glad because of the plant. But when dawn came up the next day, God appointed a worm which attacked the plant, so that it withered. When the sun rose, God appointed a sultry east wind, and the sun beat upon the head of Jonah so that he was faint; and he asked that he might die, and said, "It is better for me to die than to live." But God said to Jonah, "Do you do well to be angry for the plant?" And he said, "I do well to be angry, angry enough to die." And the Lord said, "You pity the plant, for which you did not labor, nor did you make it grow, which came into being in a night, and perished in a night. And should not I pity Nin'eveh, that great city, in which there are more than a hundred and twenty thousand persons who do not know their right hand from their left, and also much cattle?"

Psalm 145 [page 801]   or   *145:1-8* [page 801]

A Reading (Lesson) from the Letter of Paul
to the Philippians [1:21-27]

For to me to live is Christ, and to die is gain. If it is to be
life in the flesh, that means fruitful labor for me. Yet which
I shall choose I cannot tell. I am hard pressed between the
two. My desire is to depart and be with Christ, for that is
far better. But to remain in the flesh is more necessary on
your account. Convinced of this, I know that I shall remain
and continue with you all, for your progress and joy in the
faith, so that in me you may have ample cause to glory in
Christ Jesus, because of my coming to you again. Only let
your manner of life be worthy of the gospel of Christ, so
that whether I come and see you or am absent, I may hear
of you that you stand firm in one spirit, with one mind
striving side by side for the faith of the gospel.

✝ *The Holy Gospel of Our Lord Jesus Christ*
According to Matthew [20:1-16]

Jesus said, "The kingdom of heaven is like a householder
who went out early in the morning to hire laborers for his
vineyard. After agreeing with the laborers for a denarius a
day, he sent them into his vineyard. And going out about
the third hour he saw others standing idle in the market
place; and to them he said, 'You go into the vineyard too,
and whatever is right I will give you.' So they went. Going
out again about the sixth hour and the ninth hour, he did
the same. And about the eleventh hour he went out and
found others standing; and he said to them, 'Why do you
stand here idle all day?' They said to him, 'Because no one
has hired us.' He said to them, 'You go into the vineyard
too.' And when evening came, the owner of the vineyard
said to his steward, 'Call the laborers and pay them their
wages, beginning with the last, up to the first.' And when
those hired about the eleventh hour came, each of them

received a denarius. Now when the first came, they thought they would receive more; but each of them also received a denarius. And on receiving it they grumbled at the householder, saying, 'These last worked only one hour, and you have made them equal to us who have borne the burden of the day and the scorching heat.' But he replied to one of them, 'Friend, I am doing you no wrong; did you not agree with me for a denarius? Take what belongs to you, and go; I choose to give to this last as I give to you. Am I not allowed to do what I choose with what belongs to me? Or do you begrudge my generosity?' So the last will be first, and the first last."

Proper 21 *The Sunday closest to September 28*

A Reading (Lesson) from the Book of Ezekiel
[18:1-4, 25-32]

The word of the Lord came to me again: "What do you mean by repeating this proverb concerning the land of Israel, 'The fathers have eaten sour grapes, and the children's teeth are set on edge'? As I live, says the Lord God, this proverb shall no more be used by you in Israel. Behold, all souls are mine; the soul of the father as well as the soul of the son is mine: the soul that sins shall die. Yet you say, 'The way of the Lord is not just.' Hear now, O house of Israel: Is my way not just? Is it not your ways that are not just? When a righteous man turns away from his righteousness and commits iniquity, he shall die for it; for the iniquity which he has committed he shall die. Again, when a wicked man turns away from the wickedness he has committed and does what is lawful and right, he shall save his life. Because he considered and turned away from all the transgressions which he had committed, he shall surely live, he shall not die. Yet the house of Israel says, 'The way of the Lord is not just.' O house of Israel, are my ways not just? Is it not your ways that are not just? Therefore I will judge you, O house of Israel, every one according to his ways, says the Lord God. Repent and turn from all your transgressions, lest iniquity be your ruin. Cast away from you all the transgressions which you have committed against me, and get yourselves a new heart and a new spirit! Why will you die, O house of Israel? For I have no pleasure in the death of any one, says the Lord God; so turn, and live."

Psalm 25:1-14 [page 614] or *25:3-9* [page 614]

A Reading (Lesson) from the Letter of Paul to the Philippians [2:1-13]

If there is any encouragement in Christ, any incentive of love, any participation in the Spirit, any affection and sympathy, complete my joy by being of the same mind, having the same love, being in full accord and of one mind. Do nothing from selfishness or conceit, but in humility count others better than yourselves. Let each of you look not only to his own interests, but also to the interests of others. Have this mind among yourselves, which is yours in Christ Jesus, who, though he was in the form of God, did not count equality with God a thing to be grasped, but emptied himself, taking the form of a servant, being born in the likeness of men. And being found in human form he humbled himself and became obedient unto death, even death on a cross. Therefore God has highly exalted him and bestowed on him the name which is above every name, that at the name of Jesus every knee should bow, in heaven and on earth and under the earth, and every tongue confess that Jesus Christ is Lord, to the glory of God the Father. Therefore, my beloved, as you have always obeyed, so now, not only as in my presence but much more in my absence, work out your own salvation with fear and trembling; for God is at work in you, both to will and to work for his good pleasure.

✝ *The Holy Gospel of Our Lord Jesus Christ According to Matthew* [21:28-32]

Jesus said, "What do you think? A man had two sons; and he went to the first and said, 'Son, go and work in the vineyard today.' And he answered, 'I will not'; but afterward he repented and went. And he went to the second and said the same; and he answered, 'I go, sir,' but did not go. Which of the two did the will of his father?" They said, "The first." Jesus said to them, "Truly, I say to you, the tax collectors and the harlots go into the kingdom of God before you. For John came to you in the way of righteousness, and you did not believe him, but the tax collectors and the harlots believed him; and even when you saw it, you did not afterward repent and believe him."

Proper 22 *The Sunday closest to October 5*

A Reading (Lesson) from the Book of Isaiah [5:1-7]

Let me sing for my beloved a love song concerning his vineyard: My beloved had a vineyard on a very fertile hill. He digged it and cleared it of stones, and planted it with choice vines; he built a watchtower in the midst of it, and hewed out a wine vat in it; and he looked for it to yield grapes, but it yielded wild grapes. And now, O inhabitants of Jerusalem and men of Judah, judge, I pray you, between me and my vineyard. What more was there to do for my vineyard, that I have not done in it? When I looked for it to yield grapes, why did it yield wild grapes? And now I will tell you what I will do to my vineyard. I will remove its hedge, and it shall be devoured; I will break down its wall, and it shall be trampled down. I will make it a waste; it shall not be pruned or hoed, and briers and thorns shall grow up; I will also command the clouds that they rain no rain upon it. For the vineyard of the Lord of hosts is the house of Israel, and the men of Judah are his pleasant planting; and he looked for justice, but behold, bloodshed; for righteousness, but behold, a cry!

Psalm 80 [page 702]   or   *80:7-14* [page 703]

A Reading (Lesson) from the Letter of Paul to the Philippians [3:14-21]

I press on toward the goal for the prize of the upward call of God in Christ Jesus. Let those of us who are mature be thus minded; and if in anything you are otherwise minded, God will reveal that also to you. Only let us hold true to what we have attained. Brethren, join in imitating me, and mark those who so live as you have an example in us. For many, of whom I have often told you and now tell you even with tears, live as enemies of the cross of Christ. Their end is destruction, their god is the belly, and they glory in their shame, with minds set on earthly things. But our commonwealth is in heaven, and from it we await a Savior, the Lord Jesus Christ, who will change our lowly body to be like his glorious body, by the power which enables him even to subject all things to himself.

✝ *The Holy Gospel of Our Lord Jesus Christ According to Matthew* [21:33-43]

Jesus said, "Hear another parable. There was a householder who planted a vineyard, and set a hedge around it, and dug a wine press in it, and built a tower, and let it out to tenants, and went into another country. When the season of fruit drew near, he sent his servants to the tenants, to get his fruit; and the tenants took his servants and beat one, killed another, and stoned another. Again he sent other servants, more than the first; and they did the same to them. Afterward he sent his son to them, saying, 'They will respect my son.' But when the tenants saw the son, they said to themselves,'This is the heir; come, let us kill him and have his inheritance.' And they took him and cast him out of the vineyard, and killed him. When therefore the owner of the vineyard comes, what will he do to those tenants?" They said to him,"He will put those wretches to a miserable death, and let out the vineyard to other tenants who will give him the fruits in their seasons." Jesus said to them,"Have you never read in the scriptures: 'The very stone which the builders rejected has become the head of the corner; this was the Lord's doing, and it is marvelous in our eyes'? Therefore I tell you, the kingdom of God will be taken away from you and given to a nation producing the fruits of it."

Proper 23   *The Sunday closest to October 12*

A Reading (Lesson) from the Book of Isaiah [25:1-9]

O Lord, thou art my God; I will exalt thee, I will praise thy name; for thou hast done wonderful things, plans formed of old, faithful and sure. For thou hast made the city a heap, the fortified city a ruin; the palace of aliens is a city no more, it will never be rebuilt. Therefore strong peoples will glorify thee; cities of ruthless nations will fear thee. For thou hast been a stronghold to the poor, a stronghold to the needy in his distress, a shelter from the storm and a shade from the heat; for the blast of the ruthless is like a storm against a wall, like heat in a dry place. Thou dost subdue the noise of the aliens; as heat by the shade of a cloud, so the song of the ruthless is stilled. On this mountain the Lord of hosts will make for all peoples a feast of fat things, a feast of wine on the lees, of fat things full of marrow, of wine on the lees well refined. And he will destroy on this mountain the covering that is cast over all peoples, the veil that is spread over all nations. He will swallow up death for ever, and the Lord God will wipe away tears from all faces, and the reproach of his people he will take away from all the earth; for the Lord has spoken. It will be said on that day, "Lo, this is our God; we have waited for him, that he might save us. This is the Lord; we have waited for him; let us be glad and rejoice in his salvation."

Psalm 23 [page 612]

A Reading (Lesson) from the Letter of Paul to the Philippians [4:4-13]

Rejoice in the Lord always; again I will say, Rejoice. Let all men know your forbearance. The Lord is at hand. Have no anxiety about anything, but in everything by prayer and supplication with thanksgiving let your requests be made known to God. And the peace of God, which passes all understanding, will keep your hearts and your minds in Christ Jesus. Finally, brethren, whatever is true, whatever is honorable, whatever is just, whatever is pure, whatever is lovely, whatever is gracious, if there is any excellence, if there is anything worthy of praise, think about these things. What you have learned and received and heard and seen in me, do; and the God of peace will be with you. I rejoice in the Lord greatly that now at length you have revived your concern for me; you were indeed concerned for me, but you had no opportunity. Not that I complain of want; for I have learned, in whatever state I am, to be content. I know how to be abased, and I know how to abound; in any and all circumstances I have learned the secret of facing plenty and hunger, abundance and want. I can do all things in him who strengthens me.

✝ *The Holy Gospel of Our Lord Jesus Christ*
According to Matthew [22:1-14]

Again Jesus spoke to the people in parables, saying, "The kingdom of heaven may be compared to a king who gave a marriage feast for his son, and sent his servants to call those who were invited to the marriage feast; but they would not come. Again he sent other servants, saying, 'Tell those who are invited, Behold, I have made ready my dinner, my oxen and my fat calves are killed, and everything is ready; come to the marriage feast.' But they made light of it and went off, one to his farm, another to his business, while the rest seized his servants, treated them shamefully, and killed them. The king was angry, and he sent his troops and destroyed those murderers and burned their city. Then he said to his servants, 'The wedding is ready, but those invited were not worthy. Go therefore to the thoroughfares, and invite to the marriage feast as many as you find.' And those servants went out into the streets and gathered all whom they found, both bad and good; so the wedding hall was filled with guests. But when the king came in to look at the guests, he saw there a man who had no wedding garment; and he said to him, 'Friend, how did you get in here without a wedding garment?' And he was speechless. Then the king said to the attendants, 'Bind him hand and foot, and cast him into the outer darkness; there men will weep and gnash their teeth.' For many are called, but few are chosen."

Proper 24 *The Sunday closest to October 19*

A Reading (Lesson) from the Book of Isaiah [45:1-7]

"Thus says the Lord to his anointed, to Cyrus, whose right hand I have grasped, to subdue nations before him and ungird the loins of kings, to open doors before him that gates may not be closed: 'I will go before you and level the mountains, I will break in pieces the doors of bronze and cut asunder the bars of iron, I will give you the treasures of darkness and the hoards in secret places, that you may know that it is I, the Lord, the God of Israel, who call you by your name. For the sake of my servant Jacob, and Israel my chosen, I call you by your name, I surname you, though you do not know me. I am the Lord, and there is no other, besides me there is no God; I gird you, though you do not know me, that men may know, from the rising of the sun and from the west, that there is none besides me; I am the Lord, and there is no other. I form light and create darkness, I make weal and create woe, I am the Lord, who do all these things.' "

Psalm 96 [page 725]   or   *96:1-9* [page 725]

A Reading (Lesson) from the First Letter of Paul to the Thessalonians [1:1-10]

Paul, Silva'nus, and Timothy, To the church of the Thessalo'nians in God the Father and the Lord Jesus Christ: Grace to you and peace. We give thanks to God always for you all, constantly mentioning you in our prayers, remembering before our God and Father your work of faith and labor of love and steadfastness of hope in our Lord Jesus Christ. For we know, brethren beloved by God, that he has chosen you; for our gospel came to you not only in word, but also in power and in the Holy Spirit and with full conviction. You know what kind of men we proved to be among you for your sake. And you became imitators of us and of the Lord, for you received the word in much affliction, with joy inspired by the Holy Spirit; so that you became an example to all the believers in Macedo'nia and in Acha'ia. For not only has the word of the Lord sounded forth from you in Macedo'nia and Acha'ia, but your faith in God has gone forth everywhere, so that we need not say anything. For they themselves report concerning us what a welcome we had among you, and how you turned to God from idols, to serve a living and true God, and to wait for his Son from heaven, whom he raised from the dead, Jesus who delivers us from the wrath to come.

✝ *The Holy Gospel of Our Lord Jesus Christ According to Matthew* [22:15-22]

The Pharisees went and took counsel how to entangle Jesus in his talk. And they sent their disciples to him, along with the Hero'di-ans, saying,"Teacher, we know that you are true, and teach the way of God truthfully, and care for no man; for you do not regard the position of men. Tell us, then, what you think. Is it lawful to pay taxes to Caesar, or not?" But Jesus, aware of their malice, said,"Why put me to the test, you hypocrites? Show me the money for the tax." And they brought him a coin. And Jesus said to them,"Whose likeness and inscription is this?" They said,"Caesar's." Then he said to them,"Render therefore to Caesar the things that are Caesar's, and to God the things that are God's." When they heard it, they marveled; and they left him and went away.

Proper 25 *The Sunday closest to October 26*

A Reading (Lesson) from the Book of Exodus [22:21-27]

God said,"You shall not wrong a stranger or oppress him, for you were strangers in the land of Egypt. You shall not afflict any widow or orphan. If you do afflict them, and they cry out to me, I will surely hear their cry; and my wrath will burn, and I will kill you with the sword, and your wives shall become widows and your children fatherless. If you lend money to any of my people with you who is poor, you shall not be to him as a creditor, and you shall not exact interest from him. If ever you take your neighbor's garment in pledge, you shall restore it to him before the sun goes down; for that is his only covering, it is his mantle for his body; in what else shall he sleep? And if he cries to me, I will hear, for I am compassionate."

Psalm 1 [page 585]

A Reading (Lesson) from the First Letter of Paul to the Thessalonians [2:1-8]

You yourselves know, brethren, that our visit to you was not in vain; but though we had already suffered and been shamefully treated at Philippi, as you know, we had courage in our God to declare to you the gospel of God in the face of great opposition. For our appeal does not spring from error or uncleanness, nor is it made with guile; but just as we have been approved by God to be entrusted with the gospel, so we speak, not to please men, but to please God who tests our hearts. For we never used either words of flattery, as you know, or a cloak for greed, as God is witness; nor did we seek glory from men, whether from you or from others, though we might have made demands as apostles of Christ. But we were gentle among you, like a nurse taking care of her children. So, being affectionately desirous of you, we were ready to share with you not only the gospel of God but also our own selves, because you had become very dear to us.

✝ *The Holy Gospel of Our Lord Jesus Christ According to Matthew* [22:34-46]

When the Pharisees heard that Jesus had silenced the Sad'ducees, they came together. And one of them, a lawyer, asked him a question, to test him. "Teacher, which is the great commandment in the law?" And he said to him, "You shall love the Lord your God with all your heart, and with all your soul, and with all your mind. This is the great and first commandment. And a second is like it, You shall love your neighbor as yourself. On these two commandments depend all the law and the prophets." Now while the Pharisees were gathered together, Jesus asked them a question, saying, "What do you think of the Christ? Whose son is he?" They said to him, "The son of David." He said to them, "How is it then that David, inspired by the Spirit, calls him Lord, saying, 'The Lord said to my Lord, Sit at my right hand, till I put thy enemies under thy feet'? If David thus calls him Lord, how is he his son?" And no one was able to answer him a word, nor from that day did any one dare to ask him any more questions.

Proper 26   *The Sunday closest to November 2*

A Reading (Lesson) from the Book of Micah [3:5-12]

Thus says the Lord concerning the prophets who lead my people astray, who cry "Peace" when they have something to eat, but declare war against him who puts nothing into their mouths. Therefore it shall be night to you, without vision, and darkness to you, without divination. The sun shall go down upon the prophets, and the day shall be black over them; the seers shall be disgraced, and the diviners put to shame; they shall all cover their lips, for there is no answer from God. But as for me, I am filled with power, with the Spirit of the Lord, and with justice and might, to declare to Jacob his transgression and to Israel his sin. Hear this, you heads of the house of Jacob and rulers of the house of Israel, who abhor justice and pervert all equity, who build Zion with blood and Jerusalem with wrong. Its heads give judgment for a bribe, its priests teach for hire, its prophets divine for money; yet they lean upon the Lord and say, "Is not the Lord in the midst of us? No evil shall come upon us." Therefore because of you Zion shall be plowed as a field; Jerusalem shall become a heap of ruins, and the mountain of the house a wooded height.

Psalm 43 [page 644]

A Reading (Lesson) from the First Letter of Paul to the Thessalonians [2:9-13, 17-20]

You remember our labor and toil, brethren; we worked night and day, that we might not burden any of you, while we preached to you the gospel of God. You are witnesses, and God also, how holy and righteous and blameless was our behavior to you believers; for you know how, like a father with his children, we exhorted each one of you and encouraged you and charged you to lead a life worthy of God, who calls you into his own kingdom and glory. And we also thank God constantly for this, that when you received the word of God which you heard from us, you accepted it not as the word of men but as what it really is, the word of God, which is at work in you believers. But since we were bereft of you, brethren, for a short time, in person not in heart, we endeavored the more eagerly and with great desire to see you face to face; because we wanted to come to you—I, Paul, again and again—but Satan hindered us. For what is our hope or joy or crown of boasting before our Lord Jesus at his coming? Is it not you? For you are our glory and joy.

✝ *The Holy Gospel of Our Lord Jesus Christ According to Matthew* [23:1-12]

Jesus said to the crowds and to his disciples, "The scribes and the Pharisees sit on Moses' seat; so practice and observe whatever they tell you, but not what they do; for they preach, but do not practice. They bind heavy burdens, hard to bear, and lay them on men's shoulders; but they themselves will not move them with their finger. They do all their deeds to be seen by men; for they make their phylacteries broad and their fringes long, and they love the place of honor at feasts and the best seats in the synagogues, and salutations in the market places, and being called rabbi by men. But you are not to be called rabbi, for you have one teacher, and you are all brethren. And call no man your father on earth, for you have one Father, who is in heaven. Neither be called masters, for you have one master, the Christ. He who is greatest among you shall be your servant; whoever exalts himself will be humbled, and whoever humbles himself will be exalted."

Proper 27 *The Sunday closest to November 9*

A Reading (Lesson) from the Book of Amos [5:18-24]

Thus says the Lord, the God of hosts, the Lord: "Woe to you who desire the day of the Lord! Why would you have the day of the Lord? It is darkness, and not light; as if a man fled from a lion, and a bear met him; or went into the house and leaned with his hand against the wall, and a serpent bit him. Is not the day of the Lord darkness, and not light, and gloom with no brightness in it? I hate, I despise your feasts, and I take no delight in your solemn assemblies. Even though you offer me your burnt offerings and cereal offerings, I will not accept them, and the peace offerings of your fatted beasts I will not look upon. Take away from me the noise of your songs; to the melody of your harps I will not listen. But let justice roll down like waters, and righteousness like an ever-flowing stream."

Psalm 70 [page 682]

*A Reading (Lesson) from the First Letter of Paul
to the Thessalonians* [4:13-18]

We would not have you ignorant, brethren, concerning those who are asleep, that you may not grieve as others do who have no hope. For since we believe that Jesus died and rose again, even so, through Jesus, God will bring with him those who have fallen asleep. For this we declare to you by the word of the Lord, that we who are alive, who are left until the coming of the Lord, shall not precede those who have fallen asleep. For the Lord himself will descend from heaven with a cry of command, with the archangel's call, and with the sound of the trumpet of God. And the dead in Christ will rise first; then we who are alive, who are left, shall be caught up together with them in the clouds to meet the Lord in the air; and so we shall always be with the Lord. Therefore comfort one another with these words.

✠ *The Holy Gospel of Our Lord Jesus Christ
According to Matthew* [25:1-13]

Jesus said, "The kingdom of heaven shall be compared to ten maidens who took their lamps and went to meet the bridegroom. Five of them were foolish, and five were wise. For when the foolish took their lamps, they took no oil with them; but the wise took flasks of oil with their lamps. As the bridegroom was delayed, they all slumbered and slept. But at midnight there was a cry, 'Behold, the bridegroom! Come out to meet him.' Then all those maidens rose and trimmed their lamps. And the foolish said to the wise, 'Give us some of your oil, for our lamps are going out.' But the wise replied, 'Perhaps there will not be enough for us and for you; go rather to the dealers and buy for yourselves.' And while they went to buy, the bridegroom came, and those who were ready went in with him to the marriage feast; and the door was shut. Afterward the other maidens came also, saying, 'Lord, lord, open to us.' But he replied, 'Truly, I say to you, I do not know you.' Watch therefore, for you know neither the day nor the hour."

Proper 28 *The Sunday closest to November 16*

A Reading (Lesson) from the Book of Zephaniah
[1:7, 12-18]

Be silent before the Lord God! For the day of the Lord is at hand; the Lord has prepared a sacrifice and consecrated his guests. "At that time," says the Lord, "I will search Jerusalem with lamps, and I will punish the men who are thickening upon their lees, those who say in their hearts, 'The Lord will not do good, nor will he do ill.' Their goods shall be plundered, and their houses laid waste. Though they build houses, they shall not inhabit them; though they plant vineyards, they shall not drink wine from them." The great day of the Lord is near, near and hastening fast; the sound of the day of the Lord is bitter, the mighty man cries aloud there. A day of wrath is that day, a day of distress and anguish, a day of ruin and devastation, a day of darkness and gloom, a day of clouds and thick darkness, a day of trumpet blast and battle cry against the fortified cities and against the lofty battlements. I will bring distress on men, so that they shall walk like the blind, because they have sinned against the Lord; their blood shall be poured out like dust, and their flesh like dung. Neither their silver nor their gold shall be able to deliver them on the day of the wrath of the Lord. In the fire of his jealous wrath, all the earth shall be consumed; for a full, yea, sudden end he will make of all the inhabitants of the earth.

Psalm 90 [page 717]   or   *90:1-8, 12* [page 717]

*A Reading (Lesson) from the First Letter of Paul
to the Thessalonians* [5:1-10]

As to the times and the seasons, brethren, you have no
need to have anything written to you. For you yourselves
know well that the day of the Lord will come like a thief in
the night. When people say,"There is peace and security,"
then sudden destruction will come upon them as travail
comes upon a woman with child, and there will be no
escape. But you are not in darkness, brethren, for that day
to surprise you like a thief. For you are all sons of light and
sons of the day; we are not of the night or of darkness. So
then let us not sleep, as others do, but let us keep awake
and be sober. For those who sleep sleep at night, and those
who get drunk are drunk at night. But, since we belong to
the day, let us be sober, and put on the breastplate of faith
and love, and for a helmet the hope of salvation. For God
has not destined us for wrath, but to obtain salvation
through our Lord Jesus Christ, who died for us so that
whether we wake or sleep we might live with him.

✝ *The Holy Gospel of Our Lord Jesus Christ
According to Matthew* [25:14-15, 19-29]

Jesus said,"The kingdom of God will be as when a man
going on a journey called his servants and entrusted to
them his property; to one he gave five talents, to another
two, to another one, to each according to his ability. Then
he went away. Now after a long time the master of those
servants came and settled accounts with them. And he who
had received the five talents came forward, bringing five
talents more, saying,'Master, you delivered to me five
talents; here I have made five talents more.' His master said
to him,'Well done, good and faithful servant; you have
been faithful over a little, I will set you over much; enter
into the joy of your master.' And he also who had the two
talents came forward, saying,'Master, you delivered to me

two talents; here I have made two talents more.' His master said to him, 'Well done, good and faithful servant; you have been faithful over a little, I will set you over much; enter into the joy of your master.' He also who had received the one talent came forward saying, 'Master, I knew you to be a hard man, reaping where you did not sow, and gathering where you did not winnow; so I was afraid, and I went and hid your talent in the ground. Here you have what is yours.' But his master answered him, 'You wicked and slothful servant! You knew that I reap where I have not sowed, and gather where I have not winnowed? Then you ought to have invested my money with the bankers, and at my coming I should have received what was my own with interest. So take the talent from him and give it to him who has the ten talents. For to every one who has will more be given, and he will have abundance; but from him who has not, even what he has will be taken away."

Proper 29 *The Sunday closest to November 23*

A Reading (Lesson) from the Book of Ezekiel [34:11-17]

Thus says the Lord God: "Behold, I, I myself will search for my sheep, and will seek them out. As a shepherd seeks out his flock when some of his sheep have been scattered abroad, so will I seek out my sheep; and I will rescue them from all places where they have been scattered on a day of clouds and thick darkness. And I will bring them out from the peoples, and gather them from the countries, and will bring them into their own land; and I will feed them on the mountains of Israel, by the fountains, and in all the inhabited places of the country. I will feed them with good pasture, and upon the mountain heights of Israel shall be their pasture; there they shall lie down in good grazing land, and on fat pasture they shall feed on the mountains of Israel. I myself will be the shepherd of my sheep, and I will make them lie down, says the Lord God. I will seek the lost, and I will bring back the strayed, and I will bind up the crippled, and I will strengthen the weak, and the fat and the strong I will watch over; I will feed them in justice. As for you, my flock, thus says the Lord God: Behold, I judge between sheep and sheep, rams and he-goats."

Psalm 95:1-7 [page 724]

A Reading (Lesson) from the First Letter of Paul to the Corinthians [15:20-28]

In fact Christ has been raised from the dead, the first fruits of those who have fallen asleep. For as by a man came death, by a man has come also the resurrection of the dead. For as in Adam all die, so also in Christ shall all be made alive. But each in his own order: Christ the first fruits, then at his coming those who belong to Christ. Then comes the end, when he delivers the kingdom to God the Father after destroying every rule and every authority and power. For he must reign until he has put all his enemies under his feet. The last enemy to be destroyed is death. "For God has put all things in subjection under his feet." But when it says, "All things are put in subjection under him," it is plain that he is excepted who put all things under him. When all things are subjected to him, then the Son himself will also be subjected to him who put all things under him, that God may be everything to every one.

✝ *The Holy Gospel of Our Lord Jesus Christ According to Matthew* [25:31-46]

Jesus said, "When the Son of man comes in his glory, and all the angels with him, then he will sit on his glorious throne. Before him will be gathered all the nations, and he will separate them one from another as a shepherd separates the sheep from the goats, and he will place the sheep at his right hand, but the goats at the left. Then the King will say to those at his right hand, 'Come, O blessed of my Father, inherit the kingdom prepared for you from the foundation of the world; for I was hungry and you gave me food, I was thirsty and you gave me drink, I was a stranger and you welcomed me, I was naked and you clothed me, I was sick and you visited me, I was in prison and you came to me.' Then the righteous will answer him, 'Lord, when did we see thee hungry and feed thee, or thirsty and give thee drink? And when did we see thee a stranger and welcome thee, or naked and clothe thee? And when did we see thee sick or in prison and visit thee? And the King will answer them, 'Truly, I say to you, as you did it to one of the least of these my brethren, you did it to me.' Then he will say to those at his left hand, 'Depart from me, you cursed, into the eternal fire prepared for the devil and his angels; for I was hungry and you gave me no food, I was thirsty and you gave me no drink, I was a stranger and you did not welcome me, naked and you did not clothe me, sick and in prison and you did not visit me.' Then they also will answer, 'Lord, when did we see thee hungry or thirsty or a stranger or naked or sick or in prison, and did not minister to thee?' Then he will answer them, 'Truly, I say to you, as you did it not to one of the least of these, you did it not to me.' And they will go away into eternal punishment, but the righteous into eternal life."

Holy Days

Saint Andrew   *November 30*

A Reading (Lesson) from the Book of Deuteronomy
[30:11-14]

Moses summoned all Israel and said to them: "This commandment which I command you this day is not too hard for you, neither is it far off. It is not in heaven, that you should say,'Who will go up for us to heaven, and bring it to us, that we may hear it and do it?' Neither is it beyond the sea, that you should say,'Who will go over the sea for us, and bring it to us, that we may hear it and do it?' But the word is very near you; it is in your mouth and in your heart, so that you can do it."

Psalm 19 [page 606]   or   *19:1-6* [page 606]

A Reading (Lesson) from the Letter of Paul to the Romans [10:8b-18]

The word is near you, on your lips and in your heart (that is, the word of faith which we preach); because, if you confess with your lips that Jesus is Lord and believe in your heart that God raised him from the dead, you will be saved. For man believes with his heart and so is justified, and he confesses with his lips and so is saved. The scripture says,"No one who believes in him will be put to shame."

For there is no distinction between Jew and Greek; the same Lord is Lord of all and bestows his riches upon all who call upon him. For, "every one who calls upon the name of the Lord will be saved." But how are men to call upon him in whom they have not believed? And how are they to believe in him of whom they have never heard? And how are they to hear without a preacher? And how can men preach unless they are sent? As it is written, "How beautiful are the feet of those who preach good news!" But they have not all obeyed the gospel; for Isaiah says, "Lord, who has believed what he has heard from us?" So faith comes from what is heard, and what is heard comes by the preaching of Christ. But I ask, have they not heard? Indeed they have; for "Their voice has gone out to all the earth, and their words to the ends of the world."

✝ *The Holy Gospel of Our Lord Jesus Christ According to Matthew* [4:18-22]

As Jesus walked by the Sea of Galilee, he saw two brothers, Simon who is called Peter and Andrew his brother, casting a net into the sea; for they were fishermen. And he said to them, "Follow me, and I will make you fishers of men." Immediately they left their nets and followed him. And going on from there he saw two other brothers, James the son of Zeb'edee and John his brother, in the boat with Zeb'edee their father, mending their nets, and he called them. Immediately they left the boat and their father, and followed him.

Saint Thomas   *December 21*

A Reading (Lesson) from the Book of Habak'kuk [2:1-4]

I will take my stand to watch, and station myself on the tower, and look forth to see what he will say to me, and what I will answer concerning my complaint. And the

Lord answered me, "Write the vision; make it plain upon tablets, so he may run who reads it. For still the vision awaits its time; it hastens to the end—it will not lie. If it seem slow, wait for it; it will surely come, it will not delay. Behold, he whose soul is not upright in him shall fail, but the righteous shall live by his faith."

Psalm 126 [page 782]

A Reading (Lesson) from the Letter to the Hebrews [10:35—11:1]

Do not throw away your confidence, which has a great reward. For you have need of endurance, so that you may do the will of God and receive what is promised. "For yet a little while, and the coming one shall come and shall not tarry; but my righteous one shall live by faith, and if he shrinks back, my soul has no pleasure in him." But we are not of those who shrink back and are destroyed, but of those who have faith and keep their souls. Now faith is the assurance of things hoped for, the conviction of things not seen.

✝ *The Holy Gospel of Our Lord Jesus Christ According to John* [20:24-29]

Thomas, one of the twelve, called the Twin, was not with the other disciples when Jesus came. So the other disciples told him, "We have seen the Lord." But he said to them, "Unless I see in his hands the print of the nails, and place my finger in the mark of the nails, and place my hand in his side, I will not believe." Eight days later, his disciples were again in the house, and Thomas was with them. The doors were shut, but Jesus came and stood among them, and said, "Peace be with you." Then he said to Thomas, "Put your finger here, and see my hands; and put out your hand, and place it in my side; do not be faithless, but believing."

Thomas answered him, "My Lord and my God!" Jesus said to him, "Have you believed because you have seen me? Blessed are those who have not seen and yet believe."

Saint Stephen   *December 26*

A Reading (Lesson) from the Book of Jeremiah   [26:1-9, 12-15]

In the beginning of the reign of Jehoi'akim the son of Josi'ah, king of Judah, this word came from the Lord, "Thus says the Lord: Stand in the court of the Lord's house, and speak to all the cities of Judah which come to worship in the house of the Lord all the words that I command you to speak to them; do not hold back a word. It may be they will listen, and every one turn from his evil way, that I may repent of the evil which I intend to do to them because of their evil doings. You shall say to them, 'Thus says the Lord: If you will not listen to me, to walk in my law which I have set before you, and to heed the words of my servants the prophets whom I send to you urgently, though you have not heeded, then I will make this house like Shiloh, and I will make this city a curse for all the nations of the earth.' " The priests and the prophets and all the people heard Jeremiah speaking these words in the house of the Lord. And when Jeremiah had finished speaking all that the Lord had commanded him to speak to all the people, then the priests and the prophets and all the people laid hold of him, saying, "You shall die! Why have you prophesied in the name of the Lord, saying, 'This house shall be like Shiloh, and this city shall be desolate, without inhabitant'?" And all the people gathered about Jeremiah in the house of the Lord. Then Jeremiah spoke to all the princes and all the people, saying, "The Lord sent me to prophesy against this house and this city all the words you have heard. Now therefore amend your ways and your doings, and obey the voice of the Lord your God and the

Lord will repent of the evil which he has pronounced against you. But as for me, behold, I am in your hands. Do with me as seems good and right to you. Only know for certain that if you put me to death, you will bring innocent blood upon yourselves and upon this city and its inhabitants, for in truth the Lord sent me to you to speak all these words in your ears."

Psalm 31 [page 622] or *31:1-5* [page 622]

A Reading (Lesson) from the Acts of the Apostles [6:8 — 7:2a, 51c-60]

Stephen, full of grace and power, did great wonders and signs among the people. Then some of those who belonged to the synagogue of the Freedmen (as it was called), and of the Cyre'nians, and of the Alexandrians, and of those from Cili'cia and Asia, arose and disputed with Stephen. But they could not withstand the wisdom and the Spirit with which he spoke. Then they secretly instigated men, who said,"We have heard him speak blasphemous words against Moses and God." And they stirred up the people and the elders and the scribes, and they came upon him and seized him and brought him before the council, and set up false witnesses who said,"This man never ceases to speak words against this holy place and the law; for we have heard him say that this Jesus of Nazareth will destroy this place, and will change the customs which Moses delivered to us." And gazing at him, all who sat in the council saw that his face was like the face of an angel. And the high priest said,"Is this so?" And Stephen said, "Brethren and fathers, hear me. As your fathers did, so do you. Which of the prophets did not your fathers persecute? And they killed those who announced beforehand the coming of the Righteous One, whom you have now betrayed and murdered, you who received the law as delivered by angels and did not keep it." Now when they heard these things they were enraged, and they ground their teeth against him. But he, full of the Holy Spirit, gazed into heaven and saw the glory of God, and Jesus standing at the right hand of God; and he said, "Behold, I see the heavens opened, and the Son of man standing at the right hand of God." But they cried out with a loud voice and stopped their ears and rushed together upon him. Then they cast him out of the city and stoned him; and the witnesses laid down their garments at the feet of a young man named Saul. And as they were stoning Stephen, he prayed, "Lord Jesus, receive my spirit." And he knelt down and cried with a loud voice, "Lord, do not hold this sin against them." And when he had said this, he fell asleep.

✝ *The Holy Gospel of Our Lord Jesus Christ*
According to Matthew [23:34-39]

Jesus said, "I will send you prophets and wise men and scribes, some of whom you will kill and crucify, and some you will scourge in your synagogues and persecute from town to town, that upon you may come all the righteous blood shed on earth, from the blood of innocent Abel to the blood of Zechari'ah the son of Barachi'ah, whom you murdered between the sanctuary and the altar. Truly, I say to you, all this will come upon this generation. O Jerusalem, Jerusalem, killing the prophets and stoning those who are sent to you! How often would I have gathered your children together as a hen gathers her brood under her wings, and you would not! Behold, your house is forsaken and desolate. For I tell you, you will not see me again, until you say, 'Blessed is he who comes in the name of the Lord.' "

Saint John   *December 27*

A Reading (Lesson) from the Book of Exodus [33:18-23]

Moses said to God,"I pray thee, show me thy glory." And
he said,"I will make all my goodness pass before you, and
will proclaim before you my name 'The Lord'; and I will be
gracious to whom I will be gracious, and will show mercy
on whom I will show mercy. But," he said,"you cannot see
my face; for man shall not see me and live." And the Lord
said,"Behold, there is a place by me where you shall stand
upon the rock; and while my glory passes by I will put you
in a cleft of the rock, and I will cover you with my hand
until I have passed by; then I will take away my hand, and
you shall see my back; but my face shall not be seen."

Psalm 92 [page 720]   or   *92: 1-4, 11-14* [page 720]

A Reading (Lesson) from the First Letter of John [1:1-9]

That which was from the beginning, which we have heard,
which we have seen with our eyes, which we have looked
upon and touched with our hands, concerning the word of
life—the life was made manifest, and we saw it, and testify
to it, and proclaim to you the eternal life which was with
the Father and was made manifest to us—that which we
have seen and heard we proclaim also to you, so that you
may have fellowship with us; and our fellowship is with
the Father and with his Son Jesus Christ. And we are
writing this that our joy may be complete. This is the
message we have heard from him and proclaim to you, that
God is light and in him is no darkness at all. If we say we
have fellowship with him while we walk in darkness, we lie
and do not live according to the truth; but if we walk in the
light, as he is in the light, we have fellowship with one
another, and the blood of Jesus his Son cleanses us from all
sin. If we say we have no sin we deceive ourselves, and the

truth is not in us. If we confess our sins, he is faithful and just, and will forgive our sins and cleanse us from all unrighteousness.

☩ *The Holy Gospel of Our Lord Jesus Christ According to John* [21:19b-24]

Jesus said to Peter, "Follow me." Peter turned and saw following them the disciple whom Jesus loved, who had lain close to his breast at the supper and had said, "Lord, who is it that is going to betray you?" When Peter saw him, he said to Jesus, "Lord, what about this man?" Jesus said to him, "If it is my will that he remain until I come, what is that to you? Follow me!" The saying spread abroad among the brethren that this disciple was not to die; yet Jesus did not say to him that he was not to die, but, "If it is my will that he remain until I come, what is that to you?" This is the disciple who is bearing witness to these things, and who has written these things; and we know that his testimony is true.

The Holy Innocents   *December 28*

A Reading (Lesson) from the Book of Jeremiah [31:15-17]

Thus says the Lord: "A voice is heard in Ramah, lamentation and bitter weeping. Rachel is weeping for her children; she refuses to be comforted for her children, because they are not." Thus says the Lord: "Keep your voice from weeping, and your eyes from tears; for your work shall be rewarded, says the Lord, and they shall come back from the land of the enemy. There is hope for your future, says the Lord, and your children shall come back to their own country."

Psalm 124 [page 781]

A Reading (Lesson) from the Revelation to John [21:1-7]

I saw a new heaven and a new earth; for the first heaven
and the first earth had passed away, and the sea was no
more. And I saw the holy city, new Jerusalem, coming
down out of heaven from God, prepared as a bride
adorned for her husband; and I heard a loud voice from
the throne saying,"Behold, the dwelling of God is with men.
He will dwell with them, and they shall be his people, and
God himself will be with them; he will wipe away every
tear from their eyes, and death shall be no more, neither
shall there be mourning nor crying nor pain any more, for
the former things have passed away." And he who sat upon
the throne said,"Behold, I make all things new." Also he
said,"Write this, for these words are trustworthy and
true." And he said to me,"It is done! I am the Alpha and
the Omega, the beginning and the end. To the thirsty I will
give from the fountain of the water of life without
payment. He who conquers shall have this heritage,
and I will be his God and he shall be my son."

✝ *The Holy Gospel of Our Lord Jesus Christ*
According to Matthew [2:13-18]

When the wise men had departed, behold, an angel of the
Lord appeared to Joseph in a dream and said,"Rise, take
the child and his mother, and flee to Egypt, and remain
there till I tell you; for Herod is about to search for the
child, to destroy him." And he rose and took the child and
his mother by night, and departed to Egypt, and remained
there until the death of Herod. This was to fulfill what the
Lord had spoken by the prophet,"Out of Egypt have I
called my son." Then Herod, when he saw that he had been
tricked by the wise men, was in a furious rage, and he sent
and killed all the male children in Bethlehem and in all that
region who were two years old or under, according to the
time which he had ascertained from the wise men. Then

was fulfilled what was spoken by the prophet Jeremiah: "A voice was heard in Ramah, wailing and loud lamentation, Rachel weeping for her children; she refused to be consoled, because they were no more."

Confession of Saint Peter *January 18*

A Reading (Lesson) from the Acts of the Apostles [4:8-13]

Peter, filled with the Holy Spirit, said, "Rulers of the people and elders, if we are being examined today concerning a good deed done to a cripple, by what means this man has been healed, be it known to you all, and to all the people of Israel, that by the name of Jesus Christ of Nazareth, whom you crucified, whom God raised from the dead, by him this man is standing before you well. This is the stone which was rejected by you builders, but which has become the head of the corner. And there is salvation in no one else, for there is no other name under heaven given among men by which we must be saved." Now when they saw the boldness of Peter and John, and perceived that they were uneducated, common men, they wondered; and they recognized that they had been with Jesus.

Psalm 23 [page 612]

A Reading (Lesson) from the First Letter of Peter [5:1-4]

I exhort the elders among you, as a fellow elder and a witness of the sufferings of Christ as well as a partaker in the glory that is to be revealed. Tend the flock of God that is your charge, not by constraint but willingly, not for shameful gain but eagerly, not as domineering over those in your charge but being examples to the flock. And when the chief Shepherd is manifested you will obtain the unfading crown of glory.

✝ *The Holy Gospel of Our Lord Jesus Christ*
According to Matthew [16:13-19]

When Jesus came into the district of Caesare'a Philippi, he asked his disciples,"Who do men say that the Son of man is?" And they said,"Some say John the Baptist, others say Eli'jah, and others Jeremiah or one of the prophets." He said to them,"But who do you say that I am?" Simon Peter replied,"You are the Christ, the Son of the living God." And Jesus answered him,"Blessed are you, Simon Bar-Jona! For flesh and blood has not revealed this to you, but my Father who is in heaven. And I tell you, you are Peter, and on this rock I will build my church, and the powers of death shall not prevail against it. I will give you the keys of the kingdom of heaven, and whatever you bind on earth shall be bound in heaven, and whatever you loose on earth shall be loosed in heaven."

Conversion of Saint Paul   *January 25*

A Reading (Lesson) from the Acts of the Apostles [26:9-21]

After he was in prison for some time, Paul was permitted to state his case before King Agrippa. Paul said to the King,"I myself was convinced that I ought to do many things in opposing the name of Jesus of Nazareth. And I did so in Jerusalem; I not only shut up many of the saints in prison, by authority from the chief priests, but when they were put to death I cast my vote against them. And I punished them often in all the synagogues and tried to make them blaspheme; and in raging fury against them, I persecuted them even to foreign cities. Thus I journeyed to Damascus with the authority and commission of the chief priests. At midday, O king, I saw on the way a light from heaven, brighter than the sun, shining round me and those who journeyed with me. And when we had all fallen to the ground, I heard a voice saying to me in the Hebrew language,'Saul, Saul, why do you persecute me? It hurts you to kick against the goads.' And I said,'Who are you, Lord?' And the Lord said,'I am Jesus whom you are persecuting. But rise and stand upon your feet; for I have appeared to you for this purpose, to appoint you to serve and bear witness to the things in which you have seen me and to those in which I will appear to you, delivering you from the people and from the Gentiles—to whom I send you to open their eyes, that they may turn from darkness to light and from the power of Satan to God, that they may receive forgiveness of sins and a place among those who are sanctified by faith in me.' Wherefore, O King Agrippa, I was not disobedient to the heavenly vision, but declared first to those at Damascus, then at Jerusalem and throughout all the country of Judea, and also to the Gentiles, that they should repent and turn to God and perform deeds worthy of their repentance. For this reason the Jews seized me in the temple and tried to kill me."

Psalm 67 [page 675]

A Reading (Lesson) from the Letter of Paul to the Galatians [1:11-24]

I would have you know, brethren, that the gospel which was preached by me is not man's gospel. For I did not receive it from man, nor was I taught it, but it came through a revelation of Jesus Christ. For you have heard of my former life in Judaism, how I persecuted the church of God violently and tried to destroy it; and I advanced in Judaism beyond many of my own age among my people, so extremely zealous was I for the traditions of my fathers. But when he who had set me apart before I was born, and had called me through his grace, was pleased to reveal his Son to me, in order that I might preach him among the Gentiles, I did not confer with flesh and blood, nor did I go up to Jerusalem to those who were apostles before me, but

I went away into Arabia; and again I returned to Damascus. Then after three years I went up to Jerusalem to visit Cephas, and remained with him fifteen days. But I saw none of the other apostles except James the Lord's brother. (In what I am writing to you, before God, I do not lie!) Then I went into the regions of Syria and Cili'cia. And I was still not known by sight to the churches of Christ in Judea; they only heard it said, "He who once persecuted us is now preaching the faith he once tried to destroy." And they glorified God because of me.

✝ The Holy Gospel of Our Lord Jesus Christ According to Matthew [10:16-22]

Jesus said, "Behold, I send you out as sheep in the midst of wolves; so be wise as serpents and innocent as doves. Beware of men; for they will deliver you up to councils, and flog you in their synagogues, and you will be dragged before governors and kings for my sake, to bear testimony before them and the Gentiles. When they deliver you up, do not be anxious how you are to speak or what you are to say; for what you are to say will be given to you in that hour; for it is not you who speak, but the Spirit of your Father speaking through you. Brother will deliver up brother to death, and the father his child, and children will rise against parents and have them put to death; and you will be hated by all for my name's sake. But he who endures to the end will be saved."

The Presentation   February 2

A Reading (Lesson) from the Book of Malachi [3:1-4]

Thus says the Lord, "Behold, I send my messenger to prepare the way before me, and the Lord whom you seek will suddenly come to his temple; the messenger of the covenant in whom you delight, behold, he is coming, says the Lord of hosts. But who can endure the day of his coming, and who can stand when he appears? For he is like a refiner's fire and like fullers' soap; he will sit as a refiner and purifier of silver, and he will purify the sons of Levi and refine them like gold and silver, till they present right offerings to the Lord. Then the offering of Judah and Jerusalem will be pleasing to the Lord as in the days of old and as in former years."

Psalm 84 [page 707]   or   *84:1-6* [page 707]

A Reading (Lesson) from the Letter to the Hebrews [2:14-18]

Since God's children share in flesh and blood, Jesus himself likewise partook of the same nature, that through death he might destroy him who has the power of death, that is, the devil, and deliver all those who through fear of death were subject to lifelong bondage. For surely it is not with angels that he is concerned but with the descendants of Abraham. Therefore he had to be made like his brethren in every respect, so that he might become a merciful and faithful high priest in the service of God, to make expiation for the sins of the people. For because he himself has suffered and been tempted, he is able to help those who are tempted.

✝ *The Holy Gospel of Our Lord Jesus Christ According to Luke* [2:22-40]

When the time came for their purification according to the law of Moses, the parents of Jesus brought him up to Jerusalem to present him to the Lord (as it is written in the law of the Lord, "Every male that opens the womb shall be called holy to the Lord") and to offer a sacrifice according to what is said in the law of the Lord, "a pair of turtledoves, or two young pigeons." Now there was a man in Jerusalem, whose name was Simeon, and this man was righteous and devout, looking for the consolation of Israel, and the Holy Spirit was upon him. And it had been revealed to him by the Holy Spirit that he should not see death before he had seen the Lord's Christ. And inspired by the Spirit he came into the temple; and when the parents brought in the child Jesus, to do for him according to the custom of the law, he took him up in his arms and blessed God and said, "Lord, now lettest thou thy servant depart in peace, according to thy word; for mine eyes have seen thy salvation which thou hast prepared in the presence of all peoples, a light for revelation to the Gentiles, and for glory to thy people Israel." And his father and his mother marveled at what was said about him; and Simeon blessed them and said to Mary his mother, "Behold, this child is set for the fall and rising of many in Israel, and for a sign that is spoken against (and a sword will pierce through your own soul also), that thoughts out of many hearts may be revealed." And there was a prophetess, Anna, the daughter of Pha'nu-el, of the tribe of Asher; she was of great age, having lived with her husband seven years from her virginity, and as a widow till she was eighty-four. She did not depart from the temple, worshiping with fasting and prayer night and day. And coming up at that very hour she gave thanks to God, and spoke of him to all who were looking for the redemption of Jerusalem. And when they had performed everything according to the law of the Lord, they returned into Galilee, to their own city, Nazareth. And the child grew and became strong, filled with wisdom; and the favor of God was upon him.

Saint Matthias *February 24*

A Reading (Lesson) from the Acts of the Apostles [1:15-26]

Peter stood up among the brethren (the company of persons was in all about a hundred and twenty), and said, "Brethren, the scripture had to be fulfilled, which the

Holy Spirit spoke beforehand by the mouth of David, concerning Judas who was guide to those who arrested Jesus. For he was numbered among us, and was allotted his share in this ministry. (Now this man bought a field with the reward of his wickedness; and falling headlong he burst open in the middle and all his bowels gushed out. And it became known to all the inhabitants of Jerusalem, so that the field was called in their language Akel′dama, that is, Field of Blood.) For it is written in the book of Psalms,'Let his habitation become desolate, and let there be no one to live in it; and 'His office let another take.' So one of the men who have accompanied us during all the time that the Lord Jesus went in and out among us, beginning from the baptism of John until the day when he was taken up from us—one of these men must become with us a witness to his resurrection." And they put forward two, Joseph called Barsab′bas, who was surnamed Justus, and Matthi′as. And they prayed and said,"Lord, who knowest the hearts of all men, show which one of these two thou hast chosen to take the place in this ministry and apostleship from which Judas turned aside, to go to his own place." And they cast lots for them, and the lot fell on Matthi′as; and he was enrolled with the eleven apostles.

Psalm 15 [page 599]

*A Reading (Lesson) from the Letter of Paul
to the Philippians* [3:13b-21]

One thing I do, forgetting what lies behind and straining forward to what lies ahead, I press on toward the goal for the prize of the upward call of God in Christ Jesus. Let those of us who are mature be thus minded; and if in anything you are otherwise minded, God will reveal that also to you. Only let us hold true to what we have attained. Brethren, join in imitating me, and mark those who so live as you have an example in us. For many, of whom I have often told you and now tell you even with tears, live as enemies of the cross of Christ. Their end is destruction, their god is the belly, and they glory in their shame, with minds set on earthly things. But our commonwealth is in heaven, and from it we await a Savior, the Lord Jesus Christ, who will change our lowly body to be like his glorious body, by the power which enables him even to subject all things to himself.

✝ *The Holy Gospel of Our Lord Jesus Christ According to John* [15:1, 6-16]

Jesus said, "I am the true vine, and my Father is the vinedresser. If a man does not abide in me, he is cast forth as a branch and withers; and the branches are gathered, thrown into the fire and burned. If you abide in me, and my words abide in you, ask whatever you will, and it shall be done for you. By this my Father is glorified, that you bear much fruit, and so prove to be my disciples. As the Father has loved me, so have I loved you; abide in my love. If you keep my commandments, you will abide in my love, just as I have kept my Father's commandments and abide in his love. These things I have spoken to you, that my joy may be in you, and that your joy may be full. This is my commandment, that you love one another as I have loved you. Greater love has no man than this, that a man lay down his life for his friends. You are my friends if you do what I command you. No longer do I call you servants, for the servant does not know what his master is doing; but I have called you friends, for all that I have heard from my Father I have made known to you. You did not choose me, but I chose you and appointed you that you should go and bear fruit and that your fruit should abide; so that whatever you ask the Father in my name, he may give it to you."

Saint Joseph   *March 19*

A Reading (Lesson) from the Second Book of Samuel
[7:4, 8-16]

The word of the Lord came to Nathan, "Thus you shall say to my servant David: 'Thus says the Lord of hosts, I took you from the pasture, from following the sheep, that you should be prince over my people Israel; and I have been with you wherever you went, and have cut off all your enemies from before you; and I will make for you a great name, like the name of the great ones of the earth. And I will appoint a place for my people Israel, and will plant them, that they may dwell in their own place, and be disturbed no more; and violent men shall afflict them no more, as formerly, from the time that I appointed judges over my people Israel; and I will give you rest from all your enemies. Moreover the Lord declares to you that the Lord will make you a house. When your days are fulfilled and you lie down with your fathers, I will raise up your offspring after you, who shall come forth from your body, and I will establish his kingdom. He shall build a house for my name, and I will establish the throne of his kingdom for ever. I will be his father, and he shall be my son. When he commits iniquity, I will chasten him with the rod of men, with the stripes of the sons of men; but I will not take my steadfast love from him, as I took it from Saul, whom I put away from before you. And your house and your kingdom shall be made sure for ever before me; your throne shall be established for ever."

Psalm 89:1-29 [page 713]   or   *Psalm 89:1-4, 26-29* [page 713]

A Reading (Lesson) from the Letter of Paul to the Romans
[4:13-18]

The promise to Abraham and his descendants, that they should inherit the world, did not come through the law but through the righteousness of faith. If it is the adherents of the law who are to be the heirs, faith is null and the promise is void. For the law brings wrath, but where there is no law there is no transgression. That is why it depends on faith, in order that the promise may rest on grace and be guaranteed to all his descendants—not only to the adherents of the law but also to those who share the faith of Abraham, for he is the father of us all, as it is written, "I have made you the father of many nations"—in the presence of the God in whom he believed, who gives life to the dead and calls into existence the things that do not exist. In hope he believed against hope, that he should become the father of many nations; as he had been told, "So shall your descendants be."

✝ *The Holy Gospel of Our Lord Jesus Christ According to Luke* [2:41-52]

Jesus' parents went to Jerusalem every year at the feast of the Passover. And when Jesus was twelve years old, they went up according to custom; and when the feast was ended, as they were returning, the boy Jesus stayed behind in Jerusalem. His parents did not know it, but supposing him to be in the company they went a day's journey, and they sought him among their kinsfolk and acquaintances; and when they did not find him, they returned to Jerusalem, seeking him. After three days they found him in the temple, sitting among the teachers, listening to them and asking them questions; and all who heard him were amazed at his understanding and his answers. And when they saw him they were astonished; and his mother said to him, "Son, why have you treated us so? Behold, your father and I have been looking for you anxiously." And he said to them, "How is it that you sought me? Did you not know that I must be in my Father's house?" And they did not understand the saying which he spoke to them. And he went down with them and came to Nazareth, and was obedient to them; and his mother kept all these things in her heart. And Jesus increased in wisdom and in stature, and in favor with God and man.

The Annunciation *March 25*

A Reading (Lesson) from the Book of Isaiah [7:10-14]

The Lord spoke to Ahaz, "Ask a sign of the Lord your God; let it be deep as Sheol or high as heaven." But Ahaz said, "I will not ask, and I will not put the Lord to the test." And he said, "Hear then, O house of David! Is it too little for you to weary men, that you weary my God also? Therefore the Lord himself will give you a sign. Behold, a young woman shall conceive and bear a son, and shall call his name Imman'u-el."

Psalm 40:1-11 [page 640]   or   *40:5-10* [page 640]   or

The Magnificat, Canticle 3 or 15 [page 50 or 91]

A Reading (Lesson) from the Letter to the Hebrews [10:5-10]

When Christ came into the world, he said, "Sacrifices and offerings thou hast not desired, but a body hast thou prepared for me; in burnt offerings and sin offerings thou hast taken no pleasure. Then I said, 'Lo, I have come to do thy will, O God,' as it is written of me in the roll of the book." When he said above, "Thou hast neither desired nor taken pleasure in sacrifices and offerings and burnt offerings and sin offerings" (these are offered according to the law), then he added, "Lo, I have come to do thy will."

He abolishes the first in order to establish the second. And by that will we have been sanctified through the offering of the body of Jesus Christ once for all.

✝ *The Holy Gospel of Our Lord Jesus Christ According to Luke* [1:26-38]

In the sixth month the angel Gabriel was sent from God to a city of Galilee named Nazareth, to a virgin betrothed to a man whose name was Joseph, of the house of David; and the virgin's name was Mary. And he came to her and said, "Hail, O favored one, the Lord is with you!" But she was greatly troubled at the saying, and considered in her mind what sort of greeting this might be. And the angel said to her, "Do not be afraid, Mary, for you have found favor with God. And behold, you will conceive in your womb and bear a son, and you shall call his name Jesus. He will be great, and will be called the Son of the Most High; and the Lord God will give to him the throne of his father David, and he will reign over the house of Jacob for ever; and of his kingdom there will be no end." And Mary said to the angel, "How shall this be, since I have no husband?" And the angel said to her, "The Holy Spirit will come upon you, and the power of the Most High will overshadow you; therefore the child to be born will be called holy, the Son of God. And behold, your kinswoman Elizabeth in her old age has also conceived a son; and this is the sixth month with her who was called barren. For with God nothing will be impossible." And Mary said, "Behold, I am the handmaid of the Lord; let it be to me according to your word." And the angel departed from her.

Saint Mark   *April 25*

A Reading (Lesson) from the Book of Isaiah [52:7-10]

How beautiful upon the mountains are the feet of him who
brings good tidings, who publishes peace, who brings good
tidings of good, who publishes salvation, who says to
Zion,"Your God reigns." Hark, your watchmen lift up
their voice, together they sing for joy; for eye to eye they
see the return of the Lord to Zion. Break forth together
into singing, you waste places of Jerusalem; for the Lord
has comforted his people, he has redeemed Jerusalem. The
Lord has bared his holy arm before the eyes of all the
nations; and all the ends of the earth shall see the salvation
of our God.

Psalm 2 [page 586]   or   *2:7-10* [page 586]

*A Reading (Lesson) from the Letter of Paul
to the Ephesians* [4:7-8, 11-16]

Grace was given to each of us according to the measure of
Christ's gift. Therefore it is said,"When he ascended on
high he led a host of captives, and he gave gifts to men."
And his gifts were that some should be apostles, some
prophets, some evangelists, some pastors and teachers, to
equip the saints for the work of ministry, for building up
the body of Christ, until we all attain to the unity of the
faith and of the knowledge of the Son of God, to mature
manhood, to the measure of the stature of the fullness of
Christ; so that we may no longer be children, tossed to and
fro and carried about with every wind of doctrine, by the
cunning of men, by their craftiness in deceitful wiles.
Rather, speaking the truth in love, we are to grow up in
every way into him who is the head, into Christ, from
whom the whole body, joined and knit together by every
joint with which it is supplied, when each part is working
properly, makes bodily growth and upbuilds itself in love.

✝ *The Holy Gospel of Our Lord Jesus Christ*
According to Mark [1:1-15]

The beginning of the gospel of Jesus Christ, the Son of God. As it is written in Isaiah the prophet, "Behold, I send my messenger before thy face, who shall prepare thy way; the voice of one crying in the wilderness: Prepare the way of the Lord, make his paths straight." John the baptizer appeared in the wilderness, preaching a baptism of repentance for the forgiveness of sins. And there went out to him all the country of Judea, and all the people of Jerusalem; and they were baptized by him in the river Jordan, confessing their sins. Now John was clothed with camel's hair, and had a leather girdle around his waist, and ate locusts and wild honey. And he preached, saying, "After me comes he who is mightier than I, the thong of whose sandals I am not worthy to stoop down and untie. I have baptized you with water; but he will baptize you with the Holy Spirit." In those days Jesus came from Nazareth of Galilee and was baptized by John in the Jordan. And when he came up out of the water, immediately he saw the heavens opened and the Spirit descending upon him like a dove; and a voice came from heaven, "Thou art my beloved Son; with thee I am well pleased." The Spirit immediately drove him out into the wilderness. And he was in the wilderness forty days, tempted by Satan; and he was with the wild beasts; and the angels ministered to him. Now after John was arrested, Jesus came into Galilee, preaching the gospel of God, and saying, "The time is fulfilled, and the kingdom of God is at hand; repent, and believe in the gospel."

or the following

✝ *The Holy Gospel of Our Lord Jesus Christ*
According to Mark [16:15-20]

Jesus said to the apostles, "Go into all the world and preach the gospel to the whole creation. He who believes and is baptized will be saved; but he who does not believe will be condemned. And these signs will accompany those who believe: in my name they will cast out demons; they will speak in new tongues; they will pick up serpents, and if they drink any deadly thing, it will not hurt them; they will lay their hands on the sick, and they will recover." So then the Lord Jesus, after he had spoken to them, was taken up into heaven, and sat down at the right hand of God. And they went forth and preached everywhere, while the Lord worked with them and confirmed the message by the signs that attended it.

Saint Philip and Saint James   *May 1*

A Reading (Lesson) from the Book of Isaiah [30:18-21]

The Lord waits to be gracious to you; therefore he exalts himself to show mercy to you. For the Lord is a God of justice; blessed are all those who wait for him. Yea, O people in Zion who dwell at Jerusalem; you shall weep no more. He will surely be gracious to you at the sound of your cry; when he hears it, he will answer you. And though the Lord give you the bread of adversity and the water of affliction, yet your Teacher will not hide himself any more, but your eyes shall see your Teacher. And your ears shall hear a word behind you, saying, "This is the way, walk in it," when you turn to the right or when you turn to the left.

Psalm 119:33-40 [page 766]

A Reading (Lesson) from the Second Letter of Paul to the Corinthians [4:1-6]

Having this ministry by the mercy of God, we do not lose heart. We have renounced disgraceful, underhanded ways; we refuse to practice cunning or to tamper with God's word, but by the open statement of the truth we would commend ourselves to every man's conscience in the sight of God. And even if our gospel is veiled, it is veiled only to those who are perishing. In their case the god of this world has blinded the minds of the unbelievers, to keep them from seeing the light of the gospel of the glory of Christ, who is the likeness of God. For what we preach is not ourselves, but Jesus Christ as Lord, with ourselves as your servants for Jesus' sake. For it is the God who said, "Let light shine out of darkness," who has shone in our hearts to give the light of the knowledge of the glory of God in the face of Christ.

✝ *The Holy Gospel of Our Lord Jesus Christ According to John* [14:6-14]

Jesus said to Thomas, "I am the way, and the truth, and the life; no one comes to the Father, but by me. If you had known me, you would have known my Father also; henceforth you know him and have seen him." Philip said to him, "Lord, show us the Father, and we shall be satisfied." Jesus said to him, "Have I been with you so long, and yet you do not know me, Philip? He who has seen me has seen the Father; how can you say, 'Show us the Father'? Do you not believe that I am in the Father and the Father in me? The words that I say to you I do not speak on my own authority; but the Father who dwells in me does his works. Believe me that I am in the Father and the Father in me; or else believe me for the sake of the works themselves. Truly, truly, I say to you, he who believes in me will also do the works that I do; and greater works than these will he do, because I go to the Father. Whatever you ask in my name, I will do it, that the Father may be glorified in the Son; if you ask anything in my name, I will do it."

The Visitation *May 31*

A Reading (Lesson) from the Book of Zephaniah [3:14-18a]

Sing aloud, O daughter of Zion; shout, O Israel! Rejoice and exult with all your heart, O daughter of Jerusalem! The Lord has taken away the judgments against you, he has cast out your enemies. The King of Israel, the Lord, is in your midst; you shall fear evil no more. On that day it shall be said to Jerusalem, "Do not fear, O Zion; let not your hands grow weak. The Lord, your God, is in your midst, a warrior who gives victory; he will rejoice over you with gladness, he will renew you in his love; he will exult over you with loud singing as on a day of festival."

Psalm 113 [page 756]   or

The First Song of Isaiah, Canticle 9 [page 86]

A Reading (Lesson) from the Letter of Paul to the Colossians [3:12-17]

Put on, as God's chosen ones, holy and beloved, compassion, kindness, lowliness, meekness, and patience, forbearing one another and, if one has a complaint against another, forgiving each other; as the Lord has forgiven you, so you also must forgive. And above all these put on love, which binds everything together in perfect harmony. And let the peace of Christ rule in your hearts, to which indeed you were called in the one body. And be thankful. Let the word of Christ dwell in you richly, teach and admonish one another in all wisdom, and sing psalms and hymns and spiritual songs with thankfulness in your hearts to God. And whatever you do, in word or deed, do everything in the name of the Lord Jesus, giving thanks to God the Father through him.

✝ *The Holy Gospel of Our Lord Jesus Christ According to Luke* [1:39-49]

Mary arose and went with haste into the hill country, to a city of Judah, and she entered the house of Zechari′ah and greeted Elizabeth. And when Elizabeth heard the greeting of Mary, the babe leaped in her womb; and Elizabeth was filled with the Holy Spirit and she exclaimed with a loud cry,"Blessed are you among women, and blessed is the fruit of your womb! And why is this granted me, that the mother of my Lord should come to me? For behold, when the voice of your greeting came to my ears, the babe in my womb leaped for joy. And blessed is she who believed that there would be a fulfillment of what was spoken to her from the Lord." And Mary said,"My soul magnifies the Lord, and my spirit rejoices in God my Savior, for he has regarded the low estate of his handmaiden. For behold, henceforth all generations will call me blessed; for he who is mighty has done great things for me, and holy is his name."

Saint Barnabas   *June 11*

A Reading (Lesson) from the Book of Isaiah [42:5-12]

Thus says God, the Lord, who created the heavens and stretched them out, who spread forth the earth and what comes from it, who gives breath to the people upon it and spirit to those who walk in it: "I am the Lord, I have called you in righteousness, I have taken you by the hand and kept you; I have given you as a covenant to the people, a light to the nations, to open the eyes that are blind, to bring out the prisoners from the dungeon, from the prison those who sit in darkness. I am the Lord, that is my name; my glory I give to no other, nor my praise to graven images. Behold, the former things have come to pass, and new things I now declare; before they spring forth I tell you of them." Sing to the Lord a new song, his praise from the end of the earth! Let the sea roar and all that fills it, the coastlands and their inhabitants. Let the desert and its cities lift up their voice, the villages that Kedar inhabits; let the inhabitants of Sela sing for joy, let them shout from the top of the mountains. Let them give glory to the Lord, and declare his praise in the coastlands.

Psalm 112 [page 755]

A Reading (Lesson) from the Acts of the Apostles
[11:19-30; 13:1-3]

Those who were scattered because of the persecution that arose over Stephen traveled as far as Phoeni'cia and Cyprus and Antioch, speaking the word to none except Jews. But there were some of them, men of Cyprus and Cyre'ne, who on coming to Antioch spoke to the Greeks also, preaching the Lord Jesus. And the hand of the Lord was with them, and a great number that believed turned to the Lord. News of this came to the ears of the church in Jerusalem, and they sent Barnabas to Antioch. When he came and saw the grace of God, he was glad; and he exhorted them all to remain faithful to the Lord with steadfast purpose; for he was a good man, full of the Holy Spirit and of faith. And a large company was added to the Lord. So Barnabas went to Tarsus to look for Saul; and when he had found him, he brought him to Antioch. For a whole year they met with the church, and taught a large company of people; and in Antioch the disciples were for the first time called Christians. Now in these days prophets came down from Jerusalem to Antioch. And one of them named Ag'abus stood up and foretold by the Spirit that there would be a great famine over all the world; and this took place in the days of Claudius. And the disciples determined, every one according to his ability, to send relief to the brethren who lived in Judea; and they did so, sending it to the elders by the hand of Barnabas and Saul. Now in the church at Antioch there were prophets and teachers, Barnabas, Simeon who was called Niger, Lucius of Cyre'ne, Man'a-en a member of the court of Herod the tetrarch, and Saul. While they were worshiping the Lord and fasting, the Holy Spirit said, "Set apart for me Barnabas and Saul for the work to which I have called them." Then after fasting and praying they laid their hands on them and sent them off.

✝ *The Holy Gospel of Our Lord Jesus Christ*
According to Matthew [10:7-16]

Jesus said to the twelve, "Preach as you go, saying, 'The kingdom of heaven is at hand.' Heal the sick, raise the dead, cleanse lepers, cast out demons. You received without paying, give without pay. Take no gold, nor silver, nor copper in your belts, no bag for your journey, nor two tunics, nor sandals, nor a staff; for the laborer deserves his food. And whatever town or village you enter, find out who is worthy in it, and stay with him until you depart. As you enter the house, salute it. And if the house is worthy, let your peace come upon it; but if it is not worthy, let your peace return to you. And if any one will not receive you or listen to your words, shake off the dust from your feet as you leave that house or town. Truly, I say to you, it shall be more tolerable on the day of judgment for the land of Sodom and Gomor'rah than for that town. Behold, I send you out as sheep in the midst of wolves; so be wise as serpents and innocent as doves."

Nativity of Saint John the Baptist *June 24*

A Reading (Lesson) from the Book of Isaiah [40:1-11]

Comfort, comfort my people, says your God. Speak
tenderly to Jerusalem, and cry to her that her warfare is
ended, that her iniquity is pardoned, that she has received
from the Lord's hand double for all her sins. A voice cries:
"In the wilderness prepare the way of the Lord, make
straight in the desert a highway for our God. Every valley
shall be lifted up, and every mountain and hill be made
low; the uneven ground shall become level, and the rough
places a plain. And the glory of the Lord shall be revealed,
and all flesh shall see it together, for the mouth of the Lord
has spoken." A voice says, "Cry!" and I said, "What shall I
cry?" All flesh is grass, and all its beauty is like the flower of
the field. The grass withers, the flower fades, when the
breath of the Lord blows upon it; surely the people is grass.
The grass withers, the flower fades; but the word of our
God will stand for ever. Get you up to a high mountain,
O Zion, herald of good tidings; lift up your voice with
strength, O Jerusalem, herald of good tidings, lift it up,
fear not; say to the cities of Judah, "Behold your God!"
Behold, the Lord God comes with might, and his arm rules
for him; behold, his reward is with him, and his recompense
before him. He will feed his flock like a shepherd,
he will gather the lambs in his arms, he will carry them in
his bosom, and gently lead those that are with young.

Psalm 85 [page 708]   or   *85:7-13* [page 709]

A Reading (Lesson) from the Acts of the Apostles
[13:14b-26]

On the sabbath day Paul and his company went into the
synagogue at Antioch and sat down. After the reading of
the law and the prophets, the rulers of the synagogue sent
to them, saying, "Brethren, if you have any word of

exhortation for the people, say it." So Paul stood up, and motioning with his hands said: "Men of Israel, and you that fear God, listen. The God of this people Israel chose our fathers and made the people great during their stay in the land of Egypt, and with uplifted arm he led them out of it. And when he had destroyed seven nations in the land of Canaan, he gave them their land as an inheritance, for about four hundred and fifty years. And after that he gave them judges until Samuel the prophet. Then they asked for a king; and God gave them Saul the son of Kish, a man of the tribe of Benjamin, for forty years. And when he had removed him, he raised up David to be their king; of whom he testified and said, 'I have found in David the son of Jesse a man after my heart, who will do all my will.' Of this man's posterity God has brought to Israel a Savior, Jesus, as he promised. Before his coming John had preached a baptism of repentance to all the people of Israel. And as John was finishing his course, he said, 'What do you suppose that I am? I am not he. No, but after me one is coming, the sandals of whose feet I am not worthy to untie.' Brethren, sons of the family of Abraham, and those among you that fear God, to us has been sent the message of this salvation."

✝ *The Holy Gospel of Our Lord Jesus Christ*
According to Luke [1:57-80]

The time came for Elizabeth to be delivered, and she gave birth to a son. And her neighbors and kinsfolk heard that the Lord had shown great mercy to her, and they rejoiced with her. And on the eighth day they came to circumcise the child; and they would have named him Zechari'ah after his father, but his mother said, "Not so; he shall be called John." And they said to her, "None of your kindred is called by this name." And they made signs to his father, inquiring what he would have him called. And he asked for a writing tablet, and wrote, "His name is John." And they all marveled. And immediately his mouth was opened and his tongue loosed, and he spoke, blessing God. And fear came on all their neighbors. And all these things were talked about through all the hill country of Judea; and all who heard them laid them up in their hearts, saying, "What then will this child be?" For the hand of the Lord was with him. And his father Zechari'ah was filled with the Holy Spirit, and prophesied, saying, "Blessed be the Lord God of Israel, for he has visited and redeemed his people, and has raised up a horn of salvation for us in the house of his servant David, as he spoke by the mouth of his holy prophets from of old, that we should be saved from our enemies, and from the hand of all who hate us; to perform the mercy promised to our fathers, and to remember his holy covenant, the oath which he swore to our father Abraham, to grant us that we, being delivered from the hand of our enemies, might serve him without fear, in holiness and righteousness before him all the days of our life. And you, child, will be called the prophet of the Most High; for you will go before the Lord to prepare his ways, to give knowledge of salvation to his people in the forgiveness of their sins, through the tender mercy of our God, when the day shall dawn upon us from on high to give light to those who sit in darkness and in the shadow of death, to guide our feet into the way of peace." And the child grew and became strong in spirit, and he was in the wilderness till the day of his manifestation to Israel.

Saint Peter and Saint Paul *June 29*

A Reading (Lesson) from the Book of Ezekiel [34:11-16]

Thus says the Lord God: "Behold, I, I myself will search for my sheep, and will seek them out. As a shepherd seeks out his flock when some of his sheep have been scattered abroad, so will I seek out my sheep; and I will rescue them from all places where they have been scattered on a day of clouds and thick darkness. And I will bring them out from the peoples, and gather them from the countries, and will bring them into their own land; and I will feed them on the mountains of Israel, by the fountains, and in all the inhabited places of the country. I will feed them with good pasture, and upon the mountain heights of Israel shall be their pasture; there they shall lie down in good grazing land, and on fat pasture they shall feed on the mountains of Israel. I myself will be the shepherd of my sheep, and I will make them lie down, says the Lord God. I will seek the lost, and I will bring back the strayed, and I will bind up the crippled, and I will strengthen the weak, and the fat and the strong I will watch over; I will feed them in justice."

Psalm 87 [page 711]

A Reading (Lesson) from the Second Letter of Paul to Timothy [4:1-8]

I charge you in the presence of God and of Christ Jesus who is to judge the living and the dead, and by his appearing and his kingdom: preach the word, be urgent in season and out of season, convince, rebuke, and exhort, be unfailing in patience and in teaching. For the time is coming when people will not endure sound teaching, but having itching ears they will accumulate for themselves teachers to suit their own likings, and will turn away from listening to the truth and wander into myths. As for you, always be steady, endure suffering, do the work of an evangelist, fulfill your ministry. For I am already on the point of being sacrificed; the time of my departure has come. I have fought the good fight, I have finished the race, I have kept the faith. Henceforth there is laid up for me the crown of righteousness, which the Lord, the righteous judge, will award to me on that Day, and not only to me but also to all who have loved his appearing.

✝ *The Holy Gospel of Our Lord Jesus Christ According to John* [21:15-19]

When they had finished breakfast, Jesus said to Simon Peter, "Simon, son of John, do you love me more than these?" He said to him, "Yes, Lord; you know that I love you." He said to him, "Feed my lambs." A second time he said to him, "Simon, son of John, do you love me?" He said to him, "Yes, Lord; you know that I love you." He said to him, "Tend my sheep." He said to him the third time, "Simon, son of John, do you love me?" Peter was grieved because he said to him the third time, "Do you love me?" And he said to him, "Lord, you know everything; you know that I love you." Jesus said to him, "Feed my sheep. Truly, truly, I say to you, when you were young, you girded yourself and walked where you would; but when you are old, you will stretch out your hands, and another will gird you and carry you where you do not wish to go." (This he said to show by what death he was to glorify God.) And after this he said to him, "Follow me."

Independence Day *July 4*

The Lessons and Psalm "For the Nation," may be used in place of the following. [See texts and citations on pages 263-265 below]

A Reading (Lesson) from the Book of Deuteronomy [10:17-21]

The Lord your God is God of gods and Lord of lords, the great, the mighty, and the terrible God, who is not partial and takes no bribe. He executes justice for the fatherless and the widow, and loves the sojourner, giving him food and clothing. Love the sojourner therefore; for you were sojourners in the land of Egypt. You shall fear the Lord your God; you shall serve him and cleave to him, and by his name you shall swear. He is your praise; he is your God, who has done for you these great and terrible things which your eyes have seen.

Psalm 145 [page 801] or *145:1-9* [page 801]

A Reading (Lesson) from the Letter to the Hebrews [11:8-16]

By faith Abraham obeyed when he was called to go out to a place which he was to receive as an inheritance; and he went out, not knowing where he was to go. By faith he sojourned in the land of promise, as in a foreign land, living in tents with Isaac and Jacob, heirs with him of the same promise. For he looked forward to the city which has foundations, whose builder and maker is God. By faith Sarah herself received power to conceive, even when she was past the age, since she considered him faithful who had promised. Therefore from one man, and him as good as dead, were born descendants as many as the stars of heaven and as the innumerable grains of sand by the seashore. These all died in faith, not having received what was promised, but having seen it and greeted it from afar, and having acknowledged that they were strangers and exiles on the earth. For people who speak thus make it clear that they are seeking a homeland. If they had been thinking of that land from which they had gone out, they would have had opportunity to return. But as it is, they desire a better country, that is, a heavenly one. Therefore God is not ashamed to be called their God, for he has prepared for them a city.

✝ *The Holy Gospel of Our Lord Jesus Christ According to Matthew* [5:43-48]

Jesus said, "You have heard that it was said, 'You shall love your neighbor and hate your enemy.' But I say to you, Love your enemies and pray for those who persecute you, so that you may be sons of your Father who is in heaven; for he makes his sun rise on the evil and on the good, and sends rain on the just and on the unjust. For if you love those who love you, what reward have you? Do not even the tax collectors do the same? And if you salute only your brethren, what more are you doing than others? Do not even the Gentiles do the same? You, therefore, must be perfect, as your heavenly Father is perfect."

For the Nation *July 4*

Alternative for Independence Day above.

A Reading (Lesson) from the Book of Isaiah [26:1-8]

In that day this song will be sung in the land of Judah: "We have a strong city; he sets up salvation as walls and bulwarks. Open the gates, that the righteous nation which keeps faith may enter in. Thou dost keep him in perfect peace, whose mind is stayed on thee, because he trusts in thee. Trust in the Lord for ever, for the Lord God is an everlasting rock. For he has brought low the inhabitants of the height, the lofty city. He lays it low, lays it low to the ground, casts it to the dust. The foot tramples it, the feet of the poor, the steps of the needy." The way of the righteous is level; thou dost make smooth the path of the righteous. In the path of thy judgments, O Lord, we wait for thee; thy memorial name is the desire of our soul.

Psalm 47 [page 650]

A Reading (Lesson) from the Letter of Paul to the Romans [13:1-10]

Let every person be subject to the governing authorities. For there is no authority except from God, and those that exist have been instituted by God. Therefore he who resists the authorities resists what God has appointed, and those who resist will incur judgment. For rulers are not a terror to good conduct, but to bad. Would you have no fear of him who is in authority? Then do what is good, and you will receive his approval, for he is God's servant for your good. But if you do wrong, be afraid, for he does not bear the sword in vain; he is the servant of God to execute his wrath on the wrongdoer. Therefore one must be subject, not only to avoid God's wrath but also for the sake of conscience. For the same reason you also pay taxes, for the authorities are ministers of God, attending to this very thing. Pay all of them their dues, taxes to whom taxes are due, revenue to whom revenue is due, respect to whom respect is due, honor to whom honor is due. Owe no one anything, except to love one another; for he who loves his neighbor has fulfilled the law. The commandments, "You shall not commit adultery, You shall not kill, You shall not steal, You shall not covet," and any other commandment, are summed up in this sentence, "You shall love your neighbor as yourself." Love does no wrong to a neighbor; therefore love is the fulfilling of the law.

✝ *The Holy Gospel of Our Lord Jesus Christ According to Mark* [12:13-17]

Some of the Pharisees and some of the Herodians were sent to Jesus to entrap him in his talk. And they came and said to him, "Teacher, we know that you are true, and care for no man; for you do not regard the position of men, but truly teach the way of God. Is it lawful to pay taxes to Caesar, or not? Should we pay them, or should we not?" But knowing their hypocrisy, he said to them, "Why put me to the test? Bring me a coin, and let me look at it." And they brought one. And he said to them, "Whose likeness and inscription is this?" They said to him, "Caesar's." Jesus said to them, "Render to Caesar the things that are Caesar's,

and to God the things that are God's." And they were
amazed at him.

Saint Mary Magdalene   *July 22*

A Reading (Lesson) from the Book of Judith   [9:1,11-14]

Judith fell upon her face, and put ashes on her head, and
uncovered the sackcloth she was wearing; and at the very
time when that evening's incense was being offered in the
house of God in Jerusalem, Judith cried out to the Lord
with a loud voice, and said, "O God my God, hear me. Thy
power depends not upon numbers, nor thy might upon
men of strength; for thou art God of the lowly, helper of
the oppressed, upholder of the weak, protector of the
forlorn, savior of those without hope. Hear, O hear me,
God of my father, God of the inheritance of Israel, Lord of
heaven and earth, Creator of the waters, King of all thy
creation, hear my prayer! Make my deceitful words to be
their wound and stripe, for they have planned cruel things
against thy covenant, and against thy consecrated house,
and against the top of Zion, and against the house
possessed by thy children. And cause thy whole nation and
every tribe to know and understand that thou art God, the
God of all power and might, and that there is no other who
protects the people of Israel but thou alone!"

Psalm 42:1-7   [page 643]

*A Reading (Lesson) from the Second Letter of Paul
to the Corinthians*   [5:14-18]

The love of Christ controls us, because we are convinced
that one has died for all; therefore all have died. And he
died for all, that those who live might live no longer for
themselves but for him who for their sake died and was
raised. From now on, therefore, we regard no one from a

human point of view; even though we once regarded Christ from a human point of view, we regard him thus no longer. Therefore, if any one is in Christ, he is a new creation; the old has passed away, behold, the new has come. All this is from God, who through Christ reconciled us to himself and gave us the ministry of reconciliation.

✝ *The Holy Gospel of Our Lord Jesus Christ According to John* [20:11-18]

Mary stood weeping outside the tomb, and as she wept she stooped to look into the tomb; and she saw two angels in white, sitting where the body of Jesus had lain, one at the head and one at the feet. They said to her, "Woman, why are you weeping?" She said to them, "Because they have taken away my Lord, and I do not know where they have laid him." Saying this, she turned round and saw Jesus standing, but she did not know that it was Jesus. Jesus said to her, "Woman, why are you weeping? Whom do you seek?" Supposing him to be the gardener, she said to him, "Sir, if you have carried him away, tell me where you have laid him, and I will take him away." Jesus said to her, "Mary." She turned and said to him in Hebrew, "Rab-bo'ni!" (which means Teacher). Jesus said to her, "Do not hold me, for I have not yet ascended to the Father; but go to my brethren and say to them, I am ascending to my Father and your Father, to my God and your God." Mary Mag'dalene went and said to the disciples, "I have seen the Lord"; and she told them that he had said these things to her.

Saint James   *July 25*

A Reading (Lesson) from the Book of Jeremiah [45:1-5]

The word that Jeremiah the prophet spoke to Baruch the son of Neri'ah, when he wrote these words in a book at the dictation of Jeremiah, in the fourth year of Jehoi'akim the son of Josi'ah, king of Judah: "Thus says the Lord, the God of Israel, to you, O Baruch: You said, 'Woe is me! For the Lord has added sorrow to my pain; I am weary with my groaning, and I find no rest.' Thus shall you say to him, Thus says the Lord: Behold, what I have built I am breaking down, and what I have planted I am plucking up—that is, the whole land. And do you seek great things for yourself? Seek them not; for, behold, I am bringing evil upon all flesh, says the Lord; but I will give you your life as a prize of war in all places to which you may go."

Psalm 7:1-10 [page 590]

A Reading (Lesson) from the Acts of the Apostles
[11:27—12:3]

In these days prophets came down from Jerusalem to Antioch. And one of them named Ag'abus stood up and foretold by the Spirit that there would be a great famine over all the world; and this took place in the days of Claudius. And the disciples determined, every one according to his ability, to send relief to the brethren who lived in Judea; and they did so, sending it to the elders by the hand of Barnabas and Saul. About that time Herod the king laid violent hands upon some who belonged to the church. He killed James the brother of John with the sword; and when he saw that it pleased the Jews, he proceeded to arrest Peter also. This was during the days of Unleavened Bread.

✝ *The Holy Gospel of Our Lord Jesus Christ According to Matthew* [20:20-28]

The mother of the sons of Zeb'edee came up to Jesus with her sons, and kneeling before him she asked him for something. And he said to her, "What do you want?" She said to him, "Command that these two sons of mine may sit, one at your right hand and one at your left, in your kingdom." But Jesus answered, "You do not know what you are asking. Are you able to drink the cup that I am to drink?" They said to him, "We are able." He said to them, "You will drink my cup, but to sit at my right hand and at my left is not mine to grant, but it is for those for whom it has been prepared by my Father." And when the ten heard it, they were indignant at the two brothers. But Jesus called them to him and said, "You know that the rulers of the Gentiles lord it over them, and their great men exercise authority over them. It shall not be so among you; but whoever would be great among you must be your servant, and whoever would be first among you must be your slave; even as the Son of man came not to be served but to serve, and to give his life as a ransom for many."

The Transfiguration   *August 6*

A Reading (Lesson) from the Book of Exodus [34:29-35]

When Moses came down from Mount Sinai, with the two tables of the testimony in his hand as he came down from the mountain, Moses did not know that the skin of his face shone because he had been talking with God. And when Aaron and all the people of Israel saw Moses, behold, the skin of his face shone, and they were afraid to come near him. But Moses called to them; and Aaron and all the leaders of the congregation returned to him, and Moses talked with them. And afterward all the people of Israel came near, and he gave them in commandment all that the Lord had spoken with him in Mount Sinai. And when Moses had finished speaking with them, he put a veil on his face; but whenever Moses went in before the Lord to speak with him, he took the veil off, until he came out; and when he came out, and told the people of Israel what he was commanded, the people of Israel saw the face of Moses, that the skin of Moses' face shone; and Moses would put the veil upon his face again, until he went in to speak with him.

Psalm 99 [page 728]   or   *99:5-9* [page 729]

A Reading (Lesson) from the Second Letter of Peter
[1:13-21]

I think it right, as long as I am in this body, to arouse you by way of reminder, since I know that the putting off of my body will be soon, as our Lord Jesus Christ showed me. And I will see to it that after my departure you may be able at any time to recall these things. For we did not follow cleverly devised myths when we made known to you the power and coming of our Lord Jesus Christ, but we were eyewitnesses of his majesty. For when he received honor and glory from God the Father and the voice was borne to him by the Majestic Glory,"This is my beloved Son, with whom I am well pleased," we heard this voice borne from heaven, for we were with him on the holy mountain. And we have the prophetic word made more sure. You will do well to pay attention to this as to a lamp shining in a dark place, until the day dawns and the morning star rises in your hearts. First of all you must understand this, that no prophecy of scripture is a matter of one's own interpretation, because no prophecy ever came by the impulse of man, but men moved by the Holy Spirit spoke from God.

✝ *The Holy Gospel of Our Lord Jesus Christ
According to Luke* [9:28-36]

Now about eight days after Jesus had foretold his death and resurrection, he took with him Peter and John and James, and went up on the mountain to pray. And as he was praying, the appearance of his countenance was altered, and his raiment became dazzling white. And behold, two men talked with him, Moses and Eli'jah, who appeared in glory and spoke of his departure, which he was to accomplish at Jerusalem. Now Peter and those who were with him were heavy with sleep, and when they wakened they saw his glory and the two men who stood with him. And as the men were parting from him, Peter said to Jesus, "Master, it is well that we are here; let us make three booths, one for you and one for Moses and one for Eli'jah"—not knowing what he said. As he said this, a cloud came and overshadowed them; and they were afraid as they entered the cloud. And a voice came out of the cloud, saying, "This is my Son, my Chosen; listen to him!" And when the voice had spoken, Jesus was found alone. And they kept silence and told no one in those days anything of what they had seen.

Saint Mary the Virgin   *August 15*

A Reading (Lesson) from the Book of Isaiah [61:10-11]

I will greatly rejoice in the Lord, my soul shall exult in my God; for he has clothed me with the garments of salvation, he has covered me with the robe of righteousness, as a bridegroom decks himself with a garland, and as a bride adorns herself with her jewels. For as the earth brings forth its shoots, and as a garden causes what is sown in it to spring up, so the Lord God will cause righteousness and praise to spring forth before all the nations.

Psalm 34 [page 627]   or   *34:1-9* [page 627]

A Reading (Lesson) from the Letter of Paul to the Galatians [4:4-7]

When the time had fully come, God sent forth his Son, born of woman, born under the law, to redeem those who were under the law, so that we might receive adoption as sons. And because you are sons, God has sent the Spirit of his Son into our hearts, crying,"Abba! Father!" So through God you are no longer a slave but a son, and if a son then an heir.

✝ *The Holy Gospel of Our Lord Jesus Christ According to Luke* [1:46-55]

Mary said,"My soul magnifies the Lord, and my spirit rejoices in God my Savior, for he has regarded the low estate of his handmaiden. For behold, henceforth all generations will call me blessed; for he who is mighty has done great things for me, and holy is his name. And his mercy is on those who fear him from generation to generation. He has shown strength with his arm, he has scattered the proud in the imagination of their hearts, he has put down the mighty from their thrones, and exalted those of low degree; he has filled the hungry with good things, and the rich he has sent empty away. He has helped his servant Israel, in remembrance of his mercy, as he spoke to our fathers, to Abraham and to his posterity for ever."

Saint Bartholomew *August 24*

A Reading (Lesson) from the Book of Deuteronomy [18:15-18]

Moses said to the people,"The Lord your God will raise up for you a prophet like me from among you, from your brethren—him you shall heed—just as you desired of the Lord your God at Horeb on the day of the assembly, when you said,'Let me not hear again the voice of the Lord my God, or see this great fire any more, lest I die.' And the Lord said to me,'They have rightly said all that they have spoken. I will raise up for them a prophet like you from

among their brethren; and I will put my words in his
mouth, and he shall speak to them all that I command him.' "

Psalm 91 [page 7 1 9]   or   *91:1-4* [page 7 1 9]

*A Reading (Lesson) from the First Letter of Paul
to the Corinthians* [4:9-1 5]

I think that God has exhibited us apostles as last of all, like
men sentenced to death; because we have become a
spectacle to the world, to angels and to men. We are fools
for Christ's sake, but you are wise in Christ. We are weak,
but you are strong. You are held in honor, but we in
disrepute. To the present hour we hunger and thirst, we are
ill-clad and buffeted and homeless, and we labor, working
with our own hands. When reviled, we bless; when
persecuted, we endure; when slandered, we try to
conciliate; we have become, and are now, as the refuse of
the world, the offscouring of all things. I do not write this
to make you ashamed, but to admonish you as my beloved
children. For though you have countless guides in Christ,
you do not have many fathers. For I became your father in
Christ Jesus through the gospel.

✝ *The Holy Gospel of Our Lord Jesus Christ
According to Luke* [22:24-30]

A dispute arose among the apostles, which of them was to
be regarded as the greatest. And Jesus said to them,"The
kings of the Gentiles exercise lordship over them; and
those in authority over them are called benefactors. But
not so with you; rather let the greatest among you become
as the youngest, and the leader as one who serves. For
which is the greater, one who sits at table, or one who
serves? Is it not the one who sits at table? But I am among
you as one who serves. You are those who have continued
with me in my trials; and I assign to you, as my Father

assigned to me, a kingdom, that you may eat and drink at my table in my kingdom, and sit on thrones judging the twelve tribes of Israel."

Holy Cross Day *September 14*

A Reading (Lesson) from the Book of Isaiah [45:21-25]

Thus says the Lord:"Declare and present your case; let them take counsel together! Who told this long ago? Who declared it of old? Was it not I, the Lord? And there is no other god besides me, a righteous God and a Savior; there is none besides me. Turn to me and be saved, all the ends of the earth! For I am God, and there is no other. By myself I have sworn, from my mouth has gone forth in righteousness a word that shall not return: 'To me every knee shall bow, every tongue shall swear.' Only in the Lord, it shall be said of me, are righteousness and strength; to him shall come and be ashamed, all who were incensed against him. In the Lord all the offspring of Israel shall triumph and glory."

Psalm 98 [page 727]   or   *98:1-4* [page 727]

A Reading (Lesson) from the Letter of Paul to the Philippians [2:5-11]

Have this mind among yourselves, which is yours in Christ Jesus, who, though he was in the form of God, did not count equality with God a thing to be grasped, but emptied himself, taking the form of a servant, being born in the likeness of men. And being found in human form he humbled himself and became obedient unto death, even death on a cross. Therefore God has highly exalted him and bestowed on him the name which is above every name, that at the name of Jesus every knee should bow, in heaven and on earth and under the earth, and every tongue confess that Jesus Christ is Lord, to the glory of God the Father.

or this

*A Reading (Lesson) from the Letter of Paul
to the Galatians* [6:14-18]

Far be it from me to glory except in the cross of our Lord Jesus Christ, by which the world has been crucified to me, and I to the world. For neither circumcision counts for anything, nor uncircumcision, but a new creation. Peace and mercy be upon all who walk by this rule, upon the Israel of God. Henceforth let no man trouble me; for I bear on my body the marks of Jesus. The grace of our Lord Jesus Christ be with your spirit, brethren. Amen.

✝ *The Holy Gospel of Our Lord Jesus Christ
According to John* [12:31-36a]

Jesus said, "Now is the judgment of this world, now shall the ruler of this world be cast out; and I, when I am lifted up from the earth, will draw all men to myself." He said this to show by what death he was to die. The crowd answered him, "We have heard from the law that the Christ remains for ever. How can you say that the Son of man must be lifted up? Who is this Son of man?" Jesus said to them, "The light is with you for a little longer. Walk while you have the light, lest the darkness overtake you; he who walks in the darkness does not know where he goes. While you have the light, believe in the light, that you may become sons of light."

Saint Matthew   *September 21*

A Reading (Lesson) from the Book of Proverbs [3:1-6]

My son, do not forget my teaching, but let your heart keep my commandments; for length of days and years of life

and abundant welfare will they give you. Let not loyalty
and faithfulness forsake you; bind them about your neck,
write them on the tablet of your heart. So you will find
favor and good repute in the sight of God and man. Trust
in the Lord with all your heart, and do not rely on your
own insight. In all your ways acknowledge him, and he
will make straight your paths.

Psalm 119:33-40 [page 766]

*A Reading (Lesson) from the Second Letter of Paul
to Timothy* [3:14-17]

As for you, continue in what you have learned and have
firmly believed, knowing from whom you learned it and
how from childhood you have been acquainted with the
sacred writings which are able to instruct you for salvation
through faith in Christ Jesus. All scripture is inspired by
God and profitable for teaching, for reproof, for
correction, and for training in righteousness, that the man
of God may be complete, equipped for every good work.

✝ *The Holy Gospel of Our Lord Jesus Christ
According to Matthew* [9:9-13]

Jesus saw a man called Matthew sitting at the tax office;
and he said to him,"Follow me." And he rose and followed
him. And as he sat at table in the house, behold, many tax
collectors and sinners came and sat down with Jesus and
his disciples. And when the Pharisees saw this, they said to
his disciples,"Why does your teacher eat with tax
collectors and sinners?"But when he heard it, he said,
"Those who are well have no need of a physician, but those
who are sick. Go and learn what this means,'I desire
mercy, and not sacrifice.'For I came not to call the
righteous, but sinners."

Saint Michael and All Angels   *September 29*

A Reading (Lesson) from the Book of Genesis   [28:10-17]

Jacob left Beer-sheba, and went toward Haran. And he came to a certain place, and stayed there that night, because the sun had set. Taking one of the stones of the place, he put it under his head and lay down in that place to sleep. And he dreamed that there was a ladder set up on the earth, and the top of it reached to heaven; and behold, the angels of God were ascending and descending on it! And behold, the Lord stood above it and said, "I am the Lord, the God of Abraham your father and the God of Isaac; the land on which you lie I will give to you and to your descendants; and your descendants shall be like the dust of the earth, and you shall spread abroad to the west and to the east and to the north and to the south; and by you and your descendants shall all the families of the earth bless themselves. Behold, I am with you and will keep you wherever you go, and will bring you back to this land; for I will not leave you until I have done that of which I have spoken to you." Then Jacob awoke from his sleep and said, "Surely the Lord is in this place; and I did not know it." And he was afraid, and said, "How awesome is this place! This is none other than the house of God, and this is the gate of heaven."

Psalm 103   [page 733]   or   *103:19-22*   [page 734]

A Reading (Lesson) from the Revelation to John   [12:7-12]

Now war arose in heaven, Michael and his angels fighting against the dragon; and the dragon and his angels fought, but they were defeated and there was no longer any place for them in heaven. And the great dragon was thrown down, that ancient serpent, who is called the Devil and Satan, the deceiver of the whole world—he was thrown down to the earth, and his angels were thrown down with him. And I heard a loud voice in heaven, saying, "Now the salvation and the power and the kingdom of our God and the authority of his Christ have come, for the accuser of our brethren has been thrown down, who accuses them day and night before our God. And they have conquered him by the blood of the Lamb and by the word of their testimony; for they loved not their lives even unto death. Rejoice then, O heaven and you that dwell therein! But woe to you, O earth and sea, for the devil has come down to you in great wrath, because he knows that his time is short!"

✝ *The Holy Gospel of Our Lord Jesus Christ According to John* [1:47-51]

Jesus saw Nathan'a-el coming to him, and said of him, "Behold, an Israelite indeed, in whom is no guile!" Nathan'a-el said to him, "How do you know me?" Jesus answered him, "Before Philip called you, when you were under the fig tree, I saw you." Nathan'a-el answered him, "Rabbi, you are the son of God! You are the King of Israel!" Jesus answered him, "Because I said to you, I saw you under the fig tree, do you believe? You shall see greater things than these." And he said to him, "Truly, truly, I say to you, you will see heaven opened, and the angels of God ascending and descending upon the Son of man."

Saint Luke   *October 18*

A Reading (Lesson) from the Book of Ecclesiasticus [38:1-4, 6-10, 12-14]

Honor the physician with the honor due him, according to your need of him, for the Lord created him; for healing comes from the Most High, and he will receive a gift from the king. The skill of the physician lifts up his head, and in the presence of great men he is admired. The Lord created medicines from the earth, and a sensible man will not despise them. And he gave skill to men that he might be glorified in his marvelous works. By them he heals and takes away pain; the pharmacist makes of them a compound. His works will never be finished; and from him health is upon the face of the earth. My son, when you are sick do not be negligent, but pray to the Lord, and he will heal you. Give up your faults and direct your hands aright, and cleanse your heart from all sin. And give the physician his place, for the Lord created him; let him not leave you, for there is need of him. There is a time when success lies in the hands of physicians, for they too will pray to the Lord that he should grant them success in diagnosis and in healing, for the sake of preserving life.

Psalm 147 [page 804] or *147:1-7* [page 804]

A Reading (Lesson) from the Second Letter of Paul to Timothy [4:5-13]

As for you, always be steady, endure suffering, do the work of an evangelist, fulfill your ministry. For I am already on the point of being sacrificed; the time of my departure has come. I have fought the good fight, I have finished the race, I have kept the faith. Henceforth there is laid up for me the crown of righteousness, which the Lord, the righteous judge, will award to me on that Day, and not only to me but also to all who have loved his appearing. Do your best to come to me soon. For Demas, in love with this present world, has deserted me and gone to Thessaloni′ca; Crescens has gone to Galatia, Titus to Dalmatia. Luke alone is with me. Get Mark and bring him with you; for he is very useful in serving me. Tych′icus I have sent to Ephesus. When you come, bring the cloak that I left with Carpus at Tro′as, also the books, and above all the parchments.

✝ *The Holy Gospel of Our Lord Jesus Christ*
According to Luke [4:14-21]

Jesus returned in the power of the Spirit into Galilee, and a report concerning him went out through all the surrounding country. And he taught in their synagogues, being glorified by all. And he came to Nazareth, where he had been brought up; and went to the synagogue, as his custom was, on the sabbath day. And he stood up to read; and there was given to him the book of the prophet Isaiah. He opened the book and found the place where it was written, "The Spirit of the Lord is upon me, because he has anointed me to preach good news to the poor. He has sent me to proclaim release to the captives and recovering of sight to the blind, to set at liberty those who are oppressed, to proclaim the acceptable year of the Lord." And he closed the book, and gave it back to the attendant, and sat down; and the eyes of all in the synagogue were fixed on him. And he began to say to them, "Today this scripture has been fulfilled in your hearing."

Saint James of Jerusalem   *October 23*

A Reading (Lesson) from the Acts of the Apostles [15:12-22a]

All the apostles and elders kept silence; and they listened to Barnabas and Paul as they related what signs and wonders God had done through them among the Gentiles. After they finished speaking, James replied, "Brethren, listen to me. Simeon has related how God first visited the Gentiles, to take out of them a people for his name. And with this the words of the prophets agree, as it is written, 'After this I will return, and I will rebuild the dwelling of David, which has fallen; I will rebuild its ruins, and I will set it up, that the rest of men may seek the Lord, and all the Gentiles who are called by my name, says the Lord, who has made these things known from of old.' Therefore my judgment is that we should not trouble those of the Gentiles who turn to God, but should write to them to abstain from the pollutions of idols and from unchastity and from what is strangled and from blood. For from early generations Moses has had in every city those who preach him, for he is read every sabbath in the synagogues." Then it seemed good to the apostles and the elders, with the whole church, to choose men from among them and send them to Antioch with Paul and Barnabas.

Psalm 1 [page 585]

A Reading (Lesson) from the First Letter of Paul to the Corinthians [15-1:11]

I would remind you, brethren, in what terms I preached to you the gospel, which you received, in which you stand, by which you are saved, if you hold it fast—unless you believed in vain. For I delivered to you as of first importance what I also received, that Christ died for our sins in accordance with the scriptures, that he was buried, that he was raised on the third day in accordance with the scriptures, and that he appeared to Cephas, then to the twelve. Then he appeared to more than five hundred brethren at one time, most of whom are still alive, though some have fallen asleep. Then he appeared to James, then to all the apostles. Last of all, as to one untimely born, he appeared also to me. For I am the least of the apostles, unfit to be called an apostle, because I persecuted the church of God. But by the grace of God I am what I am, and his grace toward me was not in vain. On the contrary, I worked harder than any of them, though it was not I, but the grace of God which is with me. Whether then it was I or they, so we preach and so you believed.

✝ *The Holy Gospel of Our Lord Jesus Christ*
According to Matthew [13:54-58]

Coming to his own country, Jesus taught them in their synagogue, so that they were astonished, and said,"Where did this man get this wisdom and these mighty works? Is not this the carpenter's son? Is not his mother called Mary? And are not his brothers James and Joseph and Simon and Judas? And are not all his sisters with us? Where then did this man get all this?" And they took offense at him. But Jesus said to them,"A prophet is not without honor except in his own country and in his own house." And he did not do many mighty works there, because of their unbelief.

Saint Simon and Saint Jude   *October 28*

A Reading (Lesson) from the Book of Deuteronomy [32:1-4]

Moses spoke the words of this song,"Give ear, O heavens, and I will speak; and let the earth hear the words of my mouth. May my teaching drop as the rain, my speech distill as the dew, as the gentle rain upon the tender grass, and as the showers upon the herb. For I will proclaim the name of the Lord. Ascribe greatness to our God! The Rock, his work is perfect; for all his ways are justice. A God of faithfulness and without iniquity, just and right is he."

Psalm 119:89-96   [page 770]

A Reading (Lesson) from the Letter of Paul to the Ephesians [2:13-22]

Now in Christ Jesus you Gentiles, who once were far off have been brought near in the blood of Christ. For he is our peace, who has made us both one, and has broken down the dividing wall of hostility, by abolishing in his flesh the law of commandments and ordinances, that he might create in himself one new man in place of the two, so making peace, and might reconcile us both to God in one body through the cross, thereby bringing the hostility to an end. And he came and preached peace to you who were far off and peace to those who were near; for through him we both have access in one Spirit to the Father. So then you are no longer strangers and sojourners, but you are fellow citizens with the saints and members of the household of God, built upon the foundation of the apostles and prophets, Christ Jesus himself being the cornerstone, in whom the whole structure is joined together and grows into a holy temple in the Lord; in whom you also are built into it for a dwelling place of God in the Spirit.

✝ *The Holy Gospel of Our Lord Jesus Christ According to John* [15:17-27]

Jesus said to his disciples, "This I command you, to love one another. If the world hates you, know that it has hated me before it hated you. If you were of the world, the world would love its own; but because you are not of the world, but I chose you out of the world, therefore the world hates you. Remember the word that I said to you, 'A servant is not greater than his master.' If they persecuted me, they will persecute you; if they kept my word, they will keep yours also. But all this they will do to you on my account, because they do not know him who sent me. If I had not come and spoken to them, they would not have sin; but now they have no excuse for their sin. He who hates me hates my Father also. If I had not done among them the works which no one else did, they would not have sin; but now they have seen and hated both me and my Father. It is to fulfill the word that is written in their law, 'They hated me without a cause.' But when the Counselor comes, whom I shall send to you from the Father, even the Spirit of truth, who proceeds from the Father, he will bear witness to me; and you also are witnesses, because you have been with me from the beginning."

All Saints' Day I *November 1*

A Reading (Lesson) from the Book of Ecclesiasticus
[44:1-10, 13-14]

Let us now praise famous men, and our fathers in their generations. The Lord apportioned to them great glory, his majesty from the beginning. There were those who ruled in their kingdoms, and were men renowned for their power, giving counsel by their understanding, and proclaiming prophecies; leaders of the people in their deliberations and in understanding of learning for the people, wise in their words of instruction; those who composed musical tunes, and set forth verses in writing; rich men furnished with resources, living peaceably in their habitations—all these were honored in their generations, and were the glory of their times. There are some of them who have left a name, so that men declare their praise. And there are some who have no memorial, who have perished as though they had not lived; they have become as though they had not been born, and so have their children after them. But these were men of mercy, whose righteous deeds have not been forgotten. Their posterity will continue for ever, and their glory will not be blotted out. Their bodies were buried in peace, and their name lives to all generations.

Psalm 149 [page 807]

A Reading (Lesson) from the Revelation to John [7:2-4, 9-17]

I saw another angel ascend from the rising of the sun, with the seal of the living God, and he called with a loud voice to the four angels who had been given power to harm earth and sea, saying, "Do not harm the earth or the sea or the trees, till we have sealed the servants of our God upon their foreheads." And I heard the number of the sealed, a hundred and forty-four thousand sealed, out of every tribe of the sons of Israel. After this I looked, and behold, a great multitude which no man could number, from every nation, from all tribes and peoples and tongues, standing before the throne and before the Lamb, clothed in white robes, with palm branches in their hands, and crying out with a loud voice, "Salvation belongs to our God who sits upon the throne, and to the Lamb!" And all the angels stood round the throne and round the elders and the four living creatures, and they fell on their faces before the throne and worshiped God, saying, "Amen! Blessing and glory and wisdom and thanksgiving and honor and power and might be to our God for ever and ever! Amen." Then one of the elders addressed me, saying, "Who are these, clothed in white robes, and whence have they come?" I said to him, "Sir, you know." And he said to me, "These are they who have come out of the great tribulation; they have washed their robes and made them white in the blood of the Lamb. Therefore are they before the throne of God, and serve him day and night within his temple; and he who sits upon the throne will shelter them with his presence. They shall hunger no more, neither thirst any more; the sun shall not strike them, nor any scorching heat. For the Lamb in the midst of the throne will be their shepherd, and he will guide them to springs of living water; and God will wipe away every tear from their eyes."

✝ *The Holy Gospel of Our Lord Jesus Christ*
According to Matthew [5:1-12]

Seeing the crowds, Jesus went up on the mountain, and when he sat down his disciples came to him. And he opened his mouth and taught them, saying: "Blessed are the poor in spirit, for theirs is the kingdom of heaven. Blessed are those who mourn, for they shall be comforted. Blessed are the meek, for they shall inherit the earth. Blessed are those who hunger and thirst for righteousness, for they shall be satisfied. Blessed are the merciful, for they shall obtain mercy. Blessed are the pure in heart, for they shall see God. Blessed are the peacemakers, for they shall be called sons of God. Blessed are those who are persecuted for righteousness' sake, for theirs is the kingdom of heaven. Blessed are you when men revile you and persecute you and utter all kinds of evil against you falsely on my account. Rejoice and be glad, for your reward is great in heaven, for so men persecuted the prophets who were before you."

All Saints' Day II   *November 1 (or the Sunday following)*

A Reading (Lesson) from the Book of Ecclesiasticus [2:(1-6)7-11]

My son, if you come forward to serve the Lord, prepare yourself for temptation. Set your heart right and be steadfast, and do not be hasty in time of calamity. Cleave to him and do not depart, that you may be honored at the end of your life. Accept whatever is brought upon you, and in changes that humble you be patient. For gold is tested in the fire, and acceptable men in the furnace of humiliation. Trust in him, and he will help you; make your ways straight, and hope in him.

You who fear the Lord, wait for his mercy; and turn not aside, lest you fall. You who fear the Lord, trust in him, and your reward will not fail; you who fear the Lord, hope for good things, for everlasting joy and mercy. Consider the ancient generations and see: who ever trusted in the Lord and was put to shame? Or who ever persevered in the fear of the Lord and was forsaken? Or who ever called upon him and was overlooked? For the Lord is compassionate and merciful; he forgives sins and saves in time of affliction.

Psalm 149 [page 807]

A Reading (Lesson) from the Letter of Paul to the Ephesians [1:(11-14) 15-23]

> In Christ, according to the purpose of him who accomplishes all things according to the counsel of his will, we who first hoped in Christ have been destined and appointed to live for the praise of his glory. In him you also, who have heard the word of truth, the gospel of your salvation, and have believed in him, were sealed with the promised Holy Spirit, which is the guarantee of our inheritance until we acquire possession of it, to the praise of his glory.

For this reason, because I have heard of your faith in the Lord Jesus and your love toward all the saints, I do not cease to give thanks for you, remembering you in my prayers, that the God of our Lord Jesus Christ, the Father of glory, may give you a spirit of wisdom and of revelation in the knowledge of him, having the eyes of your hearts enlightened, that you may know what is the hope to which he has called you, what are the riches of his glorious inheritance in the saints, and what is the immeasurable greatness of his power in us who believe, according to the working of his great might which he accomplished in Christ when he raised him from the dead and made him sit at his right hand in the heavenly places, far above all rule and authority and power and dominion, and above every name that is named, not only in this age but also in that which is to come; and he has put all things under his feet and has made him the head over all things for the church, which is his body, the fullness of him who fills all in all.

✝ *The Holy Gospel of Our Lord Jesus Christ*
According to Luke [6:20-26(27-36)]

Jesus lifted up his eyes on his disciples, and said: "Blessed are you poor, for yours is the kingdom of God. Blessed are you that hunger now, for you shall be satisfied. Blessed are you that weep now, for you shall laugh. Blessed are you when men hate you, and when they exclude you and revile you, and cast out your name as evil, on account of the Son of man! Rejoice in that day, and leap for joy, for behold, your reward is great in heaven; for so their fathers did to the prophets. But woe to you that are rich, for you have received your consolation. Woe to you that are full now, for you shall hunger. Woe to you that laugh now, for you shall mourn and weep. Woe to you, when all men speak well of you, for so their fathers did to the false prophets."

"But I say to you that hear, Love your enemies, do good to those who hate you, bless those who curse you, pray for those who abuse you. To him who strikes you on the cheek, offer the other also; and from him who takes away your coat do not withhold even your shirt. Give to every one who begs from you; and of him who takes away your goods do not ask them again. And as you wish that men would do to you, do so to them. If you love those who love you, what credit is that to you? For even sinners love those who love them. And if you do good to those who do good to you, what credit is that to you? For even sinners do the same. And if you lend to those from whom you hope to receive, what credit is that to you? Even sinners lend to sinners, to receive as much again. But love your enemies, and do good, and lend, expecting nothing in return; and your reward will be great, and you will be sons of the Most High; for he is kind to the ungrateful and the selfish. Be merciful, even as your Father is merciful."

Thanksgiving Day

A Reading (Lesson) from the Book of Deuteronomy
[8:1-3, 6-10 (17-20)]

Moses said to all Israel, "All the commandments which I command you this day you shall be careful to do, that you may live and multiply, and go in and possess the land which the Lord swore to give to your fathers. And you shall remember all the way which the Lord your God has led you these forty years in the wilderness, that he might humble you, testing you to know what was in your heart, whether you would keep his commandments, or not. And he humbled you and let you hunger and fed you with manna, which you did not know, nor did your fathers know; that he might make you know that man does not live by bread alone, but that man lives by everything that proceeds out of the mouth of the Lord. So you shall keep the commandments of the Lord your God, by walking in his ways and by fearing him. For the Lord your God is bringing you into a good land, a land of brooks of water, of fountains and springs, flowing forth in valleys and hills, a land of wheat and barley, of vines and fig trees and pomegranates, a land of olive trees and honey, a land in which you will eat bread without scarcity, in which you will lack nothing, a land whose stones are iron, and out of whose hills you can dig copper. And you shall eat and be full, and you shall bless the Lord your God for the good land he has given you.

"Beware lest you say in your heart, 'My power and the might of my hand have gotten me this wealth.' You shall remember the Lord your God, for it is he who gives you power to get wealth; that he may confirm his covenant which he swore to your fathers, as at this day. And if you forget the Lord your God and go after other gods and serve them and worship them, I solemnly warn you this day that you shall surely perish. Like the nations that the Lord makes to perish before you, so shall you perish, because you would not obey the voice of the Lord your God."

Psalm 65 [page 672] or *65:9-14* [page 673]

A Reading (Lesson) from the Letter of James [1:17-18, 21-27]

Every good endowment and every perfect gift is from above, coming down from the Father of lights with whom there is no variation or shadow due to change. Of his own will he brought us forth by the word of truth that we should be a kind of first fruits of his creatures. Therefore put away all filthiness and rank growth of wickedness and receive with meekness the implanted word, which is able to save your souls. But be doers of the word, and not hearers only, deceiving yourselves. For if any one is a hearer of the word and not a doer, he is like a man who observes his natural face in a mirror; for he observes himself and goes away and at once forgets what he was like. But he who looks into the perfect law, the law of liberty, and perseveres, being no hearer that forgets but a doer that acts, he shall be blessed in his doing. If any one thinks he is religious, and does not bridle his tongue but deceives his heart, this man's religion is vain. Religion that is pure and undefiled before God and the Father is this: to visit orphans and widows in their affliction, and to keep oneself unstained from the world.

✝ *The Holy Gospel of Our Lord Jesus Christ According to Matthew* [6:25-33]

Jesus said, "Do not be anxious about your life, what you shall eat or what you shall drink, nor about your body, what you shall put on. Is not life more than food, and the body more than clothing? Look at the birds of the air: they neither sow nor reap nor gather into barns, and yet your heavenly Father feeds them. Are you not of more value than they? And which of you by being anxious can add one cubit to his span of life? And why are you anxious about clothing? Consider the lilies of the field, how they grow; they neither toil nor spin; yet I tell you, even Solomon in all his glory was not arrayed like one of these. But if God so clothes the grass of the field, which today is alive and tomorrow is thrown into the oven, will he not much more clothe you, O men of little faith? Therefore do not be anxious, saying, 'What shall we eat?' or 'What shall we drink?' or 'What shall we wear?' For the Gentiles seek all these things; and your heavenly Father knows that you need them all. But seek first his kingdom and his righteousness, and all these things shall be yours as well."